LEADING CHANGE

"This book deserves a wide readership and is an excellent guide
to 'whole systems' thinking and the benefits it could bring to the
management of public services."
Ian Christie, Associate of New Economics Foundation and The Local Futures Group

"The authors of *Leading change* write from experience – their own and that
of others ... We should follow their suggestions – after all we know that what
we are doing now does not work so there's all to play for."
Fiona Ellis, Director, Northern Rock Foundation

LEADING CHANGE

A guide to whole systems working

Margaret Attwood, Mike Pedler, Sue Pritchard and David Wilkinson

The POLICY PRESS

First published in Great Britain in February 2003 by

The Policy Press
34 Tyndall's Park Road
Bristol BS8 1PY
UK

Tel +44 (0)117 954 6800
Fax +44 (0)117 973 7308
e-mail tpp@bristol.ac.uk
www.policypress.org.uk

British Library Cataloguing in Publication Data

A catalogue record for this book is available from the British Library

ISBN 1 86134 449 X

Margaret Attwood, **Mike Pedler**, **Sue Pritchard** and **David Wilkinson** are colleagues in Whole Systems Development, the consulting network.

Whole Systems Development Tel 01535 680537

Cover design by Qube Design Associates, Bristol.

Figure 9 on page 69 is reproduced with kind permission from the authors.

Illustration on page 111 © Karen Bowler.

Printed and bound in Great Britain by Bell & Bain Ltd, Glasgow

Contents

Contents

Foreword

David Fillingham

I recently attended a one-day conference organised by health service leaders in an industrial town in the Northwest of England. The town was once a thriving centre of manufacturing industry, but now faces social and economic decline. In line with the thinking of the authors of this book, the health service leaders had set out to tackle the problems they faced by 'getting the whole system in the room'. As a result, those attending were not only from all parts of the NHS, but also from local authorities, businesses, community groups and churches. Everyone present understood that improving the health of local people would be a long and arduous process. There would be no easy quick fixes, and many difficulties and challenges lay ahead. What is more, they recognised that hitting government targets and improving their town's position in the relevant league tables, was actually about improving the sense of wellbeing and quality of life of everyone who lived there.

All too often this isn't the face of public sector change that grabs the headlines. Instead the 'mad management virus' described by the authors of this book is perceived to be the predominant model for getting change to happen in the public sector. The myth is one of inflexible top-down targets being ruthlessly administered by faceless bureaucrats. The reality is increasingly one of public servants working creatively to develop new and effective means of implementation.

For far too long public service delivery in the UK has been characterised by policy thinking that has been unambitious and often poorly implemented. Just as risky are bold and radical ideas that are unsupported by effective implementation. This is frustrating for everyone: for politicians, who do not see the pace of progress that they would wish; for citizens who do not see services improve; and for those working in the public services who are trying their absolute hardest and yet feel criticised for not implementing ideas that they see as unrealistic and unworkable. What is needed is a new approach to the effective implementation of change in the public sector that can match the bold radicalism of new policy thinking. It is unquestionably the role of politicians and policy makers to develop effective policies that will meet the changing demands of the 21st century. Such visions need to be painted in bold colours to capture the imagination. At the same time, it is the job of public servants and public sector managers to develop new approaches to implementation that recognise the inherent complexity of bringing about change in the public sector.

The NHS is a good case in point. It is without a doubt in need of radical improvement. But we must make sure that it is not reform of the 'mad management virus' variety. As I heard one health service manager say recently, "we need to hit all the targets, but without missing the point". What the NHS needs is an implementation strategy that is able to cope with the complexities of a million-person-strong employing organisation that significantly affects the lives of every UK citizen. Leading change draws on ideas from complexity science to suggest how change can most successfully be achieved in such large complex systems.

The NHS Plan sets out a bold vision of a health service that remains based on need not the ability to pay, but which also offers world class standards of service. The implementation strategy that is beginning to deliver this is firmly in line with many of the principles of whole system development set out in *Leading change*. At a macro level, it is the role of the Department of Health to configure the whole system of healthcare delivery in such a way that will support sustainable, long-term change, while also being able to demonstrate some early signs of progress. That system does most certainly consist of 'targets' (that is, national standards, and inspection and regulation), but the other elements of the new system are equally important. These include a progressive decentralisation of control away from Westminster and Whitehall as evidenced by the creation of Primary Care Trusts and the development of foundation hospitals. Accompanying this decentralisation is the development of greater diversity of provision, with more flexibility and choice for patients. Finally, the Department of Health is seeking to encourage a new style of management and leadership across the service, and to support improvement and development through the NHS Modernisation Agency.

It is perhaps not surprising as this new system comes into being that its tensions and dilemmas are felt acutely by many managers and leaders. This is because it is the job of local leaders to resolve those tensions in the interests of staff and service users alike. This is what makes the ability to manage paradox and tolerate ambiguity such an important core competence! On a daily basis, such leaders must be able to balance the need for early progress, against that for long-term sustainable improvement. There are already some encouraging signs that these challenges are being met through the development of new and more effective approaches to leading change.

In the NHS, two areas in which dramatic results have already been achieved are in Cancer Services and in Primary Care. The Cancer Services Collaborative was established in 1999 with nine pilot sites in eight cancer networks. The aim was to help support the implementation of the National Cancer Plan. It works by engaging frontline clinical staff and managers and by helping them develop the tools and techniques of quality improvement. The philosophy is to start with small-scale changes and to test these out before repeating them on a larger scale and making them sustainable. As the name 'Collaborative' suggests, the philosophy is that everyone has something to share and everyone has something to learn. Groups of frontline staff from different hospitals and health communities across the country meet together to share their experiences and to learn from each other. The enthusiasm and sense of value created by this approach is tremendous and has had a revitalising effect on many staff. Furthermore, the tangible results have been equally impressive.

The Collaborative has spread throughout the NHS in England, involving 500 clinical project teams with an average of 102 improvements being reported every month. These are benefiting patients by reducing delays and duplication right across the healthcare system, from the GP surgery to the final stages of treatment. For example, in Leicester, patients with prostate cancer are seen, receive diagnosis and have an agreed treatment plan within one month of referral and with no more than three visits; previously, this took up to twelve months and at least six visits. Across the country, over 80% of patients are now being reviewed and treatment agreed by a multidisciplinary team; previously this was estimated to have been less than 10%.

Similarly, within Primary Care, the National Primary Care Collaborative began in a relatively small way in June 2000 with just over 100 practices. By applying the tools of quality improvement, testing out small changes and looking together at what works, the practices have been able to bring about a 65% reduction in the time patients wait to see a doctor. By the end of 2002 the Collaborative had expanded to involve approximately 3,000 practices serving over 19 million patients, which makes it the largest health improvement programme in the world. Mortality statistics have demonstrated a remarkable fourfold reduction in mortality for patients with coronary heart disease in practices involved with the Collaborative compared with those not involved.

The NHS Modernisation Agency, which supports the work of both of these collaboratives, is now engaging 100,000 staff across the NHS in leadership development and quality improvement. The principles of whole system development as set out in *Leading change* run right through the work of the Modernisation Agency. The application of these principles is both delivering tangible short-term improvements – 'hitting the targets' – but also bringing about the cultural changes required in order to make improvements sustainable in the long run. It is these practices of effective implementation that will be the key to the transformation of the NHS, whether it be in the GP surgery, community health team, the operating theatre or on the acute medical ward. Lessons for other parts of the public sector seem to be clear. Bold and radical policy ideas are important if we are to create communities in which the human spirit can thrive. But these ideas need to be implemented in the context of the messy reality of our organisational and communal lives. *Leading change* will be a help and inspiration to those countless leaders at every level who are passionate about creating public services that are truly world class.

David Fillingham
Director, NHS Modernisation Agency
January 2003

Foreword

Will Hutton

This book gets to the heart of many issues that are of concern to those seeking public service change and transformation. The aim of improving public services has become a critical one, and thus far it has eluded most efforts at change. Consider this recent scenario:

> Someone dies in a house fire. It is November 2002 and the firefighters are on strike. The army has been tasked with stepping in to direct the hoses. Woefully under-resourced and under-trained for the job, they are forced to use 40-year-old Green Goddesses in place of the up-to-date all-purpose fire-engines the public has become used to. The government, egged on by the mainstream media, tries to invoke the blitz spirit. In this head-to-head conflict the government's mantra is reform – the public sector unions' goal is higher pay. This is the frontline of the public sector reform debate at the start of the 21st century.

The firefighters' dispute neatly highlights the tensions at the heart of successive governments' attempts to transform the public services. The social contract may need rewriting but 'how to do so' is obscured by a desire to change little on one side and by a lack of clarity about exactly what the future might look like on the other. In the five years since New Labour came to office, we have witnessed a shift in the territory on which the debate about public service delivery takes place. In 1997 the focus was on levels of spending – which party could commit to spending more on key services. In 2001 the public had become more critical consumers: more money had not delivered sufficient improvement in services. Hence the focus on money linked to reform.

Demands for new standards of delivery are matched by exhortations to join up practice and involve service users, but the only means of implementation appears to be through top-down audit and inspection regimes. By contrast, *Leading change* argues that whole systems approaches and partnership working are required to achieve new service configurations. It outlines the theory behind whole systems development and gives practical guidance on developing 'systems' to improve joined-up working.

It is clear that the large increases in public spending agreed by the Chancellor in his 2002 budget – £301 billion by 2005-06 – will not result in a step change in performance without a degree of reform in working practices and work organisation. This requires improvements in the way the public sector rewards and retains its staff – particularly its high performers– and an increased focus on delivery over policy and process. As Gordon Brown told the Commons Treasury select committee earlier in 2002:

"This is not money thrown at a problem. This is money dependent on modernisation. Responsibility in pay setting is absolutely crucial to the next few years of the health service. Responsibility in pay is going to be important in the way all public services develop."

This is the government's oft-repeated mantra; rights (to more pay) accompanied by responsibilities (to reform working practices). It seems self-evidently a reasonable approach, but in truth it is racked with tensions.

The first is that in much of the public sector is a coalition of trades' unions and middle management who are deeply suspicious of reform. The entry of the private sector into health, transport and education has arguably led to a two-tier workforce, debatable efficiency gains and low morale in those parts of the public sector deemed to need private discipline. This phalanx of opposition to reform of working practices needs to be won over to avoid constipating the efforts to ally the delivery of additional resources with reform of the delivery of public services. Both sides need to close what has become a widening gap through an agreement to arbitration over pay linked to reform that binds and commits. As the Work Foundation has argued, the government needs a sustained policy for handling public sector pay and industrial relations.

The second is a point that goes to the heart of the arguments in *Leading change*: the need to innovate versus the hardening of risk-averse cultures reinforced by an obsession with target setting at the centre of government. Innovation works best where workers feel able to take risks. In too many parts of the public sector the culture is one of risk avoidance. Hence, all that is achieved is a stasis over genuine improvements in delivery and, in their place, the hitting of often over-simplistic targets.

Third, targets are too often short term in nature and built into the four-year electoral cycle. Yet, as we all know, to be sustainable improvement takes time. This type of tension is particularly difficult for politicians to handle when their jobs depend on things happening now.

Fourth, pay and pay setting needs review. The public sector remains the last bastion of collective bargaining. The government needs to pay fairly and reward the best performers wherever they sit. It needs to establish a way of monitoring public sector pay trends and establish a clear overall pay strategy. ACAS needs to be firmly in the picture when disputes might loom large with a commitment for compulsory but not binding mediation. Reward strategies need to be based on genuine partnership agreements between local employers and unions. Sclerotic national bargaining structures need to go in favour of more local flexibility around nationally set norms. Performance pay, whether team or individually based, also needs to be examined across the public sector.

Fifth, we come to the issue of Whitehall. Constitutional practice and time-honoured custom mean that senior civil servants remain unshakeable in their belief that their duties are solely to ministers rather than the public. This skews the strategy and focus of the large fiefdoms they control and militates against a genuine commitment to delivery downwards as opposed to managing upwards.

Finally, and linked to the fifth tension, is the firm entrenchment of policy over delivery in central Whitehall's hierarchy of importance. Talent within the public services moves towards the centre. Ability is interpreted as policy-making ability. This inevitably results in a two-tier approach to the public service with a wide divide between those devising policy and those implementing delivery. It is critical that this divide is closed and those good at delivering services, capable of innovating and creating new ways of serving their local 'customers' are encouraged, learnt from and rewarded.

Leading change will not resolve all of these tensions, but it offers refreshing thinking on new ways of acting to implement agreed changes, which will help resolve at least some of these difficulties. The authors have produced a valuable resource for those faced with bringing about such changes. And this focus on implementation is vital. If the above tensions remain unresolved the government and public's hoped-for improvements for our public services will remain under-delivered. A whole systems approach to public service delivery may well help plot a route to improved delivery.

Will Hutton
January 2003

Prologue

This book has been some time in the writing. It represents the dialogue, both conceptual and practical, between the four of us, as consultants, researchers and writers concerned with the integration of thinking and action across three largely disconnected fields of activity – organisation development, community development and the implementation of government policy on public services. Its context is one of a rapidly changing social and public policy landscape.

Figure 1: The scope of whole systems thinking

The pressures continue to grow for new forms and standards of delivery and for local joining up and reconnecting of services to users, citizens and communities. This demands new service configurations, and new forms of partnership and local and neighbourhood governance. The organisational challenges to meet these changing requirements are considerable. In this book our exploration of them can be summarised as a question: How can organisations fit to house the human spirit be created and sustained such that they meet the needs of communities and society at large?

Our responses to this from our various experiences have driven us to despair as well as giving a sense of the emerging possibilities.

On the dark side we see organisations whose design is still based on machine-like and territorial assumptions where:

- change is equated with restructuring, with the attendant dangers of moving the chairs around the deck of the *Titanic* and, in the process, setting back progress to improve services;
- managerial attention is focused on internal silos to the detriment of a coherent approach to stakeholder needs;
- territory is defended against the demands or wishes of partners and residents, and even against the 'unreasonable' demands of staff;

- the attention span is short and of the 'let's fix it' variety, rather than taking a longer-term and sustainable view.

Such organisations are not usually populated by bad or even incompetent people. People, we believe, are the product of the circumstances, the system, in which they find themselves. Firing the key people will not change these design assumptions; equally, developing individual competencies alone will not change the way things work.

On the brighter side some people and organisations are:

- working creatively with local residents to improve services;
- asking different questions about ways of organising that support-improved delivery;
- seeing structural change as only one ingredient of sustainable development;
- putting greater emphasis on learning from experience – individual, team, intra- and inter-organisational – and taking action as a result;
- trying to take a longer-term view, while at the same time understanding the imperatives, particularly from the government, about shorter-term improvement.

It is possible for all organisations to develop these characteristics. In this book we suggest a set of principles or keys that supports the wider relationships that will enable organisations to work effectively internally and as part of a wider system of external relationships. This includes partner organisations and local communities, and involves drawing collectively on the information needed to breathe life into these connections and networks.

This is not comfortable territory. The notion of organisation as machine gives a superficial, and illusory, sense of control and action that fits with our task-fixated culture of performance targets and indicators. Equally, organisation development approaches have implicitly emphasised the notion of single organisations with clear territory and well-defended walls. The landscape we chart here is more uncertain, being composed of phenomena that cannot be reduced to simple cause and effect. It also requires a capability to work with paradox and a tolerance of ambiguity. Magic bullets or quick fixes will not deliver change.

In drawing back from simple prescriptions, we recognise the need for frameworks that enable people to make sense of the world around them. We start the book with what passes for a public health warning. We are not unaware of the irony inherent in writing about 'whole systems development' and then disaggregating a clearly interconnected process into what we have called the Five Keys. Many long hours have been spent worrying over how we might best conceptualise and describe the elements we work with and have found to be important, even crucial, in bringing about whole systems development. Using metaphors connected with new science and change architecture, we puzzled over the most accurate and vivid ways to describe complex challenges in simple and appealing language. Like the philosophers in *Gulliver's Travels*, we debated the possibilities – none of which proved complete, comprehensive or original – and so, in the spirit of continuing the exploration and learning, we have given up on that and will test our best efforts in the doing.

So the Five Keys, summarised in Chapter Two and covered in depth and supported by 'stories' based on our experiences in Chapters Nine to Ten, are:

- leadership
- public learning
- diversity
- meeting differently
- follow-through.

In their separate but wholly interconnected ways they are central to effective whole systems development. They cannot be 'applied' separately, but nevertheless invite description separately so that we can better understand the whole.

Figure 2: The five keys of whole systems development

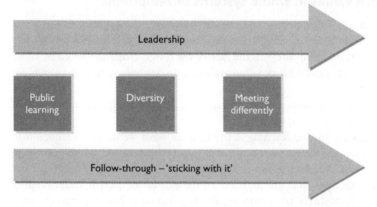

While the Five Keys constitute the framework within which we work, it is important that they are understood in conjunction with the values that guide their application. The Five Keys can become a mechanical prescription if they are applied without the backing of appropriate values. Those who purport to assist cross-system working, including the engagement of formal organisations with the communities they serve, can do much damage unless their behaviour is congruent with the principles they espouse.

Given a sense of humility, a willingness to listen and learn, and the other values we advocate, they can provide an antidote to the sorts of action hero performances sometimes erroneously equated with leadership. Public learning, working with diversity and finding ways of meeting differently all encourage the development of processes that will bring people together across the barriers and boundaries of organisations and communities. Follow-through emphasises the need to see whole systems development as a long-term process of change whose path can be mapped by the sketching of 'change architecture' (refer to

Chapter Eight: Follow-through and making it stick) and new forms of organising (see Chapter Nine: From organisations to networks).

The stories that support the Five Keys are developed from our own experiences. We have not named the organisations or individuals involved because we wanted these to be 'warts and all' glimpses of whole systems development in action rather than glossy 'here's how to do it' tales. They translate the conceptual and theoretical territory of whole systems change into the practical actions that people are taking to improve the lives of residents, service users and staff. In this sense, we hope that they may prompt new thinking and action by readers.

Over time, we have developed a number of values in respect of our own activities. Our view of whole systems development is underpinned by these values, which are as important to success as are the principles or the Keys themselves. Like the rest of this book, these ten core values are offered in the spirit of learning rather than as 'ten easy steps for consultants engaged with whole systems projects'.

Ten core values in whole systems development

(1) Optimism – that people and organisations have the capacity to learn and the commitment to tackle dilemmas and intractable 'problems'.

(2) Empathy and humility – in the face of the tough challenges faced by those who are charged with, or voluntarily take on, a whole systems development agenda.

(3) Tenacity and courage – to question assumptions and current ways of working.

(4) Learning – putting learning at the heart of what we do and a recognition that it is as important to honour what is and what works as it is to encourage new ways of thinking and acting.

(5) Relationships – that are founded on the pursuit of mutual understanding and preparedness to negotiate, sharing learning and experience from elsewhere and working through problems.

(6) Whole system perspective – resisting fragmented and 'one size fits all' approaches and seeing organisational and community issues within the wider environmental context.

(7) Local knowledge for local solutions – a bias towards the use of local knowledge, held by individuals, communities and organisations, to create locally invented solutions.

(8) Building social capital – an active appreciation of the personal qualities and experiences of the people with whom we work and a determination to involve them in designing processes that will strengthen learning and build capacity and social capital.

(9) Celebrating small steps – a welcoming of the small improvements that demonstrate the practical possibilities and potential for learning in whole systems development.

(10) The long view – being there for the long haul rather than the quick fix.

ONE

Why do we need whole systems change?

Governments the world over are desperate to find ways of delivering better services and new forms of governance that are responsive to user, citizen and community needs. Economic forces and globalisation have pushed these previously domestic matters into a wider international context. Government priorities worldwide centre on stabilising national economies and improving public services, especially health and education, in the face of electorates apparently reluctant to pay higher taxes. The clarion call of politicians is 'Delivery, delivery, delivery'. Their political lives now depend on it. But do politicians, their civil servants and managers have the conceptual, institutional and practical tools that are fit for this purpose?

The answer to the question seems to be no, at least not in any consistent sense. Top-down change initiatives increase in the hope of a 'big' answer around the corner. Private sector ideas such as internal markets, hit squads of super managers and tougher inspection regimes are imported in the hope of a fix. Yet many of these ideas are deeply flawed and not even effective in the commercial settings where they originate (Heller, 2001). However, while leaders are driven to desperate searches for big solutions, there are numerous examples of exciting innovations at the local level. Despite the persistent mantra of learning from best practice, much of this local innovation is not widely shared and gets lost.

Whole systems approaches are rooted in years of evidence-based practice in public, private, voluntary and community domains (Wilkinson, 1997; Wilkinson and Appelbee, 1999). Despite the political slogan that 'What works is what counts', service improvements are 'constructed' and delivered through organisational frameworks and practices that have not themselves been subject to evidence-based enquiry. As Robert Heller puts it:

> These schemes are devised, usually at ministerial behest, by civil servants who know little about management, and probably think less, and who are not expert in the practice of medicine, education, justice or transport. The inevitably misshapen plans are sold to politicians even less qualified than the Whitehall wizards. (Heller, 2001, p 9)

Whole systems approaches do not offer a single technique or new big answer. A large part of the problem is that we live in the continuing hope that we either have, or are about to discover, the final answer. There are no solutions that can be programmed in from the top. Whole systems approaches start from *rethinking* organisational change issues; how we *act* in relation to them, and, crucially, how we *involve both ourselves and others* in their diagnosis and treatment. Whole systems working is not another fad or series of buzz words, but is above all concerned with *implementation*, and with seeking to reconcile these dilemmas in practice.

In this chapter we:

- explore the failure of programmatic change;
- identify the imperative for implementation of sustainable change, rather than mere intervention to 'fix' problems;
- briefly examine alternative streams of activity and thinking that can create a 'different beat' in efforts to handle intractable problems;
- share our emerging thinking about the reconciliation of four linked dilemmas integral to whole systems working that must be confronted in achieving changes in public policy and service delivery.

The poverty of programmatic change

In developing our ideas about whole systems development approaches, we have worked primarily, but not exclusively, in and across the public, voluntary and community sectors. Most of our examples are taken from these sectors because the problems encountered here are likely to be complex and multi-organisational, and to require user and stakeholder involvement to find sustainable solutions. Yet, private sector businesses are an important part of the analysis. These days few organisations go it alone; most are likely to be part of supply and value chains and networks with many different partners. Commercial organisations are increasingly involved in the multi-agency mix seeking to deliver improved services. Private sector organisations are under increasing pressure to be accountable, environmentally sound and socially responsible, and this is leading to more inclusive approaches with a variety of stakeholders. As the ideas of whole systems development have often been pioneered in the public, voluntary and community sectors, private organisations have much to learn from their colleagues in these areas.

The most important lesson is the failure and poverty of programmatic change. For example, the UK government has set itself targets for achieving world-class public services because it is evident that these services have to be transformed to meet the expectations of the electorate. From the government's perspective there are unacceptable differences between the performances of, for example, schools and hospitals with comparable population characteristics. Too many public services are seen as clinging to outmoded practices and working in the interests of self-serving professions. Consequently, they are perceived as unresponsive to service users and communities alike. Despite the efforts of successive governments, a culture of complacency still dominates and the view is that putting more resources into this system will produce more of the same, rather than bringing about the transformation required. The situation calls for ever more determined resolve to find solutions to these intractable problems, which seem to be getting worse rather than better. The feeling seems to be that, if the current institutions and those leading them are not up to the job, then the private sector may be.

From this vantage point, it is easy to understand why the chosen tools of change, top-down targets, inspection and the search for the 'big' solution are so dominant. However, achieving the government's targets is no simple matter; this complex problem comprises an interlinked set of issues, as follows.

Lack of resources?

Until recently, the government has been seeking to provide Britain with the standards of public services found in Germany and France (where tax is 50% of gross domestic product, or GDP) using levels of taxation nearer to those of the US (tax 30-35% of GDP). This has also happened at a time of increasing costs imposed by the massive expansion of inspection and audit regimes, although this is being moderated by increased spending on health and education in particular. However, the extent to which increased expenditure now can compensate for the shortfalls of the previous 25 years remains an open question.

Institutional rigidity?

> Our powerlessness is not a personal failing, but an institutional one. Most of the institutions we rely upon to protect and guide us through this tumult – governments, trade unions, companies – seem paralysed. Our traditional institutions, many of which were designed for an era of railways, steelworks, factories and dockyards, are enfeebled. We are on the verge of the global twenty-first century knowledge economy, yet we rely on national institutions inherited from the nineteenth-century industrial economy. The contrast is instructive. The nineteenth century was revolutionary because the Victorians matched their scientific and technological innovations with radical institutional innovations: the extension of democracy, the creation of local government, the birth of modern savings and insurance schemes, the development of a professional civil service, the rise of trade unions and the emergence of the research-based university. We are timid and cautious where the Victorians were confident and innovative. We live within the shell of institutions the nineteenth century handed down to us. Our highly uneven capacity for innovation is the fundamental source of our unease. We are scientific and technological revolutionaries, but political and institutional conservatives. (Leadbeater, 2000, p viii)

The delivery gap?

> Bright ideas dreamt up at the centre sink time and again ... [due to] ... the absence of a grassroots delivery mechanism that is both accountable and effective.... Thanks to the Social Exclusion Unit's work we know the exact dimensions and location of deprivation. But dealing with it ... depends more critically than ever on ministers and civil servants deciding just how they are going to deliver at the micro and local levels if they will not or cannot use councils. (David Walker, quoted in Christie and Worpole, 2000)

Lack of innovative capacity and capability?

There is a need for extra investment in the public sector, and the government has both the money and the political mandate to provide it. But if it were simply to pump extra money into public services without reform it would be indistinguishable from Labour governments of yesteryear, which thought money was the answer to everything. In the end, ministers believe that consumers of public services are agnostic about the way they are delivered. If, at the time of the next election, there is a discernible improvement in the quality of education and health, voters will probably not bother that much over whether it is a local authority or a private limited company that has provided the expertise.

Current methods of implementation?

> Public services are dominated by a programmatic approach to change, which assumes that the organisation is like a machine and which therefore needs to be fixed by having off-the-shelf changes imposed from the top. The instigators of programmatic change are normally human resources staff or similar, supported by top management. Rarely are line managers the main agents of change. As the change effort impacts upon them they may find it difficult to see how it answers the real day-to-day problems that they have to address. It may appear as yet another change initiative in an apparently endless series, the meaning of each having long since become detached from the originators' intentions. Programmatic change efforts are often felt to add extra work and not be linked to the main purpose of people's real work. They often become discredited and descend into a kind of mad management disease; endless change programmes being led by different individuals, detached from each other and divorced from any connecting bigger picture. The change effort becomes an end in itself; another task to be done, a box ticked; or quietly forgotten, when top management has lost interest and moved on to the next fad. Sadly, nearly all quality initiatives suffer the same fate. (Wilkinson and Appelbee, 1999, p 36)

A Mad Management Virus (MMV)?

As we have been developing our own understanding and approaches to whole systems development, we have speculated about a 'virus' that transmits abstract and untested assertions about what management *should* be (see Chapter Ten). The virus has come to dominate much of the language and style of the management discourse of many politicians and their advisers, because it offers the promise of a simple way to control delivery outcomes from the centre and thus fulfil ambitious election promises. Its ability to worm its way into the operating system damages the genuine efforts of organisations, communities and individuals to improve the way services work on the ground.

The key strands of the virus can be characterised as follows:

- Programmatic top-down approaches always work.
- The more inspection and control, the better the outcome.
- Setting top-down targets produces specified results; there are no unintended consequences.
- These methods have no harmful effect on levels of trust, staff morale, absenteeism or turnover.
- This 'Management[1] alchemy' has an abstract language of its own, can be parachuted onto the top of any kind of organisation, and operates a system of carrots, sticks and levers by remote control, disconnected from the concrete world of doing and implementing. It is about Management, not managing.
- It uses 'hard' engineering systems approaches with negative feedback control systems. Effectively, it treats people as though they are central heating systems, and is inherently dehumanising.
- It prevents the fundamental ideas of quality systems and philosophies by turning them into top-down bureaucratic control exercises.
- It is what happens in the private sector and 'private sector disciplines' always produce better results.

This virus incubates in places of great power and defends itself within an abstract, closed world of supposedly incontrovertible truths. It is almost impossible to counteract with evidence or the experience of its application.

The implementation imperative

Programmatic, top-down approaches to change (particularly those driven by the MMV perspective) are certain to be ineffective in the face of these complex and interlocking questions. Such approaches have had little success in producing transformational change, even in the commercial context (Beer et al, 1990). Programmatic change generally attempts to focus on restructuring of one kind or another and few people believe that this brings about real and lasting change. Yet, under pressure from inspections and the need to bid for funding, which removes attention from the supposed beneficiaries, clients, users, carers, citizens and neighbourhoods, such proposals continue to be made in an ever-increasing fever of activity. The transaction costs now arising from all this, together with ever-increasing cycles and levels of distrust, is beyond calculation.

In considering any attempt at change, it is vital to clarify the key dimensions of what might be called 'the implementation landscape'. *Engagement* and *implementation* are the key words; they are far more important than the elegance of the organisational change *intervention*. Greater clarity of the implementation landscape helps to shape the processes of engagement and involvement with organisational systems and networks. Especially crucial are the processes of leadership and the creation of what is later called 'holding frameworks'.

The American W.E. Deming, who introduced the idea of quality to Japanese manufacturers in the 1950s, would, if he were alive today, be horrified by what is being inflicted on the British public sector in the name of quality. He advised getting rid of inspection because of its cost, wastefulness and encouragement of the status quo. 'You can't inspect quality in', he said; it is the system that people work in and under that needs to change. It is the workers themselves, aided by their managers, who should work on the analysis of cause and improvement. Deming abhorred top-down targets and managerial exhortation to best effort, seeing them as counter to the continued improvement of quality. As a statistician, he was precise about the use of numbers and would have been appalled by their innumerate use in the current obsession with counting what are often, at best, proxies for what really matters. Given the inspection regimes that operate now, Deming would have predicted the increased costs, poor quality, increased fear, lack of trust and pride in work, the sub-optimising of individual effort to the detriment of the 'whole' and the low morale, poor staff retention and culture of blame and retribution that characterises so many workplaces.

Toyota's legendary production system is a lasting example of Deming's method applied and developed for over 50 years. Despite the doldrums of Japan's economy, Toyota, which is much smaller than Daimler-Chrysler, Ford or General Motors, has the most consistent profits record. For much of this period, its market capitalisation has been greater than that of the 'big three' put together. The result of the patient refinement of the integrated production and sales system is the ability to build cars at lower cost, to higher quality and in greater variety than any other manufacturer (Johnson, 2001).

The successful implementation of sustainable change is not easy. It takes time and there are many hurdles to overcome. Over 30 years ago, Donald Schon wrote:

> ... established social systems absorb agents of change and de-fuse, dilute and turn to their own ends the energies originally directed towards change.... When processes embodying threat cannot be repelled, ignored, contained or transformed, social systems tend to respond by change – but the *least change* capable of neutralising or meeting the intrusive process. (1971, p 40)

This is a difficult cycle to break. To revitalise poor neighbourhoods means reviving the local economy, empowering the local community, improving public services and encouraging local leadership. However, years of top-down solutions have made local communities suspicious:

> The political and professional classes, who dominate the regeneration industry, are well-meaning and chant the correct mantras; 'Urban renewal must be community led'. But the more I get involved I get the more to feel we do not understand what it means. One disillusioned local group told me that it means: 'When we want your opinion we'll give it to you'.... Kensington New Deal in Liverpool has been awarded £61.9 million, which is expected to lever in a further £250 million over 10 years. But how much of that money will be spent *on* the community instead of *through* it? (Jones, 2001, p 5)

Communities of people in big organisations are as suspicious as these residents, and rightly so. The question too often asked is:

> 'How do we respond to and absorb all these changes?'

Rather than:

> 'How do we change ourselves and our institutions to better meet the social needs, challenges and demands of today?'

A great deal is known about successful sustainable change; the challenge is to do it.

Change that works: a different beat?

Positive and successful paradigms of change put users and communities at the centre, taking the view that *effective lateral cooperation around action and learning can transform communities of place, interest, practice and influence.*

There are new leaders who have learned to create these conditions and who display unusual combinations of toughness, sheer bloody-minded determination and nurturing. They create and use power in very different ways and because of this they may be experienced as threatening to those in formal authority in the old order.

Some glimpses of these new alternative streams of activity and thinking follow.

Community capacity building

For over 40 years, practice and research has pointed conclusively to community building as an essential starting point for physical, economic and environmental regeneration. Trust between residents, developed through working on local needs, creates the social cement for new partnerships with professionals.

Social and civic entrepreneurs

There has been a huge increase in innovative service provision inspired by the efforts and leadership of individuals and groups from within the community. These 'social entrepreneurs' or 'community champions' have managed to unite diverse stakeholders, such as residents and service providers, and find under-utilised resources and funding streams to deliver innovative services that bring users, communities and providers together in entirely different relationships. Where innovations have been developed within the institutions of delivery, by head teachers and GPs for example, they have been called civic entrepreneurs (Wilkinson and Appelbee, 1999). Where all those concerned have a joint stake in the ownership, delivery and evaluation of services, networks of trust are built that enhance well-being and quality of life.

Systems thinking

Globalisation, environmental awareness and the evolution of the world wide web have been some of the driving forces in a shift towards understanding problems and their resolution by looking at the interconnections between parts and wholes, and relationships of subsystems within bigger systems. Because of this interconnectedness, we can no longer afford to ignore the effects of unfettered action on environments and social conditions; we need to balance freedoms and recognise webs of mutual responsibility (Mulgan, 1997).

Joining up and partnership

New forms of organising, such as alliances, supply chains, networks and 'the associative economy', have become the order of the day in the private sector (Cooke and Morgan, 1998; Pettigrew and Fenton, 2000). Ironically, the need for a competitive edge has led to new collaborative behaviour across competitive boundaries. Maintaining competitive advantage in an interconnected world has led to a search for more temporary, flexible forms of organising around 'knowledge-intensive' products and services (Hastings, 1993). In the public services, it is still the case that some partnerships happen in order to comply with policy and funding streams, yet increasingly this new imperative is a powerful source of action and learning. 'Joining up' may be the new jargon, but those who have embarked on it now see it as raising fundamental questions and challenges to the way they work with residents, users, clients and communities.

The regional associative economy

There is growing evidence that regional economic development is best advanced through networks and frameworks of learning between collaborating enterprises and government agencies. More successful regions are marked by 'associational activity, learning capability and networking practices among firms and governance organisations' (Cooke and Morgan, 1998). Putnam (1993) has demonstrated that where a region has high levels of horizontal social trust, or social capital, this will be a stimulant and support to both economic development and good institutions of governance.

Action learning and research approaches to implementation

These approaches to organisational change and development counter the tradition of academic or expert consulting. Implementation is achieved by theories being tested in action by those who have a stake in the implementation and evaluation of outcomes. Among others, the work of Deming (1986) on quality, Revans (1982) on action learning, Weisbord (1987, 1992) on participative designs and Heifetz (1994) on leadership is central to the discussion. These writers share the belief that those who experience a problem must be core to researching, acting and learning to resolve it.

Four key dilemmas

Whole systems processes are powerful and proven tools for effective change. They can, and sometimes do, lead to effective and sustainable change. However, this sustainable change only happens when people are prepared to confront, and think radically about, these key issues and dilemmas. Effective whole systems working involves the reconciling of four key dilemmas:

* top-down and bottom-up
* consumer and citizen
* treatment and prevention
* consultation and involvement.

Dilemma one – Reconciling top-down and bottom-up

Hierarchy in some form is present in all forms of living systems and human organisations; yet, to survive, there must also be effective links between the parts and the whole. The reconciliation of vertical order and horizontal integration is crucial to collective effectiveness, never more so than when survival requires transformational change. The dominant metaphor that informs change programmes is that of the organisation as machine, where performance is optimised when work is specified in detail and shared out to distinct operating units. Whole systems processes employ the metaphor of organisations as living beings, pluralist and in transition and flux. Seen this way, the relationships between the parts are more important than detailed definition of the workings of each part: minimum specification enhances creativity.

The central problem is that hierarchy and order are needed as much as diversity and integration. Those who cleave to the former, with their emphasis on top-down targets and inspection, are likely to have pessimistic assumptions about human nature and operate on the basis of low trust. Whole systems work takes a more optimistic view of human capacity, potential and capability, and assumes that the generation of a high-trust environment is a more realistic route to implementation. This polarity was famously set out as Theory X and Theory Y by Douglas McGregor in *The human side of the enterprise*, but it is as old as history (McGregor, 1961).

Whole systems working proceeds from Ken Blanchard's dictum 'that nobody ever came to their first day at work wanting to do a bad job'. People start from positive positions, but this often dissipates on the way. Following Deming, one of the first actions is to remove fear from the workplace in order to bring about successful change. Robert Putnam has emphasised the importance of social capital in generating trust in community and organisational settings. One of his starting points is the parable by David Hume, the 18th-century Scottish philosopher:

> Your corn is ripe to-day; mine will be so to-morrow. 'Tis profitable for us both, that I shou'd labour with you to-day, and that you shou'd aid me to-morrow. I have no kindness for you, and know you have as little for me. I will not, therefore, take any pains upon your account; and should I labour with you upon my own account, in expectation of a return, I know I shou'd be disappointed, and that I shou'd in vain depend upon your gratitude. Here then I leave you to labour alone; You treat me in the same manner. The seasons change; and both of us lose our harvests for want of mutual confidence and security. (Putnam, 1993, p 163)

Strong civic societies are connected by *horizontal* networks of collaboration, renewed by virtuous cycles of reciprocity and trust. Weaker societies are likely to be held together more by vertical linkages of supplication and patronage as the best protection against neighbours who cannot be trusted. In these conditions, societies are held together by cycles of dependence and exploitation:

> It is evident of course that all forms of human collaboration and institutions involve both vertical and horizontal relationships, even the most participative of organisations. Further, it is almost always a cruel deception, especially in more formal organisations when leaders say that all have equal voices and that hierarchy does not exist. The important question here, is of course, the balance between the two; the extent to which formal authority is seen as legitimate, legal, accountable and transparent, and is used to give direction,

leadership and support to the horizontal ties of the wider civic society. It is the horizontal networks of civic society that give this legitimacy to vertical authority. It in turn needs to foster this by serving to strengthen its source. (Wilkinson and Appelbee, 1999, pp 55-6)

From this perspective, it is obvious that over-reliance on top-down change initiatives in complex systems is likely to increase distrust, promote sub-optimisation, reduce social capital and work against joining up, especially in action on the ground. Innovators employing whole systems methodologies seek to work in the uncomfortable spaces where the top-down collides with the horizontal and networked world of implementation. Restraining the top-down impulse in order to create virtuous cycles of hope, collective innovation and pride of purpose is what this book is about.

Dilemma two – Improving services to customers and citizens

These agendas are not mutually exclusive and can result in tangible improvements both for consumers *and* citizens. Collective effort between service agencies and neighbourhood groups can produce many benefits, including: less crime and vandalism; the improvement of housing and social interaction, which, in turn, produces better health; better parenting and pre-school care leading to better educational performance; more respect for persons means more respect for place, the public space, a better environment; and so on.

On the one hand, there are huge long-term gains and potential savings to be made from communities, service users and providers working together, but it does require long-term investment in both community and interagency capacity. On the other hand, short-term service delivery imperatives, especially for health, education and crime, inevitably drown out the long-term, joined-up preventative agendas. Both poles of this dilemma need support, but the second citizen pole also needs radical institutional change. This book contends that machine-like organisations with top-down ways of working cannot implement the complex agendas needed to deliver real improvements to the lives of citizens.

Dilemma three – Curative and preventative approaches

Curative approaches attempt to deal with the presenting problems, while preventative ones aim to tackle underlying causes. Again, these approaches are not mutually exclusive. Prevention may lead to the eradication of problems, such as smallpox, and the huge strides in public health and human longevity are now seen to stem almost exclusively from environmental, preventative and lifestyle improvements, with the 'curative' contribution being negligible. Sometimes attempts are made to shift the balance, as in the policy slogan 'tough on crime, tough on the causes of crime'. In dilemma two a shift to neighbourhood renewal and sustainable regeneration is a reorientation towards

Table 1: Some differences between consumerist and citizen-based approaches to improvement

The consumerist agenda	The citizen/community agenda
Emphasis is on better services for individuals at the point of delivery; hospitals, schools, and so on. The focus is on what individual hospitals, schools and agencies of delivery do to work on a person's needs/problems as they are currently manifested.	The emphasis is more on building stronger, safer communities as a basis for improving employment, education, environment and health. Improving schools and health provision, especially primary care, is supported by this changing context and in turn helps to support community building.
• works with needs and problems as they exist. Accepts demand levels and increases in them, as given	• works on a preventative agenda, dealing with issues upstream in order to decrease problems and change needs
• tends to focus on improvements within individual services, but also accepts the need for maximising one-stop shops and online services	• works for the improvement of joined-up services and their re-engineering at the neighbourhood level around community agendas
• leaves the traditional relationship between provider and user much as it is, but puts greater emphasis on better customer access, information and service • many service users might prefer this agenda, especially where services are accessible and improving, and they are confident, able to articulate demands and feel heard	• seeks a shift in the relationship and power balance between users/citizens and service providers. (Professionals on 'tap' rather than on top.) This aids sustainability by increasing the capacity for individuals to articulate their needs, and via the regeneration of communities and environments
• tends to lessen the emphasis on personal responsibility. Can lead to escalating and unrealistic expectations, for example, expecting a world-class service to provide aspirin in the middle of the night	• the move towards prevention places a greater responsibility on individuals, communities and providers to work together to take responsibility for the analysis of problems, their solutions and implementation
• some joining up necessary to provide better services within the existing paradigm. High alignment with the assumptions underpinning Best Value and audit/inspection regimes	• joining up and sustainable service improvement initiatives essential for long-term improvement. Likelihood of major difficulties with 'silo-based' Best Value and current performance management/audit/inspection regimes
• consultation – rather than involvement or participation – is carried out from the perspective of the needs and questions as perceived by the service professionals, rather than starting with the users' agendas. However, the terms consultation, involvement and participation may be used interchangeably	• focus is on genuine involvement and community participation through capacity building to develop neighbourhood and/or community interest needs and agendas. Definitely not 'citizens in committee'. Community agendas are the basis for service, redesign and integration

prevention. Arresting and reversing the interconnected causes of decay involves tackling such 'wicked issues' holistically and systemically.

However, whole systems approaches are not only relevant to upstream, preventative issues. For instance, to take a simple part of a complex issue, in many cases better intermediate care facilities, particularly for elderly people, can provide more appropriate treatment and may prevent the need for a stay in hospital or, at least, reduce the time spent there. This can result in a better transition back to the community and can free up hospital beds.

There are three significant aspects to the preventative dimension:

- behavioural and cultural changes on the part of users/citizens/communities, as well as providers, is usually required;
- multi-stakeholder collaboration in local developments is often required;
- the balance is shifted from individuals demanding services as of right towards a balance of personal responsibilities *and* rights.

Moving towards prevention usually requires behavioural change; for example, better diet improves health; observing speed limits lowers the number of road deaths; recycling lessens the effects of environmental degradation and creates jobs for others. A simple illustration of this is people throwing rubbish out of cars, without thinking about the environmental impact or the cost of removal. Yet the same people want their own neighbourhoods kept clean by publicly provided services and don't want to pay more for the service.

> A *public good*, such as clean air or safe neighbourhoods, can be enjoyed by everyone, regardless of whether he contributes to its provision. Under ordinary circumstances, therefore, no one has an incentive to contribute to providing the public good, and too little is produced, causing all to suffer. (Putnam, 1993, p 163)

Moving up the scale, Britain is faced with disposing of ever-increasing amounts of domestic waste. The long-term solution in the past has been to tip it into holes in the earth – landfill. But this 'solution' is becoming increasingly problematic because of public opposition, European directives and the recognition of land contamination. There are three broad alternatives: incineration, recycling, and waste minimisation and resource productivity – 'waste represents matter in the wrong place' (Murray, 1999). While landfill and incineration are curative, recycling and minimisation are preventative and support each other. Murray describes these two approaches to waste management as contending modernities "at odds with each other. They embody different organisational cultures, one representing the old industrial order, the other the new" (p 31). This is not to do with public versus private sector, but with the issue of individual responsibilities – a neat illustration of the implications of preventative approaches for individual behaviour.

There are also clear connections with the top-down/bottom-up dilemma; faced with a complex challenge such as waste management, top-down target setting does not work:

> Recycling is one of those activities that everybody supports in principle, but in the UK it has failed to take off. In 1995 the Government set a target of 25 per cent recycled household waste by the millennium. Since then the rate has risen by just two per cent to a miserable 8 per cent. (Murray, 1999, p 5)

However, governments and public authorities fear the accusation of acting as a nanny state; of telling 'the public' what to do. This is a key challenge and it has its parallels with those who lead organisations and partnerships. In the writing of Heifetz (1994), 'adaptive work' is core to leadership. In other words, leaders have a core role in assisting others to face up to challenges, including addressing the conflicts between the values they hold dear and the realities that they and their organisations face. But it seems that 'setting tough targets' (on things they have no control over) has become a displacement activity for proper understanding and leadership. It also passes the responsibility somewhere else – in this case to local authorities.

Dilemma four – Consulting and involving people

Do people need to be consulted or involved, or both? There are several tough questions here. What is meant by the terms consultation, participation, involvement and empowerment, as used by those concerned? Why are people being asked to contribute? What differences will this consultation or involvement make? And, when organisations consult, are they really only doing this to conform to higher authority?

Paul Brickell argues that traditional forms of public consultation actually prevent the direct, practical involvement of people in sorting out their own problems. Communities become 'citizens in committee':

> The people who attend the Ward Forum, whether residents, councillors or officers, are actually deeply concerned about the neighbourhood, but the structure casts participants in roles that leave them frustrated and unhappy with each other. The residents' role is to bring their problems along and to hand them over to the officers, with varying levels of abuse. There are no other lines in their script. It is certainly not envisaged that they might have any part in solving the problems. The officers' role is on the one hand to promise to solve the problems, and on the other to explain why they were unable to solve the problems brought to the previous meeting. Since the same types of problem are endlessly recycled from one meeting to the next, this can be a challenging part to play. The officers are not failing to solve the problems because they are bad or incompetent people, but rather because their resources and energies are simply outstripped by the ability of people

to generate problems. Occasionally a senior officer appears as a *deus ex machina* to explain the latest bright idea for improving service delivery or for regenerating the neighbourhood. The script says that the residents' role in this circumstance is to comment sagely on the proposals, to own them, to adopt them and to love them. More usually, they assemble themselves into a kind of Greek chorus to rubbish the idea and to give a dozen reasons why it won't work – and in eleven of these the residents are probably right. The councillors' role is to referee, unless the officers are smart enough to make them carry the can. Instead of involving and empowering residents, the Ward Forum alienates and disempowers everybody and the Park remains derelict. The Ward Forum is neither unique nor unusual. Structures like it are strewn across the local democratic landscape of east London and elsewhere. (Brickell, 2000, pp 32-3)

The 'community in committee' scenario leads to widespread disillusionment and cynicism and blocks the contribution of local knowledge and local people. The participatory tools intended to empower people actually maintain their exclusion from decision and action on the 'wicked issues'. 'Consultation fatigue' is exacerbated by the lack of a joined-up approach as each company, department, health organisation and police authority does its own thing. Community capacity building, neighbourhood renewal and sustainable change in general requires people to work together and support each other's efforts. Joined-up action on the ground fundamentally alters the relationship between the agencies of delivery and the public and is far more cost-effective from a holistic perspective.

Leadership that counts – handling these dilemmas within organisations

To meet these challenges and reconcile these dilemmas requires a lot of leadership by a lot of people. They present general challenges to the workings of societies – to the improvement of our lives as citizens. They also present more specific challenges to leaders of individual organisations. Top-down, hierarchical leadership does not engage the hearts and minds of employees. One-way consultation through formal written documents, often written in managerial or professional jargon, is no way to engage the public in improving services or regenerating neighbourhoods. And, particularly for public and voluntary sector organisations, working in isolation to develop curative solutions for consumers means ignoring the opportunity to work 'upstream' with partners on preventative approaches that will enhance citizens' lives. In summary, old leadership recipes will not deliver the agenda explored in this book.

It is for this reason that we see the idea of 'leadership that keeps the big picture in view' as one of the Five Keys to whole systems development.

Yet, it is our contention that the practice of leadership needs to be relearnt and re-energised if whole systems development is to become a reality rather than fine rhetoric and empty promises. In too many organisations we see the spread of managerialist, low-trust cultures that store up great long-term problems for both public and private organisations:

- According to a Gallup poll, 80% of UK workers lack any real commitment to their jobs. The survey estimates the cost to the UK economy of poor employee retention, high absenteeism and low productivity at billions of pounds (Scase, 2001a).
- Organisation design by itself is not an answer to deep-seated problems of disengagement. In a low-trust culture, apparently enlightened changes can produce quite opposite outcomes. Instead of positive, engaged leaders, the result can be despotic little Hitlers. Instead of committed, productive employees, cynical timekeepers. As is now becoming apparent, this new British disease is as devastating for public-sector organisations as it is in large corporations (Scase, 2001b).
- McKinsey figures show that in manufacturing the UK lags behind the US by 39 per cent overall – a gap that is growing. The difference, concludes McKinsey, is not investment but people management. The proof lies with lacklustre British plants taken under the wing of US or Japanese managers; these regularly outperform UK-managed rivals by up to 80% (Caulkin, 2001a).
- A Mori survey into attitudes to change among local government staff elicited the following responses:
  , 74% agreed with the statement 'I understand the need for change'
  , 55% agreed with 'I support the need for change'
  , 52% agreed with 'I look forward to change as a challenge'
  , 30% agreed that 'The reasons for change are well communicated to me'
  , only 22% said that 'Change here is well managed'
  (Audit Commission, 2001)

The quest for greater accountability for outputs and outcomes has gone so far that many people in organisations are drowning in floods of bureaucracy emanating from above, which result in compliance, meaningless number chasing and low-trust cultures. Moves towards whole systems methods and ways of working can produce remarkable results, but they need to be founded on realism about the opportunities for, and the problems and dilemmas of, implementation and change. To lead in these directions takes courage and commitment to two value-based propositions:

- *Leading as if people really matter* – reinventing change management from positive Theory Y assumptions about people and their capabilities, understandings and possibilities.
- *Meeting differently* – changing the ways in which we meet and engage with each other.

The challenge for those in top jobs can perhaps be summarised in a graphic image:

> Our constructs of leadership ... have been built around ... the powerful individual taking charge. This aspect of leadership is like the whitecaps on the sea – prominent and captivating, flashing in the sun. But to think about the sea solely in terms of the tops of the waves is to miss the far vaster and more profound phenomenon out of which such waves arise – it is to focus attention on the tops and miss the sea beneath. And so leadership may be much more than the dramatic whitecaps of the individual leader, and may be more productively understood as the deep blue water we all swim in when we work together. (Drath and Palus, 1994, p 25)

The new leadership 'game' is engagement and involvement, not hierarchical domination, and effective leadership involves the many rather than the few. These ideas are explored in more detail in Chapter Four. Chapter Two explores the notion of whole systems development in some depth.

Note

[1] Where Management is spelt with a capital 'M', this denotes the use of the alchemical and abstract form driven by the MMV. Where management – or more usually managing – starts with a lower case, it refers to an active engagement with the concrete world of doing.

TWO

How do we put these fine words into action? An overview of whole systems development

Business is 5% strategy, 95% implementation.

As emphasised in Chapter One, it is implementation, and not vision or strategy, that is the biggest challenge for leaders seeking to bring about change. Whole systems development is a set of propositions, tools and practices that aims to engage all the people in the system in designing and implementing change. There is nothing magical or mysterious about this. Sustainable change, in contrast to that which is temporary and superficial, is only brought about by involving all those who are part of the problem in creating and implementing the solutions.

In this chapter we:

- outline our practice of whole systems development at the three levels of philosophy, operating principles and processes;
- emphasise the importance of a pragmatic approach to change, action and learning
- develop some principles for the whole systems way of working;
- explain how these are underpinned by five working processes, which we term the Five Keys of whole systems development.

Philosophies – useful action and learning in the context of the whole system

Our standpoint is a pragmatic one: what works best in helping people bring about the changes they seek. As a philosophical movement, pragmatism flourished in the later 19th and early 20th century and is associated with people like Charles Peirce, William James, John Dewey and George Herbert Mead. Like many philosophers before them, pragmatists sought to unite reason and values, and their particular contribution was to ally scientific knowledge and the ideals of human conduct in an era characterised by rapid social and intellectual change. This led them to focus on the possibilities for, and the consequences of, human action in a changing world. They emphasised the need for experiment, reflection and learning in working out what is most useful for us, what works best.

William James tells a story that illustrates this position. While camping in the mountains with friends, James returned from a solitary walk to find them engaged in a furious metaphysical dispute:

> The *corpus* of the dispute was a squirrel – a live squirrel supposed to be clinging to one side of a tree trunk; while over against the tree's opposite side a human being was imagined to stand. This human witness tries to get sight of the squirrel by moving rapidly round the tree, but no matter how fast he goes, the squirrel moves as fast in the opposite direction, and always keeps the tree between himself and the man, so that never a glimpse of him is caught. The resultant metaphysical problem now is this: *Does the man go round the squirrel or not?* (Thayer, 1982, p 208)

James solves this problem by saying that it depends on what is 'practically meant' by 'going round'. For practical purposes, if it means that the man has circumnavigated the squirrel's position, then yes; if it means, did the man ever pass the squirrel, then no. Although some friends thought this was hair-splitting, James explains the pragmatic method as a way of dealing with otherwise irresolvable problems. Is the world one or many? Are we fated or free? Material or spiritual? Disputes about such issues are unending. Pragmatism interrupts this dispute and interprets each notion in terms of its possible consequences. What difference would it make if this rather than that were true? If no practical difference can be traced, then the alternatives mean practically the same, and dispute is idle.

Such thinking underpins the way that human learning has been understood more recently. George Kelly, who developed Personal Construct Psychology from his experience of helping depressed farmers in the mid-west of America get on with their lives, talked about the need for 'propositional behaviour' as the basis for practical learning. Act as if such and such a notion is true and see what you learn from it – what does this help you to do? (Dalton and Dunnet, 1992). Pragmatism is also central to Revans' action learning. What are you trying to do? What is stopping you? Who could help you? (Revans, 1982).

But this is not to engage pointlessly in an abstract, intellectual debate: rather it is to say that even the practice of relatively prosaic things, such as management development, does not take place in a context or value-free environment. It is *always* emergent from a set of values and beliefs about the world and our place within it.

The growth of systems thinking

The way we think about society, the way we organise business and institutions, even the way we think about ourselves and our relationships is deeply rooted in a particular world view that began to emerge in the 17th century.

It can be seen as being formed in the 3-400 years we called the enlightenment. The medieval Christian worldview portrayed a world whose purpose was the glorification of a transcendental God. Bacon broke with this, making the link between knowledge and power and told us to study nature empirically. Galileo told us that nature was open to our gaze if we understood what was written in the language of mathematics. Descartes' *cogito, ergo sum* made a radical separation between the human and other modes of being and Newton formed an extraordinary powerful view essentially of the universe as a determinate machine obeying causal laws. (Reason, 2002, p 4)

This mechanistic, deterministic world view has taken root to such an extent that to question its validity or 'truth' is to ask people to question their long-held, taken-for-granted assumptions that have been embedded into the social context over centuries. For example, the idea of the body as a machine, which can be understood and managed as a set of discrete parts, has influenced and shaped Western medicine almost completely. In the West, it is only in recent years that the separation between mind and body has begun to be questioned. But it is still perfectly possible to work in specialisms that look at only one aspect of the person, indeed only one aspect of an illness.

In the world of management and organisations, the notion of the organisation as a machine, which can be 're-engineered' or 'levered' or managed by objectives to produce change, where departments 'fit together like cogs', and in which people understand, behave rationally and fit in with the part they play, is deeply embedded in our thinking. If the organisation is akin to a machine, then the systems and procedures within it will be developed as if this were true. Therefore, a machine needs an engineer to build it and an expert to keep it functioning. It will behave more or less predictably and it will be possible more or less to work out and plan for the variables (and especially in the world of Management and MMV; see page 5) that will affect it. For example, the current culture of performance management, in which systematic top-down strategies and procedures can be imposed onto otherwise complex and interconnected systems can only be conceived of within this set of beliefs. Gareth Morgan (1986) provides a vivid account of the growth and pervasiveness of this way of thinking.

However, while the scientists and philosophers of the 18th and 19th centuries developed this particular way of understanding the world, it is also from the world of science that the possibility of questioning the Newtonian world view has emerged. As Fritjof Capra describes in *The turning point*:

In the twentieth century, physicists faced, for the first time, a serious challenge to their ability to understand the universe. Each time they asked nature a question in an atomic experiment, nature answered with a paradox and the more they tried to clarify the situation, the sharper the paradoxes became. In their struggle to grasp this new reality, scientists became painfully aware that their basic concepts, their language, and their whole way of thinking were inadequate to describe atomic phenomena. Their problem was not

only intellectual but involved an intense emotional and existential experience.
(1983, p 76)

Their 'scientific', taken-for-granted truths were being challenged to their core by new discoveries, which they could not explain. Faced with problems, which their existing knowledge and science simply could not answer, they had no choice but to apply a 'questioning insight' to their dilemmas and be prepared to completely rethink their previous certainties in a way that has been described by Heisenberg (1958) as '... the foundations of physics ... moving'.

The development of a quantum physics in which the patterns of relationships and the 'spaces between' objects, or field theory, became the rich arena for inquiry enables us to move away from the Newtonian world view – focused on separate and discrete objects – to a relational world view, where the energy is located in the spaces between.

Where the machine metaphor fails, ground is opened up for alternative possibilities that make more sense in the light of our experiences. In turn, the exploration and development of new metaphors – such as the organisation as a living system – supports a paradigm shift in the way we relate to the world. This has had impact beyond physics, into biology and medicine, psychology, sociology and inevitably in thinking about the social institutions and organisations that we create.

Whole systems development can be traced back to socio-technical systems thinking (Emery and Trist, 1965). After the Second World War, UK researchers were concerned with understanding technological change in industry. Trist and Bamforth (1951) studied the introduction of long-wall methods in coal mining, noting how mechanisation disrupted the miners' informal social relationships. They concluded that every technical system has a matching human system and that successful change has to deal with both.

From these early studies, systems thinking was developed as researchers applied the idea, especially to group behaviour (Bales, 1950; Bion, 1961). In organisations, Menzies' (1960) classic study demonstrated that rigid nursing hierarchies can be understood as a defence against the endemic anxiety found in hospitals; and about the same time, von Bertalanffy (1968) elaborated the biologically-based concept of 'open systems' to create the basis for an organic metaphor of organisation.

Systems thinking is rich in ideas. It is a discipline or methodology for recognising the interrelatedness of parts in wholes and for working with these patterns and relationships in the subtle interconnectedness of living systems. The importance of this perspective is underlined by Senge's dramatic 'We are literally killing ourselves through being unable to think in wholes' (1990); and in Wheatley's 'patterns of relationships and the capacity to form them are more important than tasks, functions, roles and politics' (1999).

Most recently, Fritjof Capra (2002) explores the links between the organisation of the material and social domains. Recent scientific discoveries, he says, indicate that all life – from the level of the most primitive cells to that of human societies, corporations and nation states, even the global economy – is organised along the same basic patterns and principles: the network. From Capra's perspective:

> ... the systems view is holistic and organic, whereas conventional thinking is reductionist and blindly mechanical. One sees systems as living, cognitive networks shaped by values and purposes, whereas the other sees a complex system as merely a 'click together' collection of components. (McCrone, 2002)

Complexity science

The field of complexity science can be seen as the natural descendant of the critique of the machine-like metaphor and other elements of the deterministic world view. It is not a single theory but rather the study of 'complex adaptive systems', which are characterised largely by self-organising processes. How, complexity scientists ask, in an organisational or community context, are relationships developed and processes sustained? What influences the emergence of particular outcomes? It does not ignore the more predictable and apparently rational aspects of the leadership and management of organisations. Rather it seeks to complement this by examining the unpredictable and less orderly aspects of organisational life.

> What is a complex adaptive system (CAS)? ... 'Complex' implies diversity – a great number of connections between a wide variety of elements. 'Adaptive' suggests the capacity to alter or change – the ability to learn from experience. A 'system' is a connected set of connected or interdependent things ... [or agents. In a CAS] ... an agent may be a person, a molecule, a species or an organization, among many others. These agents act based on local knowledge and conditions. Their individual moves are not controlled by a master body.... A CAS has a densely connected web of interacting agents, each operating from their own schema or local knowledge. In human systems, schemata are the mental models individuals use to make sense of their world. (Zimmerman et al, 2001, p 8)

The assumptions underpinning whole systems development are congruent with those of complexity science. For example, they acknowledge the complex and paradoxical nature of life in organisations. The value of diversity, including competing value perspectives, is seen as central to success. Either–or thinking, embodied, for example in mechanistic and programmatic change processes, while superficially attractive to the pursuit of simple solutions is a chimera. People must be encouraged to face the, often tough, realities and conflicts of the world. As highlighted in Chapter One, this is one of the core roles of leadership. Finding ways of enabling the emergence of direction, rather than attempting to plan every little detail, is vital.

Minimum critical specification

Complexity science can seem complex! However, the ways it can be applied can be seen, for example, in the development of the concept of 'simple rules' to guide the actions needed within every part of the system, if adaptive change is to occur effectively. One UK health leader has suggested five such rules to inform his own and others' behaviour in 'modernising' UK healthcare:

- see things through patients' eyes
- find a better way of doing things
- look at the whole picture
- give frontline staff the time and the tools to tackle the problems
- take small steps as well as big leaps.
  (Fillingham, 2002)

Systems theorists describe such simple guiding rules as the minimum critical specification (for instance, see Morgan, 1986, pp 101-2). There are parallels between such efforts to guide complex adaptive systems and the notion of 'holding frameworks', a core proposition of whole systems development. By articulating the limits, values or principles implicit in a complex and therefore stressful situation, and by ensuring that appropriate processes are designed to explore the issues, leaders can develop a container within which highly charged discussions can take place. Simple rules are another ingredient of such a container. We cover this topic in more detail in Chapter Nine.

The concept 'equifinality' and its application to this book

Another important concept from open systems notions is von Bertalanffy's concept of 'equifinality'. It means different but equal paths to the same place, or, more colloquially, there are many ways to skin a cat. Marvin Weisbord gives a personal example of how he eventually tumbled to the meaning of the idea:

> So profoundly simple is the idea, in contrast to the obscure word, that I could not grasp equifinality until I read a symposium in a woodworking magazine on how to sharpen chisels. Some twenty experts swore by water stones or oil stones, artificial or natural, from the quarries of Arkansas or the factories of Japan. One expert said rub the chisel back and forth on the stone, another said side to side, a third in small arcs, a fourth in large circles, a fifth in figure eights. Each asserted his combination worked best, some with elaborate scientific rationales backed up by diagrams.
>
> 'This is no help at all', I said to my wife, a ceramic sculptor. 'Every one of those guys says their way is the only right way. I still don't know what *I* should do.'

'The answer is obvious', she said. 'They *all* work.' Equifinality! Nature arrives at the same place from many directions, and people, being part of nature, can do the same thing. (Weisbord, 1987)

This stands in contradiction to much of the theory and practice of management experts in the past, and in terms of managerial thinking today. Frederick W. Taylor, the founder of work study, first set out to show that there was always 'one best way' to tackle a problem or issue. This is essentially an idealistic or Utopian view of shaping and ordering organisations and people. (Although it may not feel particularly Utopian on the receiving end.) Open, or 'soft', systems theory presents different and far more pragmatic possibilities in keeping with our own grounded, practice-based approach to the developments of leading change and guiding whole systems development, as well as to the act of managing in general.

So this book could not be written as a simple 'how to' book of ordered tools and techniques. However, through it we develop a series of core beliefs: simple ways in which beliefs can inform action; clarification of core policy dilemmas; Five Keys of whole systems development; and some core concepts for 'change architecture'. These are pulled together in the Epilogue. There are likely to be many ways of drawing on these in any specific context – many paths to the same place.

Action learning

Before exploring whole systems development principles, it is important to highlight another key way of working, which, for many years, has furthered the theory and the practice of systems thinking.

Reg Revans, the founder of action learning, began to develop his thinking and perspectives in the Cavendish Laboratories in Cambridge in the 1920s while working with scientists who were grappling with the most complex scientific problems and who faced uncertainty and confusion.

The first glimpses of action learning appear in his writings in the 1940s. This was a result of his work in the mining industry and at a time when society was once again grappling – post-war (and after the atomic bomb) – with the profound challenges of creating organisations and societies fit for these new times. Through the 1950s and 1960s, taking as his test beds the newly nationalised mining industry and then the relatively new National Health Service, he developed the body of knowledge that underpins the practice of action learning today. Apparently simple but profoundly challenging, Revans resists definitions of action learning. However, in the *ABC of action learning* we learn that:

Action Learning is to make useful progress on the treatment of problems/ opportunities, where no solution can possibly exist already because different managers, all honest, experienced and wise, will advocate different courses of actions in accordance with their different value systems, their different past experiences and their different hopes for the future. (Revans, 1998, p 28)

He offers the equation, $L = P+Q$, which he explains thus:

> First there is the need to amass 'programmed knowledge' (technical expertise, functional specialism) or the fruits of authoritarian instruction, here designated as P.... But then, especially today [1978 – but no less true nearly 25 years on] there is the need to master the taking of decisions in circumstances of change so violent as to be confusing. This calls for an ability to pose useful questions when there can be no certainty as to what next might happen. This questioning insight we designate as Q; it is something quite different from P, and is exercised by leaders, while P is deployed by experts. (p 29)

He is known for his fondness for telling stories and anecdotes, and on one memorable occasion when he was describing his own influences, he said, 'There are no such things as "truths", only half truths, and it is our job to find out more about those other halves'. It is this search that whole systems development attempts to highlight to tackle issues that Revans felt needed 'questioning insight'.

What makes whole systems working different from more traditional approaches to change management?

There are three core assumptions about change that differentiate systemic approaches from more traditional programmatic efforts.

The first assumption is that the business or service task should be the focus of learning and change. Attitude and culture change flow from the behaviours needed to address the new agendas. This is in marked contrast to the assumptions behind programmatic change, where the focus is on the individual and distanced from the work on business agendas. Here there is a tendency to see behaviour change following attitude change, and to favour 'training' rather than 'action learning', where learning is situated in the group or community as well as in the individual.

Second, systemic approaches are based on organic and living system metaphors, which emphasise the interconnectedness of parts and the necessity of system-wide learning. Individuals are able to be self-reliant because they have knowledge of the bigger picture, which they have had a hand in creating. While some top-down direction and review is needed to check that understanding is being translated into practice, lateral organisational links and interorganisational networks are crucial in providing opportunities for education, for developing commitment and energy, for marrying top-down and bottom-up concerns, and for trust-making, bargaining and deal-making (Pettigrew and Fenton, 2000).

By contrast, programmatic approaches are likely to be based on the machine metaphor (mentioned on pages 21-2 and 70-4), where change can be anticipated and therefore planned and detailed from the top. The big picture is known only to a few central planners and it is assumed that implementation will result from cascading corporate goals into component objectives assigned clearly to each department and individual, with managers coordinating and supervising to ensure the smooth working of their parts of the machine. With the focus on vertical alignment and coordination, this approach provides little flexibility for lateral or cross-agency working. The assumption is that improvement of parts leads to improvements in the whole; but without a dialogue around the 'big picture' with those working locally, such attempts often lead to incoherent or competitive sub-optimisation.

The third core assumption is that systemic approaches take the 'change equation' seriously. This warns that all change involves pain, and because we all want to avoid pain – sometimes at almost any cost – the motivational factors have to be very strong to succeed:

$$D \times V \times M \text{ must be} > P$$

Where:

D = the current level of dissatisfaction with the status quo

V = more attractive ideas or vision of a better future

M = method or some practical first steps towards this future.

And for change to happen, the multiplier of $D \times V \times M$ must be greater than:

P = the pain and cost of change for those concerned.

If any of the three change factors is zero, then there will be no energy for change. The change equation is a metaphor rather than a formula for individual and organisational change, but it suggests a particular sequence for the whole systems development process:

- First, establish a common database from diagnosis of the organisation and its current challenges, including the perceptions, feelings, satisfactions and dissatisfactions of all those concerned.
- Then, design some ways in which everyone can 'come into the room together' to develop a captivating vision of the future.
- Finally, when people feel some ownership of a better way, develop some small steps that will enable movement in the desired direction. (Wilkinson and Pedler, 1996)

This sounds so simple – and as a set of tenets to guide change, it is! In the next section, we begin to explore the Five Keys of whole systems development that will strengthen progress through the involvement of many stakeholders.

Principles – engagement and implementation, not intervention

In interpreting these philosophies, we draw on a range of ideas, including action learning and systems thinking, backed by a rich empirical tradition of practice from organisational development and social regeneration. The focus is on engagement and implementation rather than intervention; on those who take action with all its consequences, outcomes and learning rather than the professional expertise of the consultant or facilitator.

This leads to various principles for working with whole systems development. Beginning with what works for people in the situations in which they find themselves, it is ideas that emerge from practice, rather than theories about practice, which are likely to be of most use. The instant solutions and 'magic bullets' commonly found in Management and organisation development are unlikely to work here.

Following Revans, knowledge first involves the ability to do things, to implement what we think we know. There is value in both the knowledge *about* academic study and the knowledge that comes *from* practice. Particularly important in whole systems development is the linking of the many varieties of professional knowledge with the local knowledge of people on the ground and in the situation. Without this local knowledge partnership in the service of action and learning, the best professional efforts are futile, even damaging (Pedler, 2002).

The lessons of systems thinking are that apparently separate events are connected in deeper patterns, and therefore isolated actions have unforeseen consequences. Understanding such complexities comes partly by understanding how we contribute to our own predicaments.

Whole systems development – principles of practice

In our whole systems development activities we try to ensure that our behaviour is congruent with the values listed in the Prologue. This implies that this work is best enacted by:

• Beginning by listening.

When people and their situations are approached in a spirit of humility and 'not knowing', there is more likely to be understanding and learning. Expertise can be useful and it is important to be forthright about what we know, but in a changing and problematic world, expert status is only fully sustained by limiting one's scope and excluding intractable problems.

• Approaching with humility – from 'not knowing'.

In Reg Revans' terms, this means starting from the assumption of ignorance, rather than from the presumption of expertise.

• Starting with questions.

Useful action and learning comes from questions rather than from intervention, policy development or the delivery of consultancy. The best prospects for changing things for the better are likely to come through concerted and collaborative actions.

• Always acting as if engaged on a learning journey.

Although the problems are intractable, both learning and change are possible when we work together effectively. In struggling with these problems, we are all, sooner or later, confounded in our view of how best to continue. At these points, learning is as vital as contributing. At these times, people work more from who they are, and from the lives that they lead, than from their professional knowledge or expertise. For things to change, those concerned must learn to speak from the heart as well as from the head. It is also important to understand the difference between knowledge as 'know about' and 'know-how', which is knowledge from practice.

All this implies the need to meet differently – one of the Five Keys.

The Five Keys of whole systems development

These principles and ways of working support five processes that are key to our practice. The Five Keys are illustrated below and elaborated on in later chapters:

• Leadership (Chapter Four).
• Public learning (Chapter Five).
• Valuing difference and diversity (Chapter Six).
• Meeting differently (Chapter Seven).
• Follow-through and sticking with it (Chapter Eight).

Key one – Leadership: keeping the big picture in view

Time to reorganise?

One of us was supporting a newly appointed chief executive. Our conversation for the best part of a day had focused on his sense of the current state of the organisation and the capabilities of its people, together with the expectations of its stakeholders. We had considered some first steps that might enable him to think through the agenda for change with some of the key players. This was likely to involve some work on organisational values and the gap between some of the rhetoric and the reality experienced both by staff and external stakeholders.

At the end of the day, as he dropped us off at the railway station, he suddenly said: "Do you think I will be seen as too slow in developing a new structure? After all, most people would reorganise at this point!"

This story demonstrates the pressure on senior managers to be seen to be doing something and to be decisive, despite the lip service paid to 'form following function'. To encourage this new chief executive, we told him the instructive story of the university vice chancellor who, when faced with similar issues, used the metaphor of the need to see where the footprints go, what paths are being trodden, before constructing the concrete footpaths or indeed the buildings.

Leaders are typically concerned with such questions as:

- How do I get this organisation to work more like a big team so that we can be the best?
- How do I ensure that all members of the organisation are committed to implementing the 'agreed' plan?
- How can I get them to work with my ideas and goals?

Most theories, models and definitions of leadership proceed from the assumption that leadership is about getting people to do something. Many leaders see it as their job to introduce change, and in recent times have restructured, re-engineered, delayered, downsized, rightsized, outsourced, run quality initiatives, won service awards, invested in people and empowered their staff. They have pursued shareholder value, created vision and mission statements, written strategic plans, policy statements and volumes of procedures and quality control documentation. As a result, many organisations have endured wave after wave of change initiatives. They inadvertently slip towards Management.

Yet, at the same time, research indicates that most of these change initiatives fail. This is often attributed to 'resistance to change', but these packaged approaches may be rejected because people do not see that they add any value in terms of effectiveness and satisfaction at work. Pascale charts the ebbs and flows of business fads between 1980 and 1988, observing for example that:

> 75% of all quality circles begun with enthusiasm in 1982 had been discontinued by 1986. (1991, p 21)

Some of the blame for this quest for the quick fix can be laid at the doors of consultants, who have a powerful hold on big corporations (O'Shea and Madigan, 1997). Consultants often encourage *fad surfing*:

> ... the practice of riding the crest of the latest wave and then paddling out again just in time to ride the next one; always absorbing for managers and lucrative for consultants; frequently disastrous for organisations. (Shapiro, 1996)

Such 'instant coffee' Management practices (Hilmer and Donaldson, 1997) lead to the belief that readymade techniques can solve any problem with little or no effort required. From a whole systems perspective, nothing could be wider of the mark.

People already have ways of doing things, and they quickly engage newcomers in following the same methods. This is often described as the organisational culture at work. Take the case of a new teacher starting in a school: which are they more likely to be influenced by – staffroom norms or the pronouncements from the head and senior management team? Formal induction programmes usually convey the official line, but the powerful influences in the workplace come through more informal channels. It is from this collective experience that most people make sense of what is going on.

This suggests that while the leader's concerns are valid, they can be more effectively reframed as:

> How can I best use my position (or my formal authority) to assist us all to make sense of what is going on, so that together we can contribute to sustainable change?

Top-down attempts to change, often through a mixture of pronouncements, restructurings and training packages, usually fail because they limit other people's contributions and therefore their sense of ownership. From a whole systems perspective, leadership is about creating situations where people themselves start to form the new meanings. Occasionally, there are times when it is appropriate for leaders to make sense on everyone's behalf – as Churchill was able to do in Britain during the Second World War – but usually there is a need to engage people in building new systems of meaning or cultures that promote improved ways of doing things.

As emphasised earlier in this chapter, leaders especially need to create 'holding frameworks' or environments that accelerate organisational and system-wide learning. Such frameworks reframe the urgent clamour for culture change on a new focus of creating receptive conditions for change, rather than prescribing the detail of its content. In this way, leaders can contain people's very natural anxieties about the impact of change *and* create the space for them to work on new ways to tackle previously intractable problems.

From a whole systems perspective, the leader's questions are seen in the context of a wider set of relations beyond the walls of any single organisation. For example, a good chief executive in a health organisation will set the direction and style of the organisation in the light of understanding about the potential for health improvement that can be reached with local partners such as local authorities, the voluntary sector, business, and so on. Leaders seeking a more 'joined-up' or systemic way of working will also be concerned with making sure that the voice of local people is heard in these conversations.

The new leader's questions are:

• How do I lead this organisation so that we can make the best possible contribution to the improvement of the lives and well-being of those we serve?
• How can I share my ideas and emerging goals in ways that do not stultify debate but assist learning about the 'bigger picture'?
• How do I ensure that we implement the plans that we have agreed with partners?

Key two – Public learning

In the West, learning is seen mainly as being about the development of individual knowledge, understanding and skills. Learning tends to be 'sited' in the individual. Yet, as mentioned earlier, local cultures are extremely influential in shaping people's actions. Cultures can be viewed as ways in which people come together to create their own meaning and understanding, usually as part of an unofficial system. In this sense, public learning is always happening.

In whole systems development, public learning is the central process whereby people create new meanings and insights together. As those involved hear from their colleagues and stakeholders from other departments, agencies and locations understand each other's perspectives, forge new understandings and make plans to change relationships, a collective 'making sense' takes place that acknowledges individual contributions but is shared and jointly owned.

An essential part of this process is a dialogue with leaders where views and feedback can be openly exchanged and new public commitments made. Learning in public, within a suitably diverse community of people, can ensure that the whole becomes at the very least the sum of its parts. This reverses the normal position – where organisations know less than their individual members and sometimes do not even seem to know what 'everyone knows' (Argyris and Schon, 1978).

Public learning depends on leaders, and others, having the confidence, courage and skill to think aloud, confront issues and support challenging views. This is very demanding, especially for those whose previous experience of leadership has been about decision-making behind closed doors. Conventional Management and leadership development does little to prepare people for this important work. Indeed, it often increases the distance between organisational players and other stakeholders by reinforcing differences of experience and language. Managers are often anxious about direct interaction with local residents. If opportunities for public learning are to be developed and sustained, then the arenas for learning across organisational and community boundaries need to be carefully created.

Key three – Valuing difference and diversity: getting the whole system into the room

Organisational flows of information, energy, resources and learning are blocked by barriers between people, departments and subsystems that become detached from each other. To survive, internal complexity must match the external complexity of the environment; only variety can absorb variety. This is the open systems principle of 'requisite variety'. It suggests that any attempt to insulate a system from the diversity of its environment runs the risk of atrophy and the loss of its distinctive capability to adapt.

Yet, in organisations, and indeed in our personal lives, we often seek to 'manage out' diversity or complexity. We talk about the desirability of:

- singing from the same hymn sheet
- getting people on board
- getting people on side
- keeping things simple, and so on.

But in a complex and fast-changing world the need for adaptability renders such blueprints impossible. The ability to respond to complex problems is greatly enhanced in an organisation able to draw on diverse sources of ideas, understandings and proposals for action. To value and make use of diversity, of experience, history, skill, profession, gender, race and community, requires frameworks where people can make connections and collaborative contributions to the bigger picture. Currently, this represents a hugely underused resource in most organisations that have not begun, and do not know how, to tap this diversity of knowledge and talent. This means 'getting everyone into the room together' and trusting them with more responsibility, both for improving their part of the organisation and for connecting this to the whole.

This is not an argument for deliberately designed complex organisations, but for organisations to learn to use all the intelligence and interconnections of their diverse membership. An open systems perspective emphasises the need for the parts to connect effectively and adaptively as a whole in order to exchange services with an equally diverse environment.

Yet, in valuing and making use of diversity, there will inevitably be more discussion and disagreement about how things should be done. To manage this, leaders must develop agreed principles of organisational identity and values that will inform the work of individuals without stultifying their creativity or keenness to contribute. Skilled leaders can bring out the talents of others in ways that produce extraordinary results.

Such leaders look for the best opportunities for building widening circles of inclusion, where appropriate dialogue and learning can take place. In recent years there has been a rapid growth in methods of large group intervention, such as future search, real-time strategic change and open space. (For a summary of these and other large-scale interventions, refer to Bunker and Alban, 1997.) These designs aim to represent the whole system 'in the room' and afford rich opportunities for learning across boundaries and through exposure to diverse perspectives. As such, they can be highly effective as contributions to whole systems development, but without effective follow-through they run the danger of being one-off events and a passing fad.

Some organisations and systems are so split by dispute that it takes much careful entry work even to get people into the same room together. This is most obvious in cases of religious or ethnic conflict, where no one has the legitimate authority to bring people together and where schisms are so wide that people do not see themselves as being in one system or 'sharing the same Earth'.

This situation can arise where there are deep conflicts between stakeholders, for example in regeneration projects where some people want better housing, others want to protect the natural environment and reduce pollution, and yet others believe that the prime driver must be the creation of jobs. Whole systems development provides no magic way to resolve such conflicts but proposes that as people come together to explore their hopes and aspirations and to learn about the issues involved, differences can often be worked through productively. This may involve amplifying the disagreements, so that they can be heard more clearly and used as a basis for clarifying understanding and finding common ground. However, this is not work for the faint-hearted. Whole systems development can be demanding and scary work for leaders – a white-knuckle ride, as one person put it.

Key four – Meeting differently: small and large group working

The need to be listened to runs deep in human beings. It is central to feeling valued, which is the key to feeling at ease with others and to understanding and hearing them. Where people feel connected, they can talk to each other, forge new understandings, and take responsibility and action together. This contrasts with the fragmentation and isolation experienced by many people in workplaces and in the wider society. Small groups are important because they make people feel safe, especially when confidence is low, yet they can also help build the confidence required to contribute in larger gatherings.

However, groups can also become closed – 'us against the world' – and for effective whole systems working two critical strands must be balanced:

- the effective facilitation of small groups with important tasks to do;
- ensuring that this development and facilitation takes place within the context of the wider system.

Many Management meetings originate in a need for the control of daily business, but such formats do not generate breakthroughs in creative and shared understandings. It is often hard to get away from the business meeting with its emphasis on decision and its intolerance of divergence, or for a local authority to depart from committee mode. Teams can use 'away days' to break with some conventions, but there is the risk that they can increase the gulf between those who are present and those who are not. Flexibility in meeting design is needed to get to the bottom of things and to create the shared commitment to implement agreed actions.

Team development or away days should take place in interaction with other key elements of the wider system. In large events, most work is done in small groups with structured opportunities to communicate across the room. The following glimpse of effective small group working within the wider system comes from a large health organisation:

Meeting differently

During a large event hosted by a health organisation to think through and progress 'better futures for all of us', the small groups developed a simple set of ground rules for working within their groups and across the room:

- respect for each other and our views
- honesty and openness – being non-judgemental
- equality – giving equal time to each other
- confidentiality
- listen to one another.

Over two days, the 120 people at the event developed a well-tuned sense of the implications of these ground rules for their personal interactions. Subsequently, the Finance Director suggested that they be used to inform all meetings in the organisation as a way of beginning to shift the work culture.

Occasionally, this provoked cries of, 'Oh not that stuff again!' from cynics, but generally it had the effect of improving meetings and the general ethos of the health organisation. Some months later, the woman responsible for organising a ceremonial ball for 1,250 staff, carers and other supporters to mark the closing of an institution for people with mental health problems introduced the ground rules to her committee. These were agreed and everyone helped each other out, respected each other's skills, contributions and the pressures of other work. The ball was a magnificent success and it was agreed that the new way of meeting had been a major contributor. Now the committee's main problem is how to cope with requests from other parts of the organisation for similar events!

Key five – Follow-through and sticking with it

One of the fundamental propositions of whole systems development is that change is not an event. Current situations have usually taken a long time to emerge, and, even if a change has revolutionary beginnings, it will only be sustainable over time through adaptive learning across the wider system. People in organisations appear to find it difficult to focus on and orchestrate the change momentum over the long term. Some of the underlying reasons for this have already been reviewed, such as:

• short-term perspectives;
• the tendency to see events as ends in themselves, rather than as one part of a whole pattern of efforts to respond to the complexity of the system;
• the separation of strategy or planning from implementation, both in the way key people think and in the way they act;
• anxiety, loneliness and personal insecurity on the part of those in authority, which drive the need to be doing something – anything – rather than risk accusations of spending too much time thinking.

When holistic ideas are turned into programmatic fads, the method becomes a solution to a problem that is little understood or owned by the supposed beneficiaries. As Revans has remarked, this is the danger of 'throwing answers like stones at people who haven't asked the questions yet'.

Whole systems development is likely to be more effective where there is a shared understanding of how the current system works and agreement on what appear to be the obstacles to the desired outcomes being achieved. Having identified the key questions, those involved then work with the available energy in the system to free these blockages by addressing fundamental system problems. Without this fundamental work, change is likely to be unsustainable.

Strategy without implementation is little more than deception. The prizes go to the skilled implementers – those who can turn strategic rhetoric into reality through their social strategies. A social strategy for change is as important as a business strategy. The social strategy often extends beyond the boundaries of the organisation to engage the wider system and is concerned with developing relationships in the spaces between people, organisations and the various subsystems that make up the whole.

Community retailing

A large retail organisation is beginning to recognise that they can and should contribute to the life of the communities within which they are located. To help with this new strategy, community noticeboards are used to encourage customers to sponsor local leisure activities and contribute to computer facilities within local schools. This marks the start of a social strategy to enable the business to play a role in the wider community or systems of which they are a part, in ways that also strengthen business objectives.

People will be successful in implementing change in so far as they can create communities of collaboration, especially across the boundaries between teams, departments, professions and organisations. Collaboration is often required in situations where there is also competition over resources or market share. Learning to work with both competition and collaboration is essential for whole systems work. Achieving this means grappling with two dilemmas:

- retaining the balance between reacting to short-term pressures while keeping the long-term view in mind;
- keeping the balance of top-down direction with the encouragement of bottom-up inclusion, involvement and initiative.

Holding frameworks

Holding frameworks, a notion drawn from psychotherapy, are useful in these situations. Because change provokes fear in many people, leaders can provide direction not by telling people what to do but by clearly communicating the core purpose, desired identity and values of the organisation and the system of which it is a part, together with the key challenges requiring response. These shared understandings can become fixed points in a sea of change, framing the important questions and issues. This allows people to think, explore and experiment with new roles and responsibilities. Through questioning and discussion people make their own sense of the changes as an integral part of the implementation process.

To be able to learn and make sense, those engaged in implementation need to see their own contribution to the whole as both builders and architects. This learning is as much sited in the workplace community as in the individual. Whole systems development emphasises the need to reflect and act together on the implementation of key business and service issues. It is through these processes that people can create the local knowledge that constitutes local cultures supportive of sustainable change.

This is a strikingly different process from the top-down change package with its cascading training programmes. Programmed packages of change designed from a machine perspective, allow little consideration of their connection to any other initiatives or of local circumstances. It is hard to make sense of leaders' change agendas when a number of apparently disconnected programmes are being driven through the organisation independently of one another. Furthermore, when top Managers delegate these programmes to specialists it sends a powerful signal to all concerned about their priorities.

Consistent top management attention is required to hold the change process, with its long-term focus on implementation and concern to promote public and community learning across boundaries, in the context of the bigger picture.

Stakeholder involvement will focus increasingly on implementing strategy. Although this will be mainly self-organising and across boundaries between and within organisations, it is the job of senior managers to give direction to this and facilitate its happening. This is a long step from the more traditional roles of control and coordination. Implementation requires that anyone who knows about or has a role to play in solving a problem and/or creating a new way of doing things is involved and has the necessary tools. It is about engaging the intelligence of everyone on a self-organising basis.

Examples of how these principles are applied in practice appear in the case studies in the following chapters.

THREE

The emerging practice of whole systems development

As indicated in the values statement in the Prologue, whole systems development aims to help people get things done locally. Because it is focused on local *implementation* rather than on dramatic intervention, whole systems development is not a neat, predictable process. Typically drawn in by a person or an organisation with a question, it starts from the problem and develops a change methodology in partnership with people in that setting. The principles that guide the work emerge as 'grounded theory' in particular contexts.

Nevertheless, a broad framework or 'change architecture' (see Chapter Eight) for such processes can be described. This framework has three components: context, content and process. Whole systems development operates within a *context* of change described by such dilemmas as those discussed in Chapter One – top-down and bottom-up, consumer and citizen, treatment and prevention, and consultation and participation. Within this context, the *content* or focus of the work is defined by the Five Keys of whole systems development, while the *process* is governed by some important principles of practice (see Chapter Two, pages 28-9).

In this chapter, through the case study of a courageous effort to deconstruct the old system of local government and challenge it with a structure based on resident self-governance through neighbourhood committees, we:

- illustrate the main principles and themes of whole systems development as they emerge from practice;
- demonstrate that all whole systems development activities are a process of action learning;
- develop a number of other themes and principles through the emerging story of Gladwell – working via 'widening circles of inclusivity' within multiple, overlapping systems, using action learning in the whole systems context, creating the space for leadership via 'holding frameworks' and 'middle-ground frameworks'. (These ideas are developed in more depth in the last three chapters.)

The story that emerges is more an account of our learning, than a cause–effect change intervention of what we did. This implies starting by trying something, reflecting and learning from it, and expecting to be confounded from time to time. It is vital to keep struggling to make sense, to learn, to act and to contribute.

We have also learned that it is not easy to keep hold of values and principles of practice where people have a natural expectation that they employ you to tell them what to do. There are strong pressures and temptations to provide answers and fixes. The skill lies in maintaining personal credibility, while practising what we know works for sustainable, enduring change and development.

The Gladwell story

This is the story of a bold attempt to introduce resident self-governance at neighbourhood level in Gladwell, a town of some 350,000 people on the edge of a major UK conurbation. With many disadvantaged people and alienated communities, the Council's recognition that it had failed its residents was the basis for its successful bids for funding from successive Single Regeneration Budgets (SRB). SRB monies are intended to redirect mainstream spending by the agencies involved so that service delivery reflects local priorities and contributes to the social and economic regeneration of local communities.

We worked as consultants on this project, dealing in particular with the partnership board of local statutory agencies, voluntary sector and business organisations that led the initiative and with an action-learning group of facilitators charged with 'empowering' the residents in neighbourhoods chosen to lead the way on resident self-governance. This story is told from the perspective of the facilitators' group.

Giving the Council back to the people

As part of a radical vision for decentralising, Gladwell's seven-year SRB delivery plan began with pilot community development work in several of its most deprived neighbourhoods. This culminated in the election of local neighbourhood committees to advise the partnership board on service delivery and improvement.

This plan to devolve more power to the community had been around for several, politically fraught, years. There were many criticisms of the local political system from both management and community quarters across the town. And the election of councillors on 20-30% turnouts was frequently described as scandalous. The SRB plan was about starting to do better. The SRB bid was backed regionally because of its radical aims and the unanimous view of the need to improve services for Gladwell's residents.

The community development effort began with public meetings in the pilot neighbourhoods. From these meetings, 'design teams' of local people were formed to engage representatives of the whole system of diverse people, groups and interests in each neighbourhood. This process led to two-day 'big events' to build a vision for the future neighbourhood. Interim community forums were then set up pending local elections to the neighbourhood committees. This process and these tasks were facilitated by a group of seconded officers drawn mostly from the Council.

The facilitators' action-learning group

By the time we arrived, the facilitators' group were already actively engaged on the demanding schedule of tasks comprising the SRB delivery plan. We worked with the facilitators as an action-learning group for a total of 15 days over a year. Monthly meetings, some lasting two days, were held amid the faded municipal grandeur of the town hall.

The background to this work on neighbourhood self-governance was not at all clear to most of the facilitators when they began work. Much effort in the early days went into trying to make sense of what was going on, partly because of the complexity of the system and partly because of the intriguing history of the group. Some, but not all, had met earlier on a seminar on whole systems change and referred to themselves as the Poston 12 after the location of the seminar. Some of these, but again not all, had been part of an internal bid for the consultancy contract eventually awarded to us.

In politically unstable conditions, the SRB facilitators were attempting difficult tasks with demanding deadlines, and were often also feeling personally insecure. Most people had a six-month agreement to undertake this work with the partnership board and were worried about their day jobs at a time of local government cuts. Life in the group was difficult, exciting, depressing and joyful in turns; history remained with us, usually under the surface.

Group development

Meetings were pressurised, overloaded with information and several emerging conflicts. From the outset, the imperative for urgent action created a steep learning curve for all concerned. Members had all sorts of questions:

> I'm interested in community work but I've never been out of the Council, will I cope?

> What will happen when we stand up in front of local people who are angry with us?

> My manager didn't want to release me and told me I had to carry the extra workload – how do we get them involved?

> What happens if the National Front comes to the start up in Gladwell?

> Who should be in a design team?

> What's happened to the baseline audit (being carried out by another consultant)?

How committed is the Council to all this?

What's happening with the partnership board?

What logistical support do we get?

By the second meeting, a feverish concern with start ups had changed to an urgent focus on the next stages in the process – 'design teams' and 'big events' – which felt like an ultimate goal at this point. By the third meeting, we had spent four days together in a little over three weeks, and by the fourth, two members had already dropped out citing day job demands. But by now the group felt less fractured, and more cohesive and committed. Outwardly, attention had again shifted – Can we deliver? How much is in the pot anyway? – plus a concern not to promise too much to residents.

At this time, we reflected on the rapid progression of the group from one urgent concern to the next and to the personal development already evident as individuals tackled apparently formidable tasks, overcame them and moved on. We also noticed how we only remembered what and how much had been done when we stopped and reflected in this way.

Leadership, conflict and learning

This rapid development was displayed in a growing individual and collective confidence. With a much wider perspective, the group had by now long passed the point where the big events were seen as an endpoint for the process. This maturing view emerged in a clash with the Council's chief executive, who, despite the practical difficulties of implementing the SRB Delivery Plan in each of the neighbourhoods, was insistent on sticking to the original timetable of events as promised to local politicians and the Council's regional masters. A series of discussions culminated in a visit of the entire council executive team, which listened carefully and was impressed by the facilitators' experiences. Finally, the chief executive agreed it was necessary to be more flexible.

This episode demonstrated the limits of formal leadership in complex, ambiguous situations where 'learning our way through' is the only workable course. It also crucially demonstrated a willingness to learn on the part of the executive team. By now the facilitators had acquired local knowledge that the team did not have, and were not only leading operationally but also had an important contribution to make to policy development. By understanding and accepting this, the executives demonstrated flexible leadership and recognition of the importance of local knowledge beyond the limits of professional or expert knowledge.

Some months later, there was almost a repetition of this conflict over the timetable for neighbourhood elections, and with the same result. The executive team wanted to stick to the promised May deadline, but the facilitators argued for a delay until September. At an uncomfortable meeting, the executives were

Figure 3: The development of the Gladwell SRB facilitators' group

The development idea
The development of this group

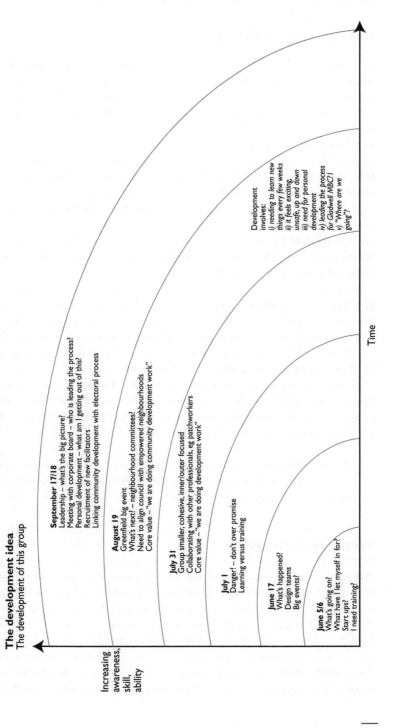

Increasing awareness, skill, ability

September 17/18
Leadership – what's the big picture?
Meeting with corporate board – who is leading the process?
Personal development – what am I getting out of this?
Recruitment of new facilitators
Linking community development with electoral process

August 19
Greenfield big event
What's next? – neighbourhood committees?
Need to align council with empowered neighbourhoods
Core value – "we are doing community development work"

July 31
Group smaller, cohesive, inner/outer focused
Collaborating with other professionals, eg patchworkers
Core value – "we are doing development work"

July 1
Danger! – don't over promise
Learning versus training

June 17
What's happened?
Design teams
Big events!

June 5/6
What's going on?
What have I let myself in for?
Start ups?
I need training?

Development involves:
i) needing to learn new things every few weeks
ii) it feels exciting, unsafe, up and down
iii) need for personal development
iv) leading the process for Gladwell MBC?!
v) "Where are we going"?

Time

experienced as prescriptive and the facilitators were left angered. Later, after various informal discussions, May was dropped in favour of September.

Widening circles of inclusivity

This discussion had the effect of setting the neighbourhood events in a yet wider context. With the timetable now agreed for elections to neighbourhood committees, another end was in sight, and so the work of the group moved on and was redefined again as part of a bigger picture. With the need to widen the scope of action and engage with other 'patchworkers' (neighbourhood-based workers) from all the agencies and also with people working on connected projects in partner organisations, working Gladwell-wide now came to the fore. Part of this was about handing work in the pilot neighbourhoods on to other mainstream officers. This involved drawing in new people, briefing them and enrolling them into this new way of working. Attention also began to move to working with the remaining neighbourhoods. Patchworker events in each neighbourhood were complemented by a two-day Action with Communities event focusing on Gladwell as a whole, which brought together some 200 residents, council officers and staff from other agencies.

Each time a goal was reached, the horizons opened further. For the SRB plan to work, the hitherto single focus of community development had to be married to organisation development work in the Council and in the other member organisations of the partnership board. If neighbourhood governance was to be a reality, it had to be complemented with changes in the functioning of all organisations with a role at community level.

In line with the continuously shifting nature of things, as we finished our contract, several key members left the group and several new facilitators were poised to join. Members of the executive team too were moving on. One of the group offered a summation of events at this point:

> "If a bomb had dropped on the Town Hall in May 1997, that would have been the end of SRB. Now, the names against the events in the neighbourhoods are not ours; it's happening without us."

Whole systems change

Whole systems development involves working with three overlapping theatres of development (Wilkinson and Appelbee, 1999, p 82), as illustrated in Figure 4.

The contextual dilemmas noted earlier (pages 9-15) are heavily present in the Gladwell situation. Here a shift was being sought from the left- to the right-hand side of these dilemmas: from top-down to bottom-up; from consumer to citizen; from treatment to prevention; and from consultation to participation. These shifts imply considerable change on the part of all those concerned – behavioural change on the part of residents and officers, and cultural change

Figure 4: Three theatres of attention

on the part of the agencies involved, including the development of new inter-organisational working.

Conventional, top-down change approaches rarely deliver these shifts. The promise of the approach explored in this book is that it can engage people and involve them in deciding upon and implementing change, thereby making it sustainable. An analysis of this case is now presented under the Five Keys of whole systems development, but in a different order from previously to tell the story in a coherent manner.

Meeting differently

Action learning is often practised with small groups of people in isolated pockets, paying little attention to the wider organisational context. In Revans' (1998) work, however, it is always clear that, while the set is perhaps the critical component of action learning, the larger task is to inspire the wider organisation and system and make of it a learning community.

When we arrived at Gladwell, the 'set' was already in existence and grappling with a difficult and highly complex task. How could it link with the whole system and especially with the partnership board, which was formally leading the project? Bringing the ideas of action learning to this situation was not straightforward. Analysing the facilitation role reveals some practices common to many management development action learning sets, but also some differences. However, the practice of action learning differs considerably here from the normal management development set where there is little organisational contact except through the actions of individuals and the focus is solely on the development of the individual members. Here, there is a collective and systemic connection.

Similarities included:

- inviting people to report on their actions since we met last;
- with others, asking questions about these reports;
- with others, encouraging people to tackle the difficult situations they were facing.

However, some different actions proved necessary:

- making short presentations about the nature of development work compared with day jobs;
- encouraging people to deal with the conflicts that surfaced in the group about their collective task;
- raising the issue of leadership – as in 'who is carrying the mission for the neighbourhood empowerment process?';
- pushing for meetings with the executive team;
- with others, continually trying to draw pictures of the 'big picture'.

In Gladwell, action learning was part of helping people meet differently. Compared with the cultural norms of management meetings or committees, an action learning approach enabled different relationships and a different way of working.

Diversity and difference

Meeting differently in Gladwell did not end with the facilitators' set. Action learning ideas informed the other ways in which diverse groups of people were brought together in a variety of settings – in neighbourhood forums and public meetings, on patchworker days and at big events. The meetings of the executive team and the facilitators' group – where the team came, by invitation, to the facilitators' meeting room – were another example of meeting differently in a way that brought a diversity of views and differences of opinion to the fore. This enabled the suspension of the 'normal organisational operating rules' in order to work from difference and consequently produce useful organisational learning and strategic direction.

One of the failures of the initiative was the inability of the partnership board to develop this level of functioning. This partnership had secured the SRB funding, but with the exception of the supportive relationship of the chief executives of the Council and the health authority, it rarely flickered into life. Developing this level of strategic partnership is a task for the future, for, if collaborative and joined-up working in mainstream services is to become a reality, these agencies must come together in all their diversity and differences.

When diversity is encouraged and differences can be openly expressed, situations and perspectives are often radically transformed. Council officers on their way to meet residents at public meetings carried many fears and preconceptions, only to find that these were mirrored in the local people they met. When it came down to specifics, people were often not expecting the earth, their requests were surprisingly modest and they were often prepared to do it themselves.

While there are usually strong and historical reasons for the barriers and constraints that hold different people and diverse views apart, it is also usually the case that it is these forces that preserve the status quo. Whole systems development is about bringing in more difference and diversity than existing organisational processes and procedures allow, in order to produce innovative solutions, action and learning.

Public learning

It is often assumed that learning is something individuals do – that it takes place at the *site* of the individual. However, this story is a graphic illustration of the difference between organisational learning and individual learning, even when the individuals who learn are members of the organisation. We examine this issue in more depth in Chapter Five. At this point, we agree strongly with Argyris and Schon that "there are too many cases in which organizations know less than their members. There are even cases in which the organization cannot seem to learn what every member knows" (1978, p 9).

There was considerable and often profound individual learning in Gladwell, but, from a whole systems development perspective, it was not the most important sort of learning taking place. Arguably the biggest problem faced in seeking change in complex situations is not individual learning but new collective understandings on the part of teams, groups, whole agencies and networks of organisations. Such collectives tend to be preoccupied by the problems of delivery and control and are not set up for organisational learning. This usually means that if change is to be successful, space or headroom has to be created to allow for such learning.

The facilitators' set serves as a small example of a learning space or 'hallway' (Dixon, 1997). In collective settings such as action learning sets, learning may take the form of a process of social construction whereby new social meanings and realities are collectively constructed (Pedler, 1997). Such collectives – groups, organisations or networks – may thus become 'communities of practice', with shared activities, knowledge and ways of knowing (Drath and Palus, 1994). In this view, it is not the individual actors who are the focus, but the collective relationship of the learning set, and by extension, the wider context.

Public learning occurs when people learn together and when changes of perception, understanding and action are observed by others. In the meetings between the executive team and the facilitators, shifts of position and movement could be seen. In the big events, when residents speak of what they have learned or a senior officer announces that he or she needs to think again, these public actions have a widespread and collective effect.

In the facilitators' group and in the neighbourhood groups with which they worked, collective learning of this sort seems as likely an explanation for what happened as any individual attribution. At the final meeting, the facilitators' group noted these things about itself:

> The corporateness of us ... lots of different people, but supporting each other; it was said that this group was the most corporate thing about Gladwell, not excluding the executive team!

> We are not trained professionals, but people willing to learn.

> Absurd deadlines, just-in-time survival ... several times the project looked like collapsing and resources arrived just in time.

> Individuals in a process of development – this was not a straight line graph, but people were always learning and moving on.

> We handled succession well – key people were allowed to leave and new ones were welcomed and supported.

> What is attracting the newcomers? Because this *is* the way we want to deliver services. The concept, the vision of the people who have the services saying what they want – that's what I've always believed in. We all knew local government wasn't working.

This is not to deny the value of individual skills and knowledge. Most people had specialist skills and knowledge, but in critical situations such expertise is rather taken for granted and somehow easily found when necessary, within or without the group. Existing knowledge moves to the background here, while a sense of ignorance and inadequacy in the face of the task comes to the fore. Expertise in housing, planning, finance and so on, essential to getting on with life in the town hall, is of limited value when faced with those who use the services and are not happy:

> I'm interested in community work but I've never been out of the Council, will I cope?

> What will happen when we stand up in front of local people who are angry with us?

When people take action in such settings, they acquire a local knowledge that is very different from their professional expertise. Local knowledge gained from direct experience of the situation is an essential requirement for effective action and learning in that context. As electricity is hard to store, best used as it is generated, so knowledge, extracted from the context in which it is created, quickly loses power and meaning (Dixon, 1994, pp 71-7). Stored and transported necessarily in a few words, which function mainly as an index, the indescribable mass of data essential to making sense of the situation is not recorded and is quickly lost. The problem of professional knowledge ('P' or 'programmed knowledge' in action learning terminology) is that it is a generalised storehouse based on the resolution of past problems somewhat similar to this one.

The reason why Gladwell (and any other organisation concerned with improving the relevance and quality of its services) wished to devolve service commissioning to local level hinges precisely on this point. The professional knowledge of, for example, social workers, leads to borough-wide plans based on 'sensible' uses of resources from a professional perspective, which when implemented in this locality or at a later date, frequently makes no sense whatsoever. Everyone knows this:

> One Gladwell story concerns the Highways team, which, in accordance with its departmental annual plan, came to a certain road on a certain estate shortly before the end of the financial year. As local government accounting rules allow no carry over of budgets, these must be spent or lost. The team started work resurfacing the road at No. 1 and reached No. 11 before the time or money ran out for that year. On 6 April, it started on the next Annual Plan elsewhere, leaving a new patch on an otherwise unimproved road. The following year it came back to the same road on the same estate at the same time and once again began resurfacing the road at No. 1, this time reaching No. 18 before the budget ran out. A third year it returned only to reach No. 6. By now the patch of road between No. 1 and No. 6 had been resurfaced 3 times but beyond No. 18 it remained unimproved.

Although this story may not be true, it acquires much of its relish because it typifies the sorts of errors that occur when professionals and leaders plough on regardless of local knowledge. One of the central problems of organisational learning concerns how to access this scattered and largely tacit local knowledge of organisation members. The Highways story is replicated daily; it is what happens where there is no dialogue between professionals and locals.

Leadership

The Gladwell case illustrates the value of different forms of knowledge, and especially the importance of local knowledge in bringing about sustainable change. Many people hold the local knowledge that is so vital to effective action and learning, but this is often not accessible to those leading the whole enterprise. It is usually blocked, withheld, filtered out and distorted. Local knowledge is potentially more accessible to an organisation if it is held in a community of practice such as an action learning set, rather than in the 'private office' of the individual (Dixon, 1997). However, this can only happen if the leadership group is bold and open enough to help create the learning space for dialogue that allows this exchange of knowledge to bypass the normal filters and barriers to vertical communication in hierarchical organisations.

The facilitators were undermined in their professional knowledge by the awareness that 'we all knew local government wasn't working'. The reward for facing up to this eventually helped the group in its dealings with the executive team. Twice the team overruled the group, only to later agree with it. This revealed the limits to its professional knowledge in leading the change process. The team did not have the local knowledge the facilitators had acquired, and this local knowledge now proved crucial not only to operational leadership, but also to policy development.

We discovered two important aspects of leadership in whole systems while working in Gladwell, which have since become core principles of our practice in whole systems development. These are the notions of 'middle-ground frameworks' and 'widening circles of inclusivity'. The first of these concerns a central problem of organisational learning; namely how to connect overall strategic direction with local knowledge and learning on the ground. The second concerns the perennial question of what comprises the whole system. To lead in a whole systems way surely means having a concept of what is included.

In Gladwell, we worked to create a middle-ground framework that linked local action with the big picture, top–down initiatives with bottom–up advice.

Figure 5: The 'middle-ground framework'

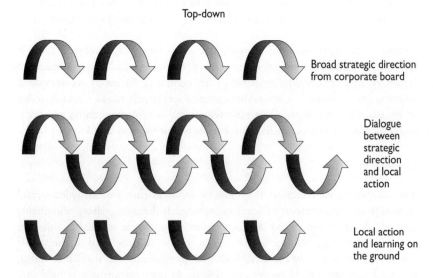

Top-down

Broad strategic direction from corporate board

Dialogue between strategic direction and local action

Local action and learning on the ground

Bottom-up

One middle-ground framework was the progressive conversation over a series of meetings between Gladwell's executive team and the facilitators' group. If this exchange is honest and if both are open to learning, then there is potential both for organisational direction to be translated into sensible local action, and for learning from local action to influence policy and direction.

In the arguments with the facilitators, the executive team held firm views derived from its understanding of government policies and its formulation of strategic direction in the face of likely changes in the environment. Similarly, the facilitators had an equally clear view based on what they thought could be done and managed effectively at the local level. While this replicates a common enough feature of organisational life, what normally happens is that the directors' view prevails and those charged with implementation fudge and filter in order to get by, being selective with the truth and their opinions. There is no learning from this process because it is not open to inspection, question or joint reflection. In contrast, a *middle-ground framework* allows for mutual exchange and public learning to take place, which then serves to guide action, both of the strategic direction and of the local tasks required.

By seeking to work with communities and agencies and promoting the interactive development of both, a middle-ground framework can assist with the dialogue of local and professional knowledge and avoid the worst excesses of miscommunication and mutual incomprehension that can characterise this interface. Middle-ground frameworks can fill a temporary leadership gap created by any change, but they are essentially holding frameworks – minimalist, loose and always being reconfigured. The dialogical process involved in producing them is one of their most useful properties, as people struggle to understand, in conversation with each other, how best to move forwards.

The middle-ground framework offers three tasks for facilitation: working with groups of action learners; engaging the leadership group or the sponsors of the work; and facilitating conversation or dialogue between them. As noted earlier, much of what passes for action learning is personal development work that does not engage the leadership in this way; but without this engagement there is likely to be little organisational change. However, this is not always an easy task. In a complex system it may be difficult to identify or to recruit 'the leadership'. The problem of how to create leadership in systems is frequently encountered, for leadership must be accepted as well as taken. The likely candidates for this role may not see themselves in this way and may not have worked with their colleagues to the point where they can operate as a leadership team. One reason for this is that simple, hierarchical models of leadership are inappropriate in these settings. Here, leadership is more of a relational concept, a culture characterised by positive and proactive relationships between people and groups. This sort of leadership often requires considerable development work if it does not already exist.

Without the development of a leadership group, the third facilitation task – encouraging and moderating the conversation between those engaged in local action and implementation and those concerned with organisational direction

Figure 6: Three facilitation tasks

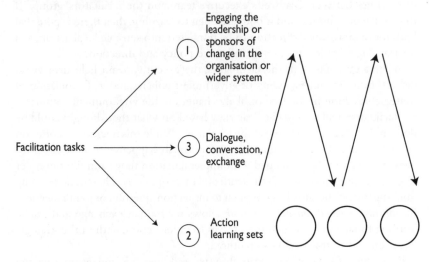

and strategy – cannot take place. The linking of micro and macro, of the operational and the strategic, is core to understanding the problem of implementation. The translation of good policy into effective practice is not achieved either by decree from above or by 'empowerment' from below, but only in a collaboration of both. As is demonstrated in the Gladwell story, this collaboration is no recipe but a considerable practical achievement, requiring resolution in the face of significant differences and conflicts of perspective.

The second important discovery about leadership in whole systems concerns the notion of 'widening circles of inclusivity'. What is the whole system? Who is included? Who else should be here? Where are the boundaries? Effective leadership and 'getting the whole system into the room together' is not possible until these questions are answered.

As this case shows, discussions in the facilitators' set were at first mainly confined to the seven pilot neighbourhoods. Yet, even after one or two meetings, it became clear that these boundaries were too limited. The whole system must include the patchworkers who worked in the neighbourhoods. To release mainstream spending, it also had to embrace their employing organisations – the Council, the health authority, the police and the other agencies in the Gladwell partnership. Later, the facilitators began to receive requests to join from other neighbourhoods in the town not included in the pilot scheme, at which point it became obvious that the boundaries between neighbourhoods were lines on an administrative map and not delineations of communities. The wider system includes business and industry, and the other towns in the conurbation making up the local economy. For Gladwell's chief executive, the big picture covered the whole of UK local government.

Figure 7: 'The big picture' – widening circles of inclusivity

The strategy that makes sense here is one of 'widening circles of inclusivity'. This starts with the people with the problem and moves progressively wider, with the limits set by available resources and short-term goals. Because width has implications for depth and focus, a continual clarification of goals is essential; for example, to focus on the transformation of local government may well result in neglecting the residents of local communities.

Another way of thinking about widening inclusivity is that there is no one system, but many. Systems thinking allows any bounded entity to function as a whole or as a part of a wider whole. Each neighbourhood can be seen as a system. The council and the probation service can be seen as separate systems or as part of a larger whole.

Middle-ground frameworks and widening circles of inclusivity are covered in more depth in Chapter Eight.

Follow-through

As indicated in Chapter Two, action learning is a core philosophy and fulfils more than one purpose in whole systems development. In Gladwell, action learning ideas were first intended to help us specifically overcome a perceived weakness in the tendency of 'whole organisation change' approaches such Jacobs' *Real time strategic change* (1994) and Weisbord's *Future search* (1992; Weisbord and Janoff, 1995).

Future search for example, seeks to involve 'everyone in improving the whole' with organisation members engaging in dialogue with their leaders to create shared meanings, joint strategies and agreed plans for action. In sharp contrast to expert consultancy or top-down approaches to change, the strength of whole systems methods is in this widespread involvement of people in the data collection, analysis and planning of change. A common characteristic of such approaches is the use of large conferences or 'big events' to create energy and commitment. Yet the power and excitement engendered are hard to sustain. A frequent criticism of whole systems approaches is that they tend to overrely on these big events, which raise expectations but share a weakness in terms of effective follow-through to action and learning.

In Gladwell, there were at least three important foci for follow-through development (see Figure 8) and more effort went into community development than into the leadership and organisation development of the participating agencies. For development of the whole systems, these three foci must be linked in the middle ground.

The shared values of action learning and whole systems thinking join a wider consensus on developmental work. Sustainable development work in a range of countries, often desperately poor, reveals that where experts paint gloomy pictures of overpopulation, environmental destruction, famine and poverty, ordinary people can work cooperatively and with great ingenuity to create better futures (Panos Institute, 1987). Similar conclusions have been reached in the UK by Rowntree researchers and others (for instance, see Taylor, 1995).

Figure 8: Three focal points for development

Without the participation of all those involved, so-called major change programmes or 'transformations' quickly run out of energy; the literature of organisation and community development is littered with examples of bright starts which faded. Thirty years ago, Donald Schon noted that social systems tend to 'dynamic conservatism' – they fight like mad to stay the same:

> ... established social systems absorb agents of change and de-fuse, dilute and turn to their own ends the energies originally directed towards change.... When processes embodying threat cannot be repelled, ignored, contained or transformed, social systems tend to respond by change – but the *least change* capable of neutralising or meeting the intrusive process. (1971, pp 49-50)

Learning systems can only develop if people are able to sustain their self-identities while at the same time learning and changing to become more of what they wish to be. In Gladwell, alongside the consistently impressive forces for dynamic conservatism, some splendid individual and collective achievements of action and learning were also apparent. There are some heartening reports from neighbourhoods: of resident groups working in teams, which have dispensed with the need for their facilitators; of local people who have moved from outright hostility to partnership with council officers; of neighbourhoods moving from domination by local 'mafias' to local electoral processes. Continuing this effort at follow-through on all the bright visions is the fifth key and challenge of whole systems development.

FOUR

Leadership: keeping the big picture in view

Our first attempts at the definition of the guiding principles for whole systems development did not include leadership. Experience of assisting with processes of change and learning across organisational boundaries suggests that this was a gross omission. Followers often express considerable anger and frustration that powerful individuals and organisations have failed to deal with issues that impact adversely on their daily lives. They are angry when a hospital blames the local social services department for the slowness of discharge procedures. They are unimpressed with the attempts of the railway companies to distance themselves from the problems of Railtrack. Explanations by car dealers about the impact of outsourcing of parts on the time taken to repair cars fall on deaf ears. It is the reality – the delivery on the ground – that matters. Effective leadership is an essential component of this.

Systemic change will not be effective if it ignores the responsibilities and accountabilities of individual organisations. Public service organisations are the servants of the public, and they should be held accountable by the politicians we elect for the resources they use. Similarly, commercial organisations are responsible to their shareholders. Collaboration or partnership across organisational boundaries runs into the sand if these constraints are not explained to those involved. This is the job of leadership. Leaders must frame these issues within a wider context, in ways that enable managers, staff, consumers and citizens to take responsibility for and begin to tackle these things themselves. Effective leadership is vital to the achievement of systemic change. These requirements are mirrored in the research on organisational renewal by Beer et al:

> Each revitalisation leader had to find a way to translate external pressures into internalised dissatisfaction with the status quo and/or excitement about a better way. Dissatisfaction is fuelled by awareness that the organisation is no longer meeting the demands of its competitive environment. Excitement can be stimulated by imagining an approach to organisation and managing that eliminates many current problems or appeals to fundamental values. (1990, p 79)

In this chapter we:

• Contend that 'hero leadership' cannot be successful in tackling 'wicked' or intractable problems.

- See leadership as something for the many rather than the few 'top' people.
- Explore the processes involved in leading across 'whole systems' – assisting sense-making, establishing 'holding frameworks', using collective intelligence and so on – and some of the paradoxes with which leaders must grapple.
- Suggest that our images of organisations – as machines, networks, jazz groups or flocks of birds – have significant influence on the expectations of leaders.
- Point the way to the link between leadership and whole systems 'public learning' processes (the subject of Chapter Five).

Within the chapter are several case examples, taken from our consultancy experiences. These are intended to make the ideas real and, more importantly, to prompt your own thinking about the issues involved.

Perspectives on leadership – what has changed?

Recent years have seen a renewed interest in leadership. However, much of the conventional wisdom focuses on the leader as 'great man' or 'action hero'. Leaders are seen as larger than life.

Abigail Adams wrote to Thomas Jefferson in 1790 that "great necessities call forth great leaders". Leaders we call 'great' have generally been strong and capable of focusing their followers' actions. Sometimes they have used fear or arbitrary authority to ensure that their will is done; at other times there has been a reliance on charisma and the communication of vision. Implicit or explicit in this is the notion of an organisation or, indeed a society, as boundaried and hierarchical, as a place where leaders exert power and influence. When thinking of organisations, we often have the image of the pyramidal organisation chart made real through systems of rules and regulations, checks and controls.

Leadership has tended to be synonymous with providing solutions. It has encouraged dependence: for example, where staff look to senior people to deal with problems or where we rely on professionals, such as doctors, lawyers or accountants, to advise on what is right.

Today, organisations face challenges to their historic identity and ways of operating. Changes in the expectations of staff, consumers and citizens, pressure on costs and changes in technology are only some of the pressures that force the clarification of organisational purposes and values, the development of new strategies and the need to learn new ways of relating to stakeholders, both internal and external. Getting people to adapt their behaviour to thrive in this different environment is the mark of leadership. No one should pretend that this is easy. In the uncertainties produced by rapid and complex change, there is a demand for leadership both by individuals and by the organisations to which they belong. Paradoxically, there is also mistrust about the wisdom of allowing our individual will and destiny to be given over to any collective, however high-minded its purpose.

In response to this, some thinking about leadership centres on notions of stewardship or servanthood. Here the leader is seen as able to articulate the visions and values of an organisation in a way that is more responsive to and respectful of the needs of followers. Leaders serve followers rather than vice versa. Charisma or drive is complemented by the gentler qualities of nurturing and caring. This quotation from William Pollard, Chairman of Service Master, is typical of the views of servant leaders:

> Our word and the promises we make to each other provide the framework for relationships to grow. Leaders must keep their promises to the people they lead, even if it is at their own personal risk and sacrifice. It is their obligation. To understand the extent of this obligation one can picture it as a debt – a liability – on the balance sheet of every leader. The opportunities, jobs, and families of the leader's followers need to be considered a debt in the same way that a mortgage is considered a debt. It is every bit as real, every bit as important. (1996, p 245)

The role of leadership in whole systems development

However, is this more humanising form of leadership sufficient in the face of challenges of change and learning across the whole system? Are other leadership qualities necessary? What kind of leadership is required to tackle poverty in our cities? How can leaders steer commercial partnerships through the complexities of oil exploration and production in the North Sea? Our experience of working with clients on these complex problems suggests that the rhetoric of change is unlikely to become a reality if leaders merely seek to control parallel streams of activity within single organisational 'silos'. Leaders need to help others to define problems and opportunities, and to frame questions across rather than within organisational boundaries. They need to be able to assist people to feel and make sense of external pressures, for example of public expectations, while at the same time supporting processes of learning and adaptation. Leaders can help to maintain focus on the important issues in the face of continued uncertainty.

Jane's dilemma

Jane Foster has recently been appointed to lead a project team of four, whose task it is to develop new networks for marketing children's books. This is her first job as a team leader. Her anxiety about handling the job well is fed both by the competitive challenges in children's book publishing and by her own experiences of working within marketing teams. Rarely has she felt that her talents have been used well; often her sense has been one of being confined to a narrow set of tasks, closely defined by her boss.

On her first afternoon in the new role, she starts to think through how to start to work with the team for which she has responsibility. She comes up with four options:

(1) Clearly define everyone's role and responsibilities and communicate this to each individual separately.
(2) Commission external consultants to survey the current and potential market.
(3) Set up policies and procedures to manage and monitor the project.
(4) Organise a number of meetings or a 'time out' to agree the purpose of the project, build commitment to it and agree ways of working and learning together.

Which should she choose?

The thought processes that lead to her decision about the most effective way of moving into the new role are that:

- Each member of the team has a clear job description. While this describes the individual tasks to be performed, it gives no sense of the collective contribution that an effective team could make to the marketing challenges facing Jane.
- External consultants might be able to scope the market very effectively. However, the team members all have publishing experience and will have their own ideas about whether or not consultants can help and, if they are to be hired, the issues that the survey should cover.
- There will need to be policies and procedures to guide the management of the project. However, there are risks that if they are devised too early and by Jane alone, they give the impression that Jane believes that only she knows what is needed. This is likely to lead team members to believe that Jane will use her authority over them to ensure conformance with her rules for the running of the project
- She cannot and should not establish the way the team will work without dialogue with the team. Once the team has thought through its purpose and begun to develop an identity and sense of direction, issues such as those identified in the first three questions can be worked through in ways that include rather than exclude people. This will enable the team to use its collective intelligence to develop the networks it will need to complete its task successfully.

In our assessment of this situation, we are working from the assumption that if Jane is to be a good team leader, she must both recognise the distinctive responsibilities of her role within the team and work with the team to ensure that everyone's talents are utilised to best effect. Leadership is not about acting alone; but equally, it is not about abdicating responsibility for determining direction and taking action. Hence, the first three options are all important issues for Jane and the team as they move into the project, but Jane acting alone in making decisions about them is unlikely to gain the collective commitment of her staff, or to use their capabilities to best effect. Equally, where there are differences of view about the approach to be taken, Jane has a responsibility to ensure that a clear way forward is agreed and implemented.

'Holding frameworks'

This thinking is in line with the whole systems development questions identified in Chapter Two. Leaders need to develop coherent frameworks within which people can decide what should remain the same and what should change. Many of the organisations we have worked recently have suffered from what we have rather flippantly called the 'Mad Management Virus' or 'death by a thousand initiatives'. The latest 'management solution' – Total Quality Management, Investors in People, re-engineering, and so on – can get in the way of staff or other stakeholders making sense together of the 'big picture' of which their organisation and they themselves are but a part. Effective leaders are able to see this picture, to helicopter above the local scene, to make sense of the 'mess' and to help others involved to do likewise. Heifetz and Laurie describe this as the challenge to leaders to 'get on the balcony':

> Business leaders have to be able to view patterns as if they were on the balcony. It does them no good to be swept up in the field of action. Leaders have to see a context for change or create one. They should give employees a strong sense of the history of the enterprise, of what's good about its past, as well as an idea about the market forces at work today and the responsibility people must take in shaping the future. (1997, p 125)

In the whole systems development context, leaders must be able to think systemically – to 'map the system' – and to help others to make sense of these realities. Theirs is not a heroic form of leadership. Neither is it a nurturing form of leadership, although there are likely to be elements of this. In order to facilitate whole systems working, leaders should seek to encourage others to take responsibility for their own actions, to enable them to act rather than rely on others. However, the essence of effective leadership across the whole system is a 'learningful' leadership, where leaders with followers are involved in activities to create a shared sense of purpose and direction, or holding framework.

This idea is important. In traditional bureaucracies, leaders own knowledge and communicate it to followers so that the latter can take action. Knowledge is power and power mainly belongs to those at the top. Effective leadership, which facilitates systemic change, creates frameworks within which followers can be 'free' to make sense and take action. This notion of holding frameworks has its origins in psychotherapy. In change or complexity, individuals experience considerable pain and uncertainty. A framework of purpose and values or strategic direction agreed by the major stakeholders in city poverty or oil exploration can act as a container for this complexity. It can become a set of fixed points in a sea of uncertainty. On occasion, and particularly for public services such as health or education, government policy can fulfil this function. Whatever the circumstances, the job of leadership is both to set in motion the processes by which the container or framework is established, and to ensure that it operates like a membrane so that those involved (stakeholders in the issues concerned) are affected by the uncertainties of the external environment in ways that support rather than stultify their sense-making and learning.

The story that follows illustrates the importance of these issues for whole systems development.

'What's the point of getting involved?'

A local authority is going through significant change. It is taking on the commissioning and running of a range of services, previously run by another authority. The local politicians are keen to use this change as an opportunity to become much more closely involved with the local community, to respond more effectively to the needs and demands of residents and to enter into more meaningful partnerships with other agencies and organisations in the borough. However, because of all these changes, staff are anxious about their own job security, including the location and nature of their future work.

Over the past year, the chief executive, with other members of senior management and key council members, has been doing a great deal of thinking and planning for the future. He is all too aware that leadership and the active involvement of staff in change is vital in these uncertain times. The Council's public relations staff identify the key messages. Several sessions for staff are organised in the council chambers. These are well attended. Staff listen politely to presentations about the current changes and the vision for the future of council services from the chief executive and council leader. There is little sense of excitement. Neither is any great anxiety expressed. The staff appear passively to accept what they are told.

As people file out of the council chambers they can be heard to say such things as:

'I didn't understand that, did you?'

'I had a question but I didn't like to ask it. I was afraid of sounding critical.'

'What's the point of getting involved? They'll do what they want anyway. They always do!'

This is a very realistic response from staff. History has probably taught them that, while Management may espouse the desire to involve them in decision-making, in practice they are told about what will happen after important decisions have been made. These experiences of staff get in the way for leaders who genuinely wish to encourage greater self-reliance and independent action. It also demonstrates the challenges involved in establishing the 'holding frameworks' referred to in the previous section.

Possible and impossible 'missions'

As suggested in the last section, an organisation or department's mission can act as a holding framework, supporting rather than constraining the ability of people to make sense of the 'world' around them. The elements of mission are:

- Purpose – why the organisation exists, what its primary purpose is.
- Values – the core values that underpin this sense of purpose, that guide how things are done.
- Vision – the aspirations for the future, say in five or ten years' time.
- Strategy – the key issues that will need to be sorted out to enable progress towards this vision.

You may have been party to the development of mission statements through the asking and answering of these questions. What happened as a result? Our experience is that some exercises of this kind should carry organisational health warnings! They result in the publication of a glossy mission statement embellished with elegant graphics. Yet, reality for staff or other stakeholders may have changed little. Indeed, the communication of this rhetoric may have caused those reading it to be cynical about the contrast between these espoused statements and their everyday experience.

We would also sound specific cautionary notes about the notions of 'vision' and 'strategy'.

Single visions about the future of any organisation are a chimera. The complexity and rapidly changing nature of our world mean that it is impossible to predict with any degree of certainty – 80 or 90 per cent – the demand for goods or for a public sector organisation's services. However, the reality is that leaders are charged with ensuring that their organisations have good plans and a vision for the future with which to inspire and motivate their staff and other stakeholders. What should they do? In Chapter Eight, we examine the use of scenario thinking. Here it is sufficient to say that a key challenge for leadership is to enable the contemplation of a range of possibilities and a sense of direction that moves the organisation forward in broadly the right direction. Indeed, the collective capability to respond to change – to be flexible in the face of external challenges – is a key capability that successful leaders develop in their staff.

From a whole systems perspective, working through these elements of mission is vital to the development of a 'holding framework'. Yet it is no easy task. The way in which it is undertaken (the process) is at least as important a leadership task as the substance (the issues covered). In conventional development of single organisations, the definition of mission is usually orchestrated by top management predominantly as an internal exercise. In whole systems development, definition of mission is *both* an issue for individual organisations *and* for the development of the system as a whole.

There are a number of ways in which leaders of an organisation, often with leaders in partner organisations, can orchestrate appropriate dialogue to develop a mission that is understood and, at least broadly owned, by staff and other stakeholders.

'What's on the Tin?' – building organisational identity

The chief executive of a new government agency believes that the development of identity is a key requirement of the first phase of her organisation's life. She sees identity as including core beliefs, principles, purpose, values and other elements of 'mission'. Her previous experiences of organisational 'life' have made her wary about devising mission statements behind closed doors with a management team. She wants to orchestrate a process whereby staff can explore why they have come together. By doing this, she hopes that people can better understand what the government expects of them and how this can or should connect with their individual desires for their own job satisfaction and careers. Her aspiration is that an exercise of this kind will enable the agency to develop a sense of purpose big enough to welcome everyone's contribution and fully utilise their creative capabilities.

A review group is established to take stock of the agency's development to date and to identify the challenges to which the organisation must respond if it is to establish its position within the system in which it has a key part to play. Chief among these is the 'what's on the Tin challenge' – a piece of work to clarify what staff believe must be the agency's contribution to the system of which it is a part.

The initial thinking about the 'Tin' takes place at a very large staff conference. An activity is organised called 'delivering what it says on the Tin'. Its purpose is to:

- Take stock of what the agency already says about its purpose, principles and working style (in its documents).
- Identify what the agency is offering to politicians, staff employed in the organisations it serves and the public.
- Develop the Tin – a concise statement of the practical benefits that the agency brings.

Staff are divided into groups and provided with a replica paint tin containing cards summarising the relevant statements from the agency's current literature. After reading this, they are asked as individuals to identify one contribution that will make ministers, staff and the public smile. After hearing everyone's ideas, they are asked to summarise their thinking and place it in the tin, adding brief comments about the progress they feel the agency is making to achieve these benefits.

After the conference, the review group member leading this work analyses the data. The exercise reveals a good deal of emotion about what everyone feels they want the organisation to stand for. The key themes are:

- Newer staff need hard information; those with longer service need clarity, harmony and integration in the work being done across the agency.
- The cards provided a great way to 'market test' the agency's key messages. Staff disliked 'jargon', which was seen as potentially arrogant. Some felt that there was insufficient emphasis on the needs of service users; others felt that the agency's priorities lacked clarity.
- Everyone liked the creativity inherent in the Tin activity, seeing it as a fresh angle on the agency's purpose and potential contribution.
- Recognition of the importance of making sense and developing synergy between different work programmes.
- Recognition that the agency must appear to be one organisation but, at the same time, must explicitly value and nurture the work of its constituent teams.

As the review group discusses both the material emerging from the Tin and the process used to develop it, there is a dawning recognition in the group that the Tin exercise is telling staff something valuable about the agency's current positioning within its part of the UK government's machinery. As a result, a decision is made to institute ongoing dialogue to 'take the temperature' of the agency's key internal and external relationships to create a stronger people focus to its image and message. To date, there has been too much attention on the communication of the agency's structure and too little on the values and contributions of its staff and on their networks with other stakeholders.

Chapter Five outlines many ideas for suitable processes to meet this need.

Learning leadership

Where there is complexity and uncertainty, individual leaders acting alone at the top of organisations can never be up to the challenge. This means that they must learn to utilise and further develop the capabilities of other players in the system. People in frontline services or in other roles on the periphery of organisations are often better placed to understand the needs of external stakeholders. This intelligence must be garnered and further developed. Traditionally structured organisations with lengthy chains of command are hostile environments for this way of working. There it is usually assumed that the most senior people have the most significant knowledge. This makes it difficult to listen to the voices of ordinary workers. Consumers too are unlikely to be heard, either because professionals who hold senior roles are deemed to know best, or because senior management refuses to be confused by any information that runs counter to its view of the world.

Getting people to take greater responsibility to listen to stakeholder needs and solve problems across organisational boundaries is not easy. Pyramidal organisations have often rewarded compliance and dependence; the staff of the local authority glimpsed previously are not untypical. Expecting people to be more self-reliant will not work overnight, and leaders must demonstrate their commitment to those who take responsibility to solve problems without recourse to more senior people. It is easy to say that 'we have a no-blame culture'; it is much harder to foster a climate where learning from mistakes is valued, ensuring that those who take risks and come unstuck are not punished by middle managers, who themselves have been rewarded for conformity in the past rather than for risk taking. Where the culture has explicitly or implicitly encouraged dependence on those at the top, encouraging people to take greater responsibility will not be a quick-fix task.

The pressure to rearrange the deckchairs

This is the story of an experienced NHS leader with a strong belief in the connection between high levels of involvement of key professionals and the performance of healthcare organisations. He was appointed to one of the largest hospital groups in the UK, which had a long history of benign but authoritarian leadership. After a year in the job, he reached the conclusion that restructuring was vital to improvements in services. There were too many directorates, and roles and relationships were unclear. He wanted to engage the key medical consultants in developing a federal form of organisation, comprising of six divisions with delegated authority to run clinical services and a high commitment to work together – to be 'united in purpose' in pursuit of overall organisational goals. His hope was that they would see the whole system of which their own services were but one part, working together internally and with external partners to provide the best possible healthcare.

When he explained his principles, values and aspirations for the organisation to the leaders of the then directorates, together with his aim to develop plans for change with them, he was very frustrated at the response. Firstly, many of them believed that he had a detailed plan. Secondly, they wanted him to get on with it – that is to implement the new structure quickly. Thirdly, they seemed to expect him to make the decisions about the powers to be delegated to the new divisions and the central controls to be retained. Fourthly, they expected him to define roles and responsibilities, including requirements for working with the wider health and healthcare system.

His response was to take time to reflect on the things he had heard. From this, he drew the conclusion that he probably needed to 'go with the grain of the culture' in order to change it. The legacy of the previous regime was strong; he could not pretend that history had not happened. He needed to see the world through these people's eyes and understand their perspectives on involvement. Believing that he wanted to change the way things were done, he would have to 'walk the talk', show his genuine beliefs and engage in developmental activities that would assist learning by all concerned. In this way, together they could start to develop shared understandings about agreed principles, values and directions for services.

This is an example of what Heifetz (1994) describes as the capability of effective leaders to know when to turn the heat up on people as a means of stimulating change and when to turn it down. A sensitivity to the right time to take more radical approaches to structural change as a means of engendering cultural change is core to this example.

Is ensuring that everyone 'sings from the same hymn sheet' a helpful aspiration for leaders?

One of us sings in a choir. There she accepts the conductor's interpretation of the musical score: he is clearly in charge and difference is not valued. He contends that members of the choir pay him for his expertise in creating the best fit between their collective capabilities and the composer's intentions. We understand this perspective, seeing it as congruent with the requirements of the task in hand.

In Chapter Two we noted the tendency in organisations to try to ensure that everyone 'sings from the same hymn sheet', is 'on board' or 'on message'. Yet, unlike choral performances, vibrant organisations draw strength from the different perspectives and beliefs held by professionals and managers, members of teams operating in the field and central support functions, and so on. Leadership in these circumstances requires the recognition that:

> ... this diversity is valuable because innovation and learning are the product of differences. No one learns anything without being open to contrasting points of view. Yet managers at all levels are unwilling – or unable – to address their competing perspectives collectively. They frequently avoid paying attention to issues that disturb them. They restore equilibrium quickly, often with work avoidance manoeuvres. A leader must get employees to confront tough trade-offs in values, procedures, operating styles and power. (Heifetz and Laurie, 1997, p 125)

We discussed in Chapter Two that 'Valuing difference and diversity: getting the whole system into the room' is one of the Five Key principles of whole systems development. Most UK public service organisations have pluralist cultures, where professionals have historically held much power but government performance imperatives have, recently, created a managerial ethos. A key leadership challenge is necessary to develop processes where people can learn to listen to and respect each other's perspectives across the divides of history, tradition, previous experience, education, and so on. These differences, pursued creatively, are more likely to meet real needs than is the pretence of agreement. While we all inhabit the same Earth, we often have very different images of the landscape. Only if this understanding is achieved is there any chance that shared meanings can be developed across organisational, occupational or departmental boundaries. Regrettably, too many top Managers assume that people can be fooled by glossy assertions that we can all work together, without thinking seriously about these cultural issues. Their rhetoric fools few people. It is regarded as window dressing or, worse, as a patronising desire to give up a little power over unimportant things in order to convince others of the moral rectitude of policies and practices that lack the ownership of those 'on the ground'.

The courage to listen to the heretics uncritically, whether they are customers, suppliers, residents or frontline staff, and to distil the important messages that they communicate is not easy. They create disquiet in organisations, which is all too easy to neutralise or rationalise. Yet, these voices may contain some of the most important truths.

The capability to orchestrate change throughout whole systems comes from learning to feel less defensive about these challenges and helping others to do likewise.

The paradoxical challenges to leadership

Binney and Williams (1997) helpfully frame the leadership development challenge in two paradoxes: firstly, providing a clear sense of direction combined with giving people the autonomy to think and act; and secondly, being forthright in action and listening effectively to what is happening inside and outside the organisation. Their thinking is summarised in Figure 10.

This paradox can be handled effectively only if leaders are able both to listen and to be forthright, and to develop an agreed and understood framework of values and principles underpinning the organisation's activities. This then enables individuals to have the 'space' to be creative, innovative and motivated in pursuit of both their own and organisational ends. This is not easy but we suggest that the history and traditions of many organisations, together with an increasingly competitive external environment, make it imperative that both of these polarities are handled.

By examining these behavioural requirements, leaders may begin to clarify their personal development agendas:

• How effectively do I listen to and have respect for others' views?
• How forthright am I in my assertions about the best approach to intractable questions?
• How well do I communicate my personal 'bottom lines' about the future direction of services?
• Do people have a clear sense of the direction in which we are going?
• Are their freedoms and their responsibilities well articulated?

The contribution of leadership development programmes

These and other questions derived from the framework should assist leaders' developmental journeys. Whole systems development also requires leaders to set the tone for self-development for everyone. If they themselves are seen to be learning, to be striving to improve their personal capabilities, it makes it

Figure 9: Forthright and listening leadership

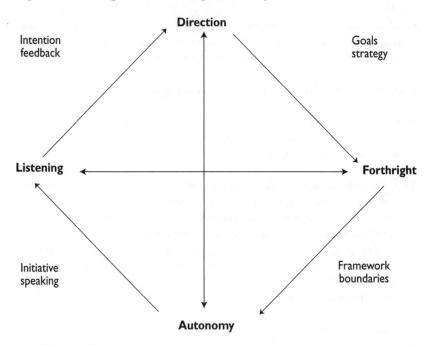

Source: Binney and Williams (1997)

'OK to be learning around here' and less likely that individual development will be seen as self-indulgence.

Designing a leadership development programme

Changes in government policy emphasised the need for collaboration and partnership to improve the health as well as the healthcare of the population. Against this background, one region of the NHS decided to launch a programme to assist high-calibre senior managers to develop the qualities required of directors operating in this policy context.

The programme aimed to enable participants to:

- clarify their understanding of the national and regional policy;
- define the characteristics, qualities and competencies of top managers who can work effectively within this context;
- take stock of personal qualities (strengths and areas for development) and of personal development so far;
- define a personal development agenda to better equip them to meet the challenges of a top management position;

- develop a portfolio for the future to enable them to obtain a more senior role;
- enhance their current contribution to the NHS in the region via successful completion of a project that contributes to improvements in the current workings of the NHS health and healthcare system.

The design principles of the programme were that participants would:

- control the content, processes and pace of their own learning;
- take collective responsibility for supporting, challenging and assessing their own progress with assistance from sponsors, managers and mentors.

The contribution to the workings of the wider system was to be achieved both through the creation of a wider learning community of participants' sponsors and members of a programme, and through a collective action learning project on the development of primary care across the region.

The first programme was independently evaluated both for its benefit to individual participants and for its impact on the health and healthcare system in the region.

The individual benefits included:

- a greater awareness of the policy context of the programme;
- an improved understanding of the current workings of the health and healthcare system in the region;
- clarity about personal development needs and ways of meeting them;
- enhanced networking and relationship-building skills.

The evaluator's report highlighted the somewhat indirect nature of the link between a leadership development programme and the improvement of health. Building a learning community of participants, sponsors and members of the programme steering group was seen as one way of strengthening and sustaining the systemic impact of the programme. Leadership that brings the key players 'into the room together', assisting people to create shared understandings about the causes of ill health and the priorities for improvement, may lead to new ways of getting competing budgets on the ground to work together, instead of against one another. Drawing participants from across the whole health and healthcare system, including social care, was recommended to strengthen this impact. Developing individuals to think systemically can have an impact on whole systems working if they feel encouraged to act in line with the principles enunciated in this book. Putting such individual learning into practice depends on the degree to which the context within which participants work is receptive to change.

The evaluator was more optimistic about the programme's benefits to individual participants than its contribution, via the action learning project, to the workings of the health and healthcare system. Creating sustainable change in this way would require a more coherent framework connecting the steering group's strategic intentions with the collective endeavours of participants in the area of primary care development.

Chapter Eight suggests how such connections can be developed through the creation of a 'middle-ground framework' that supports dialogue between, in this case, the steering group and the participants.

Whole systems team leadership

Leadership across whole systems also requires a particular focus on team working. Single leaders cannot grapple with the uncertainties of today's world. They experience loneliness, anxiety and considerable stress. One person cannot possess all the qualities required, especially where the issues to be tackled cross organisational or community boundaries. A top team that is determined to understand each member's organisation and to work in genuine partnership sets the tone for learning and working across the system.

Dysfunctional teams, where people jostle for position, voice doubts about partners' capabilities or integrity, and lack clarity of role and a shared sense of purpose and vision stultify progress on the very problems they are charged to tackle. They may need to face the challenge posited by Senge:

> How can a team of committed managers with individual IQs above 120
> have a collective IQ of 63? (1990, p 9)

Teams need to develop to the point at which their collective capabilities are greater than the sum of those that they possess as individuals. This requires self-knowledge and complementary capabilities. It also requires humility and openness to respond positively to personal or professional challenges. This does not mean that there is never any disagreement, but that those concerned have developed the capability to 'act as one'. Dissent is not managed out but rather used to enrich understanding and develop creative ways forward.

Developing supply chains

A project manager is appointed to strengthen the workings of the supply chain of a large retailing organisation. She uses her mentor to think through the characteristics of the team that will help her to deliver the project. Together they define that the team must:

• *be representative* of the system, that is, the organisation, including the stores, the depots and the support functions, and its suppliers;
• *be heterogeneous* in its age, gender and ethnic composition.

Both these characteristics are based on the assumption that homogeneity in teams reduces creativity, since the chances are that people with similar backgrounds and personal characteristics will tend to think alike.

The team must also:

- Define the roles of team members so that their qualities (as innovators, coordinators, devil's advocates and action-oriented implementers) can be fully utilised as well as their contributions to the strengthening of the supply chain as defined in their job descriptions.
- Meet together as a team frequently. If the team's existence feels important to its members, they will build the necessary confidence and trust in each other. They need to understand each others' perspectives to be able to disagree with each other, but to still generate creative ways forward.
- Be able to put itself in the 'shoes' of competitors, suppliers, company staff, and so on. This may require the use of role-playing and other techniques as part of the team development process.

The team leader also comes to recognise that to achieve these qualities in her team requires her to strengthen her own personal capabilities. A team like this will be challenging to each other and to her. She must develop her ability to manage conflict and to ensure that some team members do not voice disagreement about ways of improving the supply chain simply in the interests of a quiet life. She must be careful to check that decisions are based on real consensus, rather than apathy or disengagement. Together she and her mentor plan an initial time out for the team that will enable these issues to be explored constructively.

Images of leadership – machines, networks, birds and jazz groups

Leadership of the whole system needs to include more people than the top team. As suggested at the end of Chapter One, everyone must demonstrate leadership qualities. Conventional and machine-like organisations with classic line and staff structures operate through processes of command and control, where power and leadership is held by those at the top.

We suggest that these images of organisations have significant impact on the nature of the leadership that we expect of ourselves or others.

Whole systems development encourages us to think about organisations as part of networks of other organisations or stakeholders. Thinking through the implications of this for leadership is assisted by the use of metaphor. Gareth Morgan's (1986) seminal work encourages the reader to see organisations as machines, brains, living systems, and so on.

However, seeing our organisation at the centre of a network may be a somewhat ethnocentric view of the world. It can imply that we believe that the system revolves around us. Thinking about whole systems development challenges us to find new images for organising across systems and new images of leadership. For example, we could see the organisations and other stakeholders in a system as a flock of birds or as a jazz group (Attwood, 1994). Whatever the image, it has a significant influence on our perspectives on leadership. What, for example, do you think would be the difference between the ways in which the dialogue about 'mission' (see page 63) would be handled in a traditional hierarchical organisation, an organisation at the centre of a network, or one that is striving to resemble a jazz group or one bird in a flock?

In some ways, this is a trick question. In all cases, those in positions of power and influence are likely to have a key role in orchestrating dialogue about mission. However, the *ways* in which they do it are likely to be different, resting on very different assumptions about power and influence. In conventional hierarchies, work on mission is typically undertaken by the top management team or the board and cascaded through the organisation. Attempts are often made to get staff, and sometimes key external stakeholders, 'on board' through formal and informal communication processes or through training events.

Seeing an organisation as the centre of a network may encourage management to bring the views of partner organisations and local people on mission. However, it is likely that defining the various components of mission will be seen as an internal activity; external perspectives will be seen as useful but will be received and accepted or rejected depending on the assumptions and aspirations of the internal players.

Viewing an organisation as part of a flock of birds is congruent with whole systems development principles. Here the assumption is likely to be that leaders of individual organisations will tackle the process of orchestrating the asking and answering of these questions throughout their organisations in ways that attempt to include staff as internal stakeholders from the outset. *And* they will be conscious of the need to engage in dialogue with other 'birds' about the primary purpose of the 'flock', its direction of flight and so on. They will do this in ways that are sensitive to the individual characteristics of each 'bird'. Indeed, to complicate the metaphor, they will recognise that each bird is and is not a member of the flock: each has its own identity and internal dynamics. Flying as part of the flock cannot always be guaranteed! However, there is a shared understanding that the capabilities of the flock are much greater than those that individual birds can achieve alone. The flock is also perceived to act as a source of help and support in times of difficulty.

When listening to a good jazz group, it is apparent that every player is a great musician. However, it is the overall effect of the group that strikes you most of the time. Although many of the melodies may be familiar, the group's improvisation will also be impressive, as will be the excellence of individual solos. The implications for perspectives on leadership of this organisational metaphor may be:

- a valuing of difference and diversity – the capabilities of the different performers – within the overall identity and style of the group;
- the recognition that at times the music will sound discordant – that conflict or apparent conflict is inevitable;
- encouragement of emergent direction rather than a fixed score from which to play;
- receptiveness to external influences – requests from the audience or even a welcoming of another performer's desire to join in.

You will have other ideas to add. The flock of birds imagery can be developed similarly.

Looking at organisations through different lenses such as those suggested here assists our understanding of the challenges of organisational change for the personal behaviour of those in leadership roles. For example, if top managers accept that a machine-like, hierarchical and boundaried perspective on organisational life places impossible pressures on themselves and their colleagues to be all seeing and all knowing about the external world *and* the internal climate, they may start to utilise the imagery of networks and partnerships to describe the leadership task. This, in its turn, is likely to have an impact both on their tendency to listen to others' views and their commitment to create vision and direction more inclusively.

Our images of organisations and of their place within the system impacts on our understanding of the ways in which improvements to services or products can be made and of definitions of leadership and requirements of leaders. It is important to recognise the value of assisting people to create their own images and shared meanings through which partnerships and networks can be developed. Images invented elsewhere will not have the same power and resonance combined with personal experiences and motivations. The images depicted here of birds and jazz groups may stimulate your thinking about the systems you would like to play a part in improving. The processes you use will be more effective if you encourage people to create their own metaphors for organisations and for the system itself. Action plans to strengthen the whole will be enriched by the exploration of the themes emerging from the use of metaphors. In the case of flocks of birds and jazz groups, these would include:

- the idea of being sufficiently flexible, or even chameleon-like, to be able to work together while maintaining separate identities;
- the apparent contradiction of being leaderless as a collective, while taking the lead when circumstances demand;
- the idea that from diversity and autonomy, within the bounds of a shared sense of mission, come creativity and effective performance in pursuit of common aims.

For leaders, these themes suggest that the task is far from simple – there are no easy or fixed solutions. Leadership of an organisation seeking to improve its contribution to the system of which it is a part is very different from that required to direct from the top of a conventional hierarchy. It requires much more effort to assist people to understand the complexity and rapidly changing nature of the world beyond the organisation and to help them play their part in improving the whole, rather than defending comfortable territory over which their organisation may have control. It requires leaders to put in place processes that can help people to learn and work together to improve the system of which they are a part. This is the topic of Chapter Five, Public learning.

FIVE

Public learning

The story of Gladwell in Chapter Three illustrated that organisational learning:

> ... is not the same thing as individual learning, even when the individuals who learn are members of the organisation. There are too many cases in which organisations know less than their members. There are even cases in which the organisation cannot seem to learn what every member knows. (Argyris and Schon, 1978, p 9)

If this is true for the state of collective knowledge in organisations, it is even truer of systems. Separated by the boundaries of organisations, and with different ways of seeing based on culture, tradition and experience, people find it difficult, if not impossible, to create the shared meanings necessary to grapple effectively with the issues facing organisations as they strive to serve customers, communities and individual citizens more effectively. As a society, we have invested massively in transferring knowledge about how to organise health and social care, housing, education and other public services. Think about all the education and training processes devoted to these ends. However, most of this wisdom is created and disseminated through the separate silos of higher education institutions and professional bodies. Historically, academically, professionally and managerially, there has been territoriality or a tendency to look inward rather than to consider what to share with others so that understanding can be strengthened. "The world has problems, but universities have departments" (Brewer, 1999, p 328). We lack ways of connecting knowledge, which would assist understanding of ways in which changes in one part of society impact elsewhere. Yet, ironically, the need to develop this connectedness has never been greater. The 'closely coupled' nature of society means that changes introduced in one place quickly have an impact elsewhere.

This affects all of us. For example, the culture of long hours and the stress experienced by many parents leads to the development of 'parental time deficit', where insufficient time is spent with children. Even when families have time together, parents can be tired and stressed, with obvious consequences for the development of their children. Alongside this, many schools are reporting increased exclusions of pupils because of unacceptably disruptive behaviour. This is not just a response to the publication of league tables of exam performance. It is a result of the behavioural difficulties exhibited by some children whose parents are ill-tempered, tired and anxious about job security. Little wonder that teacher retention is an increasing problem. The long hours culture also impacts on community development. It is difficult for those working very long hours and travelling long distances to work to participate in community activities. Participants in local community organisations are increasingly comprised of those who are not in paid employment. This has implications for the life and vibrancy of local communities. On the face of it, these social factors are not the business of employers. Yet, employees with family problems or sterile lives may not contribute fully at work. A civilised society must have the capacity to understand. E.M. Forster's phrase 'only connect' has particular poignancy at the beginning of a new millennium.

A more obvious arena for learning across boundaries in the world of work is that of partnerships and other collaborative arrangements between organisations. For example, Carlisle and Parker argue that there is:

> ... a powerful case for concluding that cooperation between customer and key supplier is a far better strategy for attracting ... preferential treatment (from key suppliers) than the more traditional adversarial approach which may have produced regular short term advantages – but only so long as all customer forms played by roughly the same rules. (1989, p 169)

Private sector organisations have learnt the importance of consortia and partnerships to handle large contracts. Public services have been slow to learn these lessons.

In this chapter we:

- Examine how public learning about the impact of the long hours culture or the benefits of partnerships occurs when those who have a stake in the issue under consideration create new meanings and insights about it together.
- Explore ways in which such processes, in which those involved hear their colleagues and stakeholders from other departments, agencies and locations understand each other's perspectives, can forge new understandings by stimulating a collective 'making sense' that acknowledges individual contributions, but is shared and jointly owned.

Measurement of organisational performance and its impact on learning

Developed societies place a great deal of emphasis on measuring organisational performance. In the private sector, much of this focuses on the financial bottom line. Performance criteria for public services are more complex. Often they are comparative – hospital waiting lists and school league tables are two examples. Inspection and accreditation accompany such measurement in both sectors. But how much learning results from processes of inspection or accreditation? Too often, those who are measured and found wanting fight back with defensive criticism of the measurements, or they bury the evidence of their errors or weaknesses. The end result is rarely a positive approach to studying ways of improving – to developing a culture of learning and inquiry, where both good and not so good practices are seen as food for thought, rather than the focus of judgement, 'of naming and shaming'.

Emphasis on performance measurement, monitoring and standard setting, while important in ensuring accountability for the use of resources, both human and financial, does not hold the key to organisational or systemic learning. For example, recording the numbers attending a training course can at best only be a very crude proxy for changes in collective capability. While it is not possible to learn without an active process of 'measuring', or taking stock of experience, reflecting on the findings and thinking through ways of improvement, measurement without learning is a waste of endeavour.

The challenge is in creating the potential for learning in organisations *and* throughout the systems of which they are a part.

We so often think of learning as an activity centred on individuals. For example, as suggested in Chapter Four, leadership development often rests on assumptions about 'heroic' leaders. Training courses focus on the development of individual competencies. Yet, complex problems require a more collective process: in this case, 'many hands (can) make light(er) work'. Regrettably, it is often the case that people and groups learn within the 'boxes' of their immediate experience – in their own teams, departments, occupational or professional groups. Genuine aspirations to improve the quality of life of customers or citizens is often thwarted by the lack of connection with people occupying other 'boxes' – across the artificial boundaries of work units or organisations. The challenge is to design processes that enable people to learn together (see Chapters Eight and Nine).

We believe that, if people can identify what inhibits and what assists learning within organisations and across systems, they will be in a better position to design the conditions necessary for effective public learning.

Inhibitors of organisational learning

Within organisations, learning is often inhibited by:

- the anxiety and insecurity of those involved, which can make them reluctant to share knowledge and experience;
- the failure to treat staff as an intelligent and capable resource;
- the convergent thinking of some key groups, such as professionals, who habitually narrow down options to reach fixed solutions to intractable problems, which often do not work;
- organisations structured too much in 'silos': departments, functions and directorates with win–lose behaviour and inadequate communication across these divisions;
- rigid rules and procedures governing work;
- too much reliance on changing by restructuring or other 'engineering' approaches;

- a culture focused on achieving short-term results rather than on processes to achieve future vision;
- it's so much easier in Cleckhuddersfax; it's much more difficult here.

The power corridor

We were interviewing as part of the preparatory work for a conference involving all staff in one section of the Department of Health. Staff were telling us about their experience of work. One of the recurrent themes was the 'power corridor' inhabited by the directors, who were described as rushing along it as if dealing with the crises experienced by clinical staff in acute hospitals!

In understanding this story, we are reminded of Harrison and Dawes' description of workaholism as having its roots in:

> ... the pain of loneliness and disconnection from others; the fear of failure and inadequacy: and the despair and shame in putting one's energy, talent and creativity into an economic system that each of us intuitively know is destructive of human health and human values because it is ecologically unsustainable.

> The pain ... is eased by activity and especially by activity involving high drama. (1994, p 199)

No wonder some parents have problems with their children when this is their experience of working life.

The penultimate item on the previous list is particularly important. At the end of Chapter Four, you were encouraged to see organisations as part of networks or, indeed, metaphorically as living organisms. When organisations are seen as machines, in which restructuring is a main driver of change, there is little mention of learning. Reframing the ways in which we see organisations is usually necessary if we are to be able to think creatively about how to design processes for working and learning together effectively.

Can you identify blocks to organisational learning where you work?

We suggest that you now consider the ways in which these factors manifest themselves in organisations with which you are familiar.

- Which of the inhibitors to learning listed previously are most characteristic of your organisation?
- Which of these could you personally most influence?
- What do you think may be the three most important causes of this problem?
- How would other key players (staff, trades unions, managers, directors, customers or clients) see the problem?

Later in this chapter, suggestions are made about bringing people 'into the room together' to share perspectives and develop understanding about ways of unblocking the blockages. It may be helpful to give some initial thought to this now and to compare your own thinking with the experiences related later.

Inhibitors of learning across whole systems

Learning also takes place at the level of the whole system. Some of the blocks to systemic learning are:

- hierarchical or institutional images of single organisations as the most important places to site learning;
- difficulties in assisting people to make sense of their own roles, relationships and responsibilities as part of a wider set of community, work or other relationships;
- the lack of a 'holding framework' of purposes, principles, values and direction;
- confusion caused by rhetoric about joined-up purpose, mission and values, but a reality of competitive relationships between the organisations and the individuals within them;
- too much MMV (see Chapter One, page 5).

The rhetoric and the reality of a charitable partnership

Two independent charitable organisations, one concerned with the provision of supported housing for vulnerable people and the other with service provision, decide to form a partnership. The formal motives are economies of scale and greater competitiveness, together with a genuine desire to meet user needs. The two organisations jointly commission consultants to assess whether the benefits are likely to be delivered in practice. Based on their recommendation, a steering group of senior managers is formed to establish the partnership. An early product of their deliberations is a statement of vision and values underpinning the collaboration. However, in private, some of those involved criticised key individuals in the other organisation. There are signs that the partnership is rhetoric. The reality is mistrust, lack of respect and defence of sectional interests.

Other factors that frustrate learning across whole systems

There are a number of factors that result in deficiences in organisational learning:

- the inadequate use of the intelligence of people in 'boundary roles' on the edge of organisations about the wider environment;
- insufficient attention to the ways in which stakeholders can come to understand and value their interdependence;

- failure to develop ways in which everyone can contribute to thinking about the current and future workings of the whole;
- little or no investment in collective learning across the system.

The disillusionment of users in these charitable organisations

There is another regrettable angle on the partnership story related previously. Both organisations are committed to user involvement in their decision-making. When the formal partnership is created, a user group is set up to advise the steering group. As this group starts to experience difficulties in establishing the mutual trust necessary to make the partnership a reality, the members turn inward, focusing on their own difficulties. The user group ceases to be convened formally, but expectations had been raised by the early pronouncements from both organisations. Angry users get together and voice their mistrust through the slogan 'Nothing about us without us'. They demand to have access to the chief executives of both organisations and membership of the steering group. The partnership starts to make better progress when, due to the users' interventions, the managers realise that their actions are damaging the very people in whose interests they had formed the collaboration.

Can you identify blocks to systemic learning in contexts with which you are familiar?

Earlier, you were encouraged to identify the blocks to learning in organisations with which you are familiar. It is now time to consider some of the factors that inhibit learning about issues that cross organisational, community or occupational boundaries.

- Which of the blocks to learning listed on page 80 are most characteristic of a system with which you are familiar?
- Which of these could you personally most influence?
- What do you think may be the three most important causes of this problem?
- How would other key players (staff, trades unions, managers or directors in your own organisation; staff, trades unions, managers or directors in your other organisations; customers; service users; members of the community) see the problem?

What are your initial ideas about the ways in which you might bring these people 'into the room together' to share perspectives and develop understanding about ways of strengthening learning between them and other people within the system? Imagine the kinds of conversations you would need to have with some of those involved to persuade them to come together to work through their different perspectives on a problem and to decide on the actions to take next.

Blocks to organisational and systemic learning – a summary

Implicit in this chapter are particular facets of the ways in which learning to change is often handled. Firstly, there tends to be a heavy reliance on 'experts' – consultants and academics. These are people with credibility, who are worldly enough to provide external legitimisation, but who often remain too close to the issues to be able to challenge the status quo effectively. The result may be the illusion of learning to change, while ensuring that thinking and action remains limited to modifications within the current paradigm.

Secondly, there is a propensity towards programmatic change from the top down. While this may require new routines and skills, it does not fully utilise the capabilities of those involved to develop new external networks and other ways of working across current boundaries.

Thirdly, learning is perceived as an individual rather than a collective activity. Emphasis is placed on the development of individual competencies and processes for their assessment. It is not relational learning about connections between people and organisations: it is private rather than public. The individuals may learn (and get increasingly frustrated), but whole systems working and learning in public continues to be weak or absent.

Frustrated programme participants

One arm of a government agency whose mission is to improve joined-up working runs training programmes to enhance the competencies of key individuals in whole systems working. In a review of this work, one trainer is heard to remark:

> We get very positive feedback from the majority of participants at the end of our programmes. The trouble is that when they return to work, they get frustrated when trying to put their new learning into practice.

An interesting discussion follows about whether the agency is relying too much on individual development to improve the workings of the whole system. What could be done to integrate work and learning in ways that contribute to the strengthening of the whole?

Encouraging collective learning – a more positive perspective

The previous sections may have given the impression that the only way to strengthen learning processes in organisations and across whole systems is by removing the blocks. However, while superficially attractive, this 'Dynarod' approach is not the only way. Indeed, working only on the obstacles may act to increase resistance to change: it is also important to build on the things that are already helping organisations and systems to work well. For example, in the story about service user involvement, the users' determination to have their voices heard acts as a stimulus to the managers to act with greater integrity. The sorts of factors that are potential 'aids' to learning in organisations and across systems are often the opposite of the blocks and are likely to include:

- Leadership that can articulate the mission, values and so on, that underpin the activities of an organisation or that bind people together across organisational, community and other boundaries.
- The commitment of individuals and groups to serve customers, citizens or other stakeholders.
- Information that suggests better ways of meeting needs.
- Challenges (market pressures, legal changes, new government policies, changed expectations by staff) that create the realisation that the status quo is no longer an option.

Thinking and acting differently

In our experience, assisting the stakeholders to think and therefore to act differently on a 'wicked' problem, is a very significant prompt to organisational and systemic learning.

Many of us have become proficient at 'single-loop learning' (Bateson, 1972; Argyris and Schon, 1978). We have developed the ability to scan the external realities, to set objectives and to monitor performance using modes of thinking and operating that leave the underlying assumptions unchanged. This is predominantly error detection learning.

For example, when an organisation loses a number of employment tribunal cases because of the failure to follow its own internal disciplinary procedures, questions are likely to be asked about what is going wrong. Single-loop learning processes would probably identify such things as the need to apply the procedures more rigorously and the need for more careful record keeping on the part of managers. Steps would be taken to ensure that these errors were rectified.

By contrast, double-loop learning would be stimulated by questions such as:

- How might we manage staff performance more effectively?
- What could we do to encourage staff to feel more valued and committed, reducing the need to take disciplinary action?
- What impact would any changes have on our customers?

Exploring these issues begins to address the ways in which organisational learning occurs. As people start to understand each others' personal and organisational histories and 'worlds', to share perspectives on the issues facing them and to explore possible ways of tackling such issues, so they develop their capability to review and challenge established values and norms. In the process, their assumptions or 'theories-in-use' are changed.

In whole systems development, public learning processes strengthen the collective capacity and capability to reflect and to respond more effectively. This is not training to develop the individual skills that management or experts have decided people need. It is a collective process that assists people to make sense of things together.

Making sense together – the broad questions to address

As implied previously, public learning is at its best when we create the circumstances in which people feel able to:

- tell each other their stories of the past;
- engage in dialogue about their perspectives on the present;
- create 'stories of the future' – aspirations about what something better would be like;
- agree ways of beginning to move forward together.

This builds on the discussion of the change equation as an important way of thinking about systemic change (Chapter Two). Here we add to one of its dimensions – the need to focus on the status quo – with comments on the importance of history.

Honouring the past

J.F. Kennedy is reputed to have said, "Those who forget the past are destined to relive it".

Exploring the past together is an important foundation for public learning. Failing to attend to people's personal and organisational histories can be very damaging, making it almost impossible to work together to create new services or products. At worst, people exhibit 'survivor syndrome' – keeping their heads below the parapet in the belief that speaking out of turn may lead to their being 'shot'. However, when we work together to understand the past, we develop a sense of community where we can begin to take risks and work creatively – using double-loop learning – to build better futures for all of us.

Building a better business school

The business school of a major UK university decides to institute a major review of its effectiveness. As part of the review, a workshop is held to explore:

- how creativity, innovation and learning was managed during the various phases in the development of the school;
- how it is managed now;

Table 2: Comparing the UK higher education system: 1945 and 2001

1945	2001
14 UK universities	104 UK universities
No adverts for jobs or courses	Profusion of adverts for jobs and courses
No departmental strategies	All universities and individual departments required to have a business strategy
Very limited higher education infrastructure	Massive higher education infrastructure
Narrow homogenous studentship	Highly heterogeneous studentship

- how participants feel it should be managed in the future if the school is to respond more effectively to challenges, both internal to the university and external.

It quickly emerges that those present have different perceptions of the issues and that a major variable affecting these is the length of time that people have spent in the school.

This leads to a sketching of perspectives on the history of the UK higher education system. For example, comparing 1945 and 2001 reveals some interesting contrasts.

The workshop participants then examine the history of the school, founded about 15 years ago, in the light of these national changes. At the time the school was founded, there were no formal structures, just teams of staff developing and beginning to run courses. There was huge demand from students and therefore no need to market: 'opportunistic proliferation' was the order of the day. With growth came much more formality, including the development of marketing, much greater use of information technology and a more managerial approach to running the school. The national performance demands have increased with the introduction of systems that assess the quality of teaching and learning, and of research. Competition for students is intense. Those present felt in recent years the 'fire in the belly' – the passion about teaching and research – is somewhat diminished. This makes it more difficult to respond creatively to current pressures.

The workshop then moves on very positively to identify the key themes and patterns in this exploration of history and their implications for the strategies that the school may need to adopt if it is to thrive in the more turbulent world of 21st-century business education.

Perspectives on the present

Analysis of the reasons for the numbers of rough sleepers on our streets has emphasised the need for better integration at both policy planning and operational levels. Without better understanding of what causes people to sleep on the streets, together with more priority to coordinate efforts by government departments and other bodies to ensure that rough sleepers can receive training and ways into training, suitable accommodation and employment, the problem will remain.

There is an increasing awareness that work on this sort of problem across the departments of central government (such as education, police, probation, prison, health, local government, and so on) is not just about the joined-up development of policies. Putting money down the same fragmented channels or funding mechanisms will not solve the problem, if the necessary assistance to those sleeping rough ends up in different and disconnected places. For example, zero tolerance policing will not achieve anything where there is no housing, training or employment. The result would simply be to fill up police cells with people who are mentally ill, have drug and alcohol problems or are poor, lonely and depressed. If national policy developments are to deliver effective action on the streets, real learning, dialogue and sharing of perspectives needs to inform the process. Similarly, at the local level, ways must be found to support people working and learning together to produce local sustainable solutions.

There is a world of difference in each of the players in this situation seeking to understand its causes and manifestations in isolation, and their working together to share their different perspectives and create mutual understanding. In this way, they will build the sense that they 'inhabit the same earth' and have common concerns. The challenge to those leading whole systems development is to ensure that forums are created where people involved in this sort of issue can come together to understand it better, to deal with the anxieties of communities concerned about the impact of the problem and to make commitments to improve the lives of those sleeping rough.

Perspectives on the future

Public learning is strengthened when we create stories of the future together. There is now a general appreciation, both among managers and organisational theorists, that we cannot predict the future with a high degree of accuracy. Yet, equally, we know that predictions must be made. We must gear service provision levels to predictions of the demand for these selfsame services, including estimates of the choices that consumers will make between what we have on offer as compared with the services available from (predicted) competitors. For public services, the issues are similar, requiring some prediction of the impact of government policies and the requirements or aspirations of citizens as well as consumers.

In essence, the key issue is learning together across boundaries about the best ways to anticipate the future and to prepare everyone to respond to the uncertainties that will be generated. This sounds easy, but in practice is very difficult.

In his book, *The living company*, Ariel de Geus (1999) quotes neurobiological research showing that our brains work constantly to make sense of the future.

In our personal lives, we anticipate the time paths of our possible activities over the next few hours or days. For example, to write this chapter today will require avoiding various predictable interruptions and desisting from other possibilities for action, such as reading, gardening, and so on. Working without interruption for two more hours will allow time to see a film this evening, provided it is being shown locally today. Our plans are sequentially and hypothetically ordered: in other words, work now will give release for a leisure activity later. This example demonstrates what de Geus, quoting the scientist David Ingvar, calls a 'memory of the future'.

The message for anticipating the future is clear. Unless we have established these memories in our imaginations, we will find it difficult to be receptive to the signals from the outside world that should enable us to thrive in the complexity of the future circumstances in which we will find ourselves. To extend the trite example in the previous paragraph, unless we know where and when the film is on, and are aware of other available options, we are unlikely to experience the greatest pleasure potentially available for this chunk of leisure time.

At the level of our individual lives, this makes sense, but such memories are not easily available across the complex boundaries and tensions of whole systems. There is no collective brain process that automatically or even easily creates a sense of the future possibilities for the development or the solution of intractable problems. Developing collective memories of the future is therefore a vital element of public learning. When we create a number of such memories and articulate them to others, we begin to explore what might be done together to anticipate and prepare ourselves collectively.

The use of scenario planning as a key technique in developing and sustaining processes that strengthen working across whole systems is covered in Chapter Eight. Here, we emphasise that working together – across the divides of organisations and the communities they serve – to create stories or memories of the future is a very powerful way of building community or organisational aspirations. The future cannot be predicted, but we can link such future-based memories to dialogue about the most effective ways of 'tacking' towards agreed goals.

Creating the conditions for public learning

How do we create the conditions that enable public learning to happen? Public learning occurs when those with a stake in an issue engage in dialogue across cultural, historical, institutional and other divides. People make sense of an issue or problem and then make commitments to each other to take individual and collective action to develop purposes, plans and relationships. Planning ceases to be the province of planners alone and becomes the responsibility of all those who have a stake in creating a better future. It requires considerable effort to understand, though not necessarily to agree with, others' perspectives, mindsets and aspirations.

Our experience of working with whole systems development processes and practice leads us to contend that orchestrating public learning is not easy but can be greatly assisted by:

- The definition of the 'givens' within which learning can take place.
- The identification of the key questions to be addressed. In Chapter Four, the concept of a holding framework was used as a key means of reducing the uncertainties felt by those dealing with complex systemic issues. Here we refer not only to the definition of purposes, values and direction as a key means of guiding change.
- The encouragement for those involved to articulate their own success criteria within the 'givens' or frameworks identified for the whole exercise. These can be defined at three levels:
  › for the individual – themselves personally;
  › for any organisation of which the individual is a member;
  › for the whole system.
- Finally, framing of appropriate ways of working together encourages dialogue between all those involved to establish the territory for public learning. Effectively handled, this can help to challenge perceptions about previous relationship difficulties.

Agreeing to work as colleagues rather than competitors

The chief executives of a number of public service organisations have been persuaded by the civil service to encourage their organisations to collaborate to improve their collective contribution to the lives of residents of a major conurbation. As a precursor to this they agree a number of ground rules:

- being sensitive to and empathising with each others' roles and the pressures emanating from local contexts. This is expressed as, 'when I can genuinely stand in someone else's shoes and see the world through their eyes, I am in a much better position to learn with and from them';
- providing active understanding of the accountabilities of individuals to organisations or interest groups whose goals and interests are unlikely to be the same;
- agreeing to tell the truth as each person knows it, and accepting different perceptions of the issues at stake as legitimate for those who hold them, that is, the right to 'speak one's truth' and have it respected;
- bringing relevant information immediately to the group;
- clarifying how decisions will be made and by whom;
- establishing ways of supportively checking and challenging each other;
- limiting the time each person can speak;
- handling conflict constructively, as a positive force for change.

The Chief Executives also explore their previous and unhealthy ways of relating to each other in an attempt to ensure that these understandings become more than just rhetoric. These previous behaviours have included 'acerbic asides' and 'strikes' to defend personal positions. This leads to the recognition that some of their difficulties have emanated from personal anxieties, stress and overloaded agendas. To some degree, this was inevitable, given the public and political contexts of their work. What is important now is the open acknowledgement of these problems, together with the agreement to work together differently in the future.

Rules such as this provide a framework for improving relationships and making commitments to change. They should never become so dominant that they override the overall purposes and the learning process itself.

An underlying issue is often the need to make ways of relating to each other more transparent or understandable. Individuals have different allegiances and experience different pressures as they work within different parts of the system. This may cause them to behave in apparently contradictory ways. For example, in partnership building it is likely, or even inevitable, that the organisations involved will continue to compete for business, while their leaders are in the process of agreeing to the desirability of longer-term collaboration. Thus, at times, some people may be seen to engage in win–lose behaviour, which runs counter to the rhetoric of the importance of win–win approaches. Damage to personal relationships may be avoided by more explicit 'flagging' of behaviour in sensitive situations.

What does this mean for your own behaviour?

We hope that the example in the previous section may have prompted you to think about the implications of your personal behaviour in similar circumstances. For effective whole systems working, people, particularly those in positions of power and authority, need to be strong enough to admit that they are questioning their own perspectives, behaviour and learning. To influence change we must accept that we are part of the problem, rather than seeing it all as the fault of other people.

What challenges to your behaviour can be seen, if you are to effect improvements in the workings of systems of which you are a part?

To stimulate your thinking, we suggest that you assess the extent to which you understand the perspectives of other players in situations where you are keen to encourage commitment to different ways of working and learning together. Reflect on the challenges to your own behaviour and general personal effectiveness if you are to enhance your personal contribution to whole systems working.

These may include:

- feeling anxious about your own security or status and, therefore, seeking to over-control conversations;

- feeling personally inadequate over your lack of knowledge about certain key issues and therefore being unwilling to admit your ignorance;
- having a rather fixed view about the solution to a problem or a better way of working and therefore seeking to impose this on others;
- being keen to achieve short-term fixes rather than long-term solutions, possibly because of the pressure on you and your organisation to meet a plethora of externally imposed performance criteria;
- lacking regard for the capabilities and experiences of other people – possibly because of different histories and current roles.

The following extract, together with the issues about working with difference and diversity covered in Chapter Six, will hopefully help you to rethink some of the behaviours you adopt that are not as supportive of whole systems working as you recognise they need to be.

Quaker business practice – a prompt to strengthening public learning

Administrative processes in many organisations are, regrettably, often not a source of organisational learning. How often, for example, have you been to meetings where there is the sense that the minutes could have been written before the meeting? Whole systems development seeks guidance and experience beyond conventional business practice. One such source comes from the Quakers or Religious Society of Friends. If you have ever attended a Quaker business meeting, you will have observed that the minutes are taken during the meeting rather than afterwards. The clerk to the meeting frames the minute verbally after each item, checks it with those present and then commits it to the formal record. This process is a symbol of the value placed by Friends on openness, transparency, honesty and truth. There is also a commitment to handle conflict constructively:

> Conflict happens, and will continue to happen, even in the most peaceful of worlds. And that's good – a world where we all agreed with one another would be incredibly boring. Our differences help us to learn. Through conflict handled creatively we can change and grow: and I am not sure real change – either political or personal – can happen without it. We'll each handle conflict differently and find healing and reconciliation by different paths. (Leavitt, 1986, chapter 20, paragraph 71)

Meryl Reis Louis (1994) draws on Quaker business practice to suggest the following guidelines for renewal in the workplace. They are framed as questions in the spirit of Quaker enquiry.

- Do I seek unity on important matters? Do I recognise and strive to enable others to recognise that, while each of us has some ideas, it is likely that the best solution will come out of the collective wisdom of those closest to the problem, regardless of their formal position or group membership?
- Am I patient and genuinely present in my dealings with others? Do I refrain from over-scheduling myself, maintaining the boundaries necessary so that I have the time to be patient and present in my interactions and activities?
- Do I treat others with respect regardless of their formal position or group membership? Do I seek to know others beyond their work roles, inquiring about their lives, learning about their interests and gifts? Do I treat myself respectfully and bring more of my whole self into interactions at work?
- Am I open to the benefits of a moment of silence? At the beginning of a meeting, do I give people a chance to arrive physically and mentally?
- Do I encourage a pace of discussion that allows us to take in and consider what has been said? When differences persist, do I suggest a moment of silence to consider how we might proceed?
- Do I strive to be open, treating my position as one alternative, remaining open to being influenced by others' positions out of which we might realize a more advantageous alternative?
- Do I create opportunities for all to share responsibility for the task...? Do I recognize that shared responsibility may foster skill development, sense of ownership, and connection among us? Do I recognize that a sense of community fosters task accomplishment and the way the task is accomplished influences the sense of community that arises?
- Do I seek to strengthen the ties among people [so] ... that we can tolerate a greater measure of difference on issues in the context of ... respect and acceptance, and that out of difference can come innovation?

We feel that it is worth drawing at length from this experience, since it has much to offer to the practice of whole systems development, particularly the challenges presented by the principle of public learning.

In this chapter, we have argued that creating a climate for public learning requires:

- the definition of the givens;
- the articulation of individual and collective success criteria;
- the framing of appropriate ways of working together.

Finally, public learning may also be assisted by *explicit discussion of sources of power.*

Power and public learning

Individuals have recourse to:

- coercive power as a result of the resources at their disposal;
- persuasive power, which comes from their understanding of, and information about, the workings of the system;
- personal power, which emanates from their personal capability, for example, to influence others.

Power relationships are core to the working of systems. If power is never discussed, it will be part of the dark underbelly of efforts to improve the system and will frustrate change. Efforts to make it part of the more normal discourse between people are likely to pay dividends in the form of increased trust, mutuality and commitment to change. Learning can include enhancing understanding that power sharing can lead to more synergy in the use of resources and therefore a better outcome for most people.

Putting the elephant on the table

A difficult discussion is going on between a number of organisations concerned with the care of people with learning disabilities about organisational arrangements that will support better daily living for service users. The conversation is somewhat desultory and there is a clear sense that important things are not being said. Suddenly, the person in charge of the provision of social services says: 'There is an elephant in the corner of this room! I think I had better put it on the table!'. He then explains that the elected members of his local authority will not countenance any new organisational solution to the problems under discussion that result in social services staff being employed by any one other than the local authority. There is an uncomfortable silence, followed by a general acknowledgement that, though this is difficult, knowing that this is the case releases everyone to think about what is practically possible given the power realities of the situation.

Top teamworking

Top teams play an important role in the development of a climate of public learning, both within their own organisations and across organisational boundaries.

'Our leadership has been a disgrace'

At a staff conference, the admission by the management team that 'our collective leadership has been a disgrace' contributed significantly to the atmosphere of frankness and determination to improve the contribution by the organisation to the system in which it is a key player. The leaders' admission of their need to learn encouraged everyone else to see learning as legitimate and even desirable.

The influence that leaders can have on the quality of public learning is not restricted to admitting that they too are learning. In particular, they can assist public learning by:

- demonstrating their intent to involve the 'whole system' to develop a shared understanding of current realities and to create a collective vision of the future;
- developing key questions about the ways in which the gaps between current and desired future state can be bridged so that stakeholders can work together in public to agree the best ways forward;
- developing a climate within their own organisations, or parts of the system over which they have influence, which fosters commitment and combats coercion;
- challenging gaps between a rhetoric of collaboration and partnership, and a reality that supports competition as the prime driver of organisational relationships;
- developing human resource management processes (for example, for appraisal and performance management) that place a high value on learning with and from peers, bosses and subordinates;
- establishing an ethos within the team in which learning and development is actively valued and action-fixated behaviour discouraged;
- adopting pay and reward systems for senior people that reinforce learning and discourage unhelpful competition or short-term target setting.

For top teamworking, partnerships and networks, see Chapter Nine, particularly 'developing partnerships across whole systems'.

SIX

Valuing difference and diversity: getting the whole system into the room

We are seeing a societal learning curve where people are moving from a tendency to rely on experts to solve problems or to improve whole systems to individuals themselves wanting more control over issues that critically affect their lives. We see this in demands to be involved: by parents in decisions about the education of their children; by patients and carers in decisions about their personal health and social care; by communities in debates about the future of institutions such as hospitals or schools and in planning decisions. People are disenchanted with their inability to have a real voice in a society. This is also reflected in the apparent apathy of many people, often reflected by low turnouts at local and national elections.

Marvin Weisbord has characterised this as a historical trend over the last century:

- 1900 – experts solve problems
- 1950 – 'everybody' solves problems
- 1965 – experts improve whole systems
- 2000 – 'everybody' improves whole systems (Weisbord and Janoff, 1995, p 2)

We are not suggesting that whole systems development is the universal panacea for all these ills. However, the principle that anyone affected by a change should be an architect of it does assist thinking about ways in which diverse perspectives and aspirations can be incorporated into decisions to improve the circumstances in which people live and work. People of all political persuasions and social and economic circumstances can have a hand in painting the big picture. They can start to align their own actions with those of colleagues or fellow citizens to bring this into being.

In this chapter we:

- explore how the difference and diversity within the whole system can be utilised to the benefit of all stakeholders;
- address how the whole system can come 'into the room together' to work on complex issues such as partnerships between organisations, ways of improving education or healthcare or dealing with urban poverty;

- discuss ways of ensuring that the voices of disadvantaged groups on the margin of society are heard, if not directly at least indirectly, in whole systems development.

Inviting local residents to plan the future of their communities

Your Community Tomorrow
A Better Future For All

We are forging a new direction, where local people have a say in their tomorrow. If you are an individual or part of a group interested in building the future together, we need to hear your views.

We are running a two-day event on the weekend of 28/29 September where your voice can be heard – so why not come along?

Do please register by returning the attached form.

With the development of the new council for your town there will be many differences ... many changes.

... but real, meaningful differences to our future will be achieved with your help.

A local authority in partnership with other organisations in its area is leading a process to develop a community picture of a better future for local residents. A 'big event' is planned to bring together a cross section of residents. The organising group decides to issue invitations through eye-catching coverage in the local press.

It hopes that this will enable local residents of all backgrounds, age groups, employment status, ethnicity and so on to join together to make sense of the current state of things and make decisions about ways of improving life in future. In the event, it proves difficult to encourage participation by the long-term unemployed and other people who tend to be uninvolved in community life. Young people are disinclined to attend, as are members of ethnic minority groups, the residents of tower blocks and other severely deprived residential areas.

As the 200 or so people gather for the event, they ask questions such as, 'who are we?', 'where do we come from?', 'what do we do?', and 'who is not here?'. On a map of the borough, each person places a dot to locate their home. Other information about the mix of people present is available from the database created as people responded to the invitation to attend. It is quickly apparent that people from the most deprived parts of the community are not present.

As participants work together to think through ways in which everyone's lives could be better in future, ways of strengthening contacts with these groups to enable their voices to be heard are identified. Connections between the council, other agencies and voluntary networks in these areas are strengthened.

During the next few years new networks and partnerships are created. For example, a cross-borough environmental network emerges from the realisation by members of very local networks at the event that their success in greening the borough will be greater by combining their efforts. Another result is the commitment of a number of statutory and non-statutory organisations to integrate their activities so that there is better focus on the regeneration of an area of the borough with very high unemployment due to the decline of its traditional industries. At a meeting soon after the big event, the few young people present are supported by some adult participants to decide whether and how they could take a lead in developing ways of involving others more formally in the life of the borough. The following year a youth council is formed.

The value of maximum diversity or 'requisite variety'

The key principle at work in events and processes of this kind is that of the value of maximum diversity. Frequently, information on decisions becomes homogenised as it is fed up organisational 'silos' and disconnected from its sources or origin. Chapter Two summarised some of the main tenets of systems theory and one that is particularly relevant to this chapter is the assumption that heterogeneity produces energy. This is related to the ecological notion of 'sufficient difference', which suggests that for an organism or the system of which it is part to continue to exist there must be sufficient difference within it to enable it to cope with change in its environment. Ashby's 'law of requisite variety' has:

> ... important implications for the design of almost every aspect of organisation. Whether we are talking about the creation of a corporate planning group, a research department, or a work group in a factory, it argues in favour of a pro-active embracing of the environment in all its diversity. Very often managers do the reverse, reducing variety in order to achieve greater internal consensus. For example, corporate planning teams are often built around people who think along the same lines, rather than around a diverse set of stakeholders who could actually represent the complexity of the problems with which the team ultimately has to deal. (Morgan, 1986, p 101)

Too much similarity reduces the ability to adapt and learn, since a closed system will increasingly develop a homogenous view. Diversity is created by opening organisational or community boundaries to let in new views. Maturana and Varela (1980) take systems thinking further, coining the term 'autopoesis' to suggest that systems are self-designing and have tendencies to become more complex as they try to absorb more variety from the environment. This is highly relevant for working with difference and diversity, since it challenges the notion of the separation between an organisation and the environment of which it is a part. If we are to work effectively across systems in ways that deal effectively with the challenges of the social, political, economic or technological forces that affect their functioning, then, as individuals and as groups, we must develop mindsets that enable us to cope effectively with such diversity.

Seeking common ground rather than a forced consensus

Perhaps the core idea of working with difference is that of seeking common ground between people who may 'come into the room' with obvious differences. The idea and practices associated with this have been developed by a number of systems thinkers and practitioners, but perhaps the idea is most associated with Marvin Weisbord. However, he attributes three other significant innovators with developing the theory and practice of creating the conditions for dialogue – the prerequisite for finding and extending common ground. He writes:

> [Frederick] Emery had two … conceptual frameworks he believed would increase the probability for success. One was Philip Selznick's (1957) criteria for an effective organization: (a) clear mission; (b) 'distinctive competencies' to serve its market; (c) shared internal values among leaders to assure integrity despite dispersed authority.
>
> The second framework was social psychologist Solomon Asch's (1956) 'conditions for effective dialogue'. Asch's research into perception and consensus had convinced Emery that these conditions would make the discovery of shared mission, competencies and values more probable in any group that could achieve them. Asch's conditions, framed by Emery, were shared assumptions that:
>
> (a) all parties are 'talking about the same world' – requiring that people back up their generalizations with concrete examples;
> (b) all human beings have basic psychological similarities, as regards 'laughing, loving, working, desiring, thinking, perceiving, etc'.
> (c) As a result of a and b, then 'the facts of one person's world become part of the other's' and they develop 'a shared psychological field'.
>
> Only then, Emery believed, could a genuine dialogue proceed. Its success would depend on how much people perceived an increase in freedom of choice along with increased understanding. If they did, reasoned Emery, then we could assume – final condition – that:
>
> (d) People will experience their common dilemmas in the external demands, events, trends, developments shaping all of their lives, and plan accordingly.
> (Weisbord, 1992, pp 21-2)

Clearly, this needs time. Weisbord's classic Search Conference process spans three days, deliberately allowing two 'sleepovers' to help participants digest and make sense of their own intense involvement and discussion. All too frequently, breaking through to new understanding and action is constrained through lack of time and the convention of holding meetings with limited diversity and run according to the straightjackets of formal convention.

In order to promote conditions for dialogue and seeking common ground, both whole systems processes and large events move through a series of stages. Firstly, there is a time for participants to introduce themselves in small mixed groups – mixed to produce maximum diversity (see Chapter Seven). They are then encouraged to listen to each other's stories, histories and perspectives about how they have experienced the issue they have come together to explore. Secondly, they individually and collectively gather information and diagnose the current state of things. Thirdly, they explore visions – or what 'better' would look like. Finally, they start to seek common ground and agree actions to begin moving in the direction of better. This sequence links to that implicit in the change equation (see Chapter Two, page 27).

Great emphasis is placed on listening to other people's perceptions of events and experience: 'everybody's truth is their truth'. There is encouragement to seek common ground through this way of talking and listening, as well as to acknowledge and note differences. It is usual for people, who come together from apparently very different backgrounds, histories and experiences, to find they have far more in common that they anticipate. Once they find this, it becomes much easier to appreciate different perspectives, while not necessarily agreeing with them. From this vantage point, disagreements may come to be resolved. However, whole systems processes do not place their primary emphasis on reconciling difference. The starting point is searching for what people can hold in common, giving them freedoms and responsibilities for appreciating differences of view and working for reconciliation as appropriate to them. This runs counter to the typical pressure of so many conventional meetings to seek a forced consensus that breaks down as soon as people part and go their own way. This is, of course, the basic cause of why so often so little implementation of apparent agreements takes place. The 'team together' fails to be a 'team apart'. Implementation happens when groups and 'whole systems' become 'teams apart'.

Again, it was Marvin Weisbord who first raised the significance of meeting differently, the subject of Chapter Seven. What is now seemingly obvious was not so before – meetings are just meetings, aren't they? Describing what he calls 'applied common sense', he states:

> The equation is something like THE RIGHT TASK + THE RIGHT PEOPLE + THE RIGHT SETTING = UNPRECEDENTED ACTIONS. That sounds a lot like applied common sense. Why, in most institutions, is it not commonly applied? I have to keep reminding myself that the (probably unconscious) function of old paradigm meetings is not breakthroughs, but control.

By hanging tight to the status quo, we maintain our control fantasies. There are two ways we use our normal meetings to maintain an illusion of control. The first is appreciating the WHOLE SYSTEM, but having only experts, staff managers, or top executives in the room to do it. They get the exercise right *cognitively*, that is, their heads are in the right place. But there are too few heads, so they never fully get the whole picture. More, they cannot easily implement what they learn from each other. They equate 'understanding' with control, something that does not necessarily follow. The 'big picture' is more than a static snapshot of information exchanged. It also is a moving picture dependent on how many people participate. (Weisbord, 1992, p 8)

Weisbord goes on to say that, to implement effectively, we need shared pictures of the 'whole system' and that this requires broad face-to-face planning. The frequent absence of this is why so much 'corporate strategy comes apart'.

Learning to work with diversity and difference

Whole systems development designs in diversity and difference, rather than managing them out. This is contrary to conventional management reporting and communications. Efforts are made to include voices from the range of professional and occupational groupings, grade and status, gender, ethnicity, age, disability, area of residence and any other relevant criteria in dialogue. In so doing, we are creating frameworks for seeing and working with interrelationships rather than things. We are encouraging people to see patterns and opportunities for change together. As people create new relationships, so they develop new behaviours, skills and cultural sensitivities. These are the foundations for tackling the intractable problems found in communities and organisations.

However, we should not glibly assume that working with difference and diversity is easy. We need to remember that each of us brings who we are to every interaction – our gender, racial identity, sexual orientation, class, spiritual beliefs, age, physical and mental abilities, and cultural history. Similarly, the way in which others see us is affected by these same factors. For example, we live in a society that still tends to see women workers as wives and mothers, current or prospective, and as less likely than men to see work as a central life interest. For white people, for black people and for people of mixed racial heritage, race affects every individual's daily experience at work and, more generally, in everyday life.

To use difference and diversity creatively, we first need to learn to communicate about it. As children, we receive messages about what is OK to talk about and what not. And while we were not all taught the same rules, we all received verbal and non-verbal cues. The teenage daughter of one of us worked in a newspaper shop where someone came into the shop one day dressed as a woman and the next dressed as a man. What kind of person was this? How should she relate to him or her? These kinds of experiences and conversations influence the way we relate to people different from ourselves in later life.

In whole systems development, the challenge is to recognise that differences play a role in everyone's interactions and experiences, rather than acting as if everyone is treated the same. We then must learn to use these differences creatively to solve the problems that face us all. In our experience, it is relatively easy for people to understand the importance of embedding principles of maximum diversity into whole systems working. It is more difficult to put this into practice.

For example, many personal health and social services are now delivered by multidisciplinary teams. The rhetoric of this is that it produces seamless and effective care. The reality can be that, as professionals are exposed directly to each other's different value systems, assumptions about care and methods of working, and terms and conditions of employment, they may be driven back into their own boxes, mentally refusing to be exposed to mindsets different from their own. It is folly to ignore personal and professional histories, which have more often been about working as a single profession and ignoring or even devaluing the professional perspectives of others.

'Nothing about us without us'

This phrase, now frequently used, to stress the importance of service user involvement in decision-making was referred to earlier (page 82).

A progressive service for people with mental health problems appoints a woman who uses its services to its board. For the first year of her appointment as a non-executive director, her health is good. She becomes very competent, taking the chair of one of the main board subcommittees that oversees the organisation's clinical effectiveness. Unfortunately, shortly after taking on this role, she becomes unwell and receives regular treatment from a psychiatrist. She continues to attend board meetings and to chair the subcommittee. It is apparent to the chair and chief executive that she is not well. They are concerned about her illness and its impact on the board's execution of its responsibilities. In addition, members of the clinical team responsible for her care are expressing some disquiet about her reactions to them, which seem, on occasion, to be confusing her role as a service user with that as a board member. The chair of the board decides that his paramount responsibility is to ensure that the board can properly exercise its stewardship of the organisation. He, therefore, tells the service user that he cannot allow her to chair the subcommittee until he is satisfied that she is fully recovered from her current illness. She accuses him of discrimination against her as a service user. The whole board becomes very upset by the issue and finds it difficult to conduct its business.

This story is not told to ask the question 'what should happen next?', but rather to illustrate the dilemmas sometimes created by a determination to embed principles of difference and diversity into processes for running organisations or working with complex systems. The lessons are probably three:

- It is helpful for those in positions of responsibility for the leadership of organisations to be provided with guidance on the general principles of service-user involvement and their application in practice. National advisory bodies can be a source of such information.
- Every situation will be different. Therefore it is useful for boards or other groups to try to anticipate the issues involved. The co-creation of 'memories of the future' (see Chapter Five, page 86) can be very useful in this respect. The principles underpinning such 'what if' thinking must be honesty, transparency and a willingness to put the 'elephant on the table' (see Chapter Five, page 91), recognising the realities of power and responsibility in difficult situations.
- Service users taking on these roles need some assistance to think through the issues involved before taking on the role. Independent and confidential support may be useful.

Putting these lessons into practice will not resolve all the difficulties of this sort of situation, but it should prevent those involved from feeling out of control and guilty if things get very difficult.

The role of design teams in working out how 'the whole system' can 'come into the room together'

One way of developing processes that assist working across a complex system is to set up a diagonal slice group or design team. Such teams are a microcosm or diagonal slice of the system of which they are a part. This is important for two reasons.

Firstly, these diverse perspectives are necessary so that everyone can get a picture of the complex whole. Jacobs describes such teams as using:

> A consensus process to figure out *what* needs to be discussed, *how* it should be discussed and *when* it should be discussed to achieve the purpose. In short, everyone must agree – a sometimes difficult standard, but one that is essential. (1994, p 207)

Secondly, direct contact between stakeholders within these groups across the system builds or strengthens relationships and networks that will be powerful forces for change.

High-quality consultancy support is required if design teams are to fulfil their potential.

In considering the composition of the team, it is vital to think about the diversity of the system with which it is to work:

- the organisations
- the occupational or professional groups
- the interest groups

- the community groups
- young and older people
- the ethnic mix
- the gender mix
- disabled as well as able-bodied people
- the geography of the territory to be worked, and so on.

It is also important to select people for some personal qualities, such as a willingness to listen and learn, ability to influence others in the system and creativity. Scepticism can be useful; cynicism can be corrosive. Obviously, it will not be possible to get an exact representation, but developing a good diagonal slice is important.

For more information on the roles and workings of design teams, see Chapter Seven (pages 118-19).

Developing design teams

Because of the significance of design teams to the success of whole systems development approaches, we recommend that a great deal of care is given to their development.

They can be quite large. We have worked with teams of 20 or more. The larger the team, the more possible it is to explore the major issues in the system. However, large teams also require more time and consultancy support to their task. Developed effectively, they come to reflect and work with the challenges presented when the whole system comes into the room at a large event or through other processes. In experiencing these pressures and tensions, they become experts in the design of ways in which large events or other whole systems processes can make effective decisions. In our experience, this often creates a type of 'learning laboratory' that is powerfully developmental of the skills and qualities of those involved. Sometimes the experience prompts people from design teams to take on roles in the implementation of the changes that result from the processes for which they have taken responsibility. Occasionally, the personal development opportunity inherent in team membership results in considerable career development.

At the beginning of the team's life, care needs to be taken to assist all members to recognise their differences and similarities and to think through how these may be used to enrich the task. The following is an example of an introductory activity that will accelerate design team development.

Aim: To get to know more about each other and to decide how to work together Spend a few minutes introducing yourselves to each other. Say who you are and what encouraged you to join the team. Say what you would like to get out of this experience. Then form a pair with someone you don't know. Find out from each other things that you have in common (or think similarly about) and things that make you different. List up to three similarities and three differences on a flipchart. Be ready to share these with the whole group. When the similarities and differences have been shared, discuss as a group how these can be used to assist the team to work well together on its task. Develop a list of ground rules that will support the team to work in this way.

At this point, we need to strike a note of caution. Learning to use difference constructively is often not easy, as illustrated by the account about service-user involvement (page 101).

For these reasons, a key role for consultants is to ensure that design teams learn to use tensions productively. This will enable them to foresee and constructively explore the tensions inherent in the processes that they are designing. In this way, processes for exploring difference and diversity can be consciously designed into events in which the whole system comes into the room together. This should enable tensions to be explored constructively, rather than swept under the carpet or experienced as a source of antagonism that inhibits learning and change. In our experience, resources devoted to the establishment and development of design teams pay great dividends for these reasons because they build individual capabilities within the system to assist subsequent processes of development.

How do design teams decide which stakeholders to involve in the processes they are designing?

Teams must scope the diversity of the stakeholders in a system and organise ways in which their different perspectives can be shared.

First, it is necessary to clarify the issues on which the whole system needs to work during a big event or series of other processes. It may be helpful for the design team to summarise these in a circle on the middle of a flipchart. The names of the key people and groups that have a stake in the way in which the system operates can then be drawn like the spokes of a wheel at appropriate points around this circle.

It is very unlikely that there will be ways in which all these individuals and groups can be involved in a whole systems development intervention. Therefore, the design team must decide which people are key to the successful implementation of the issues under consideration. It is particularly important to focus carefully on the implications of neglecting any individual or group.

Members of the team will then have to think about the nature of relationships between themselves, their organisations and these key stakeholders. What actions will be needed to get them constructively involved? Whose help might be needed to ensure that this is the case? Hard-to-reach groups such as those identified in the community planning example at the beginning of this chapter (page 96), require particularly creative thinking in this respect.

Getting the whole system into the room – exploring differences, directly and indirectly, with interest groups and community members

Organisations are often wary of engaging in direct dialogue with suppliers, service users or the public at large, feeling that they must first put their own house in order. This can be misplaced anxiety. Hearing the views of external stakeholders may act to communicate the real adaptive challenges facing an organisation more powerfully than could be explained by leaders alone. In addition, excluding stakeholders at the outset may later prove to be a barrier to ownership of change.

Nevertheless, there will be whole organisation change processes in which all participants are internal. In these cases, it is vital that people are not insulated altogether from external perspectives. Systematic data gathering and its communication to staff can help to generate a climate conducive to the sharing of perspectives across the boundaries of the organisation.

In sum, the greater the diversity of views in a gathering, the more likely it is that creative ways forward will result.

Data gathering about the workings of the whole system

Data can be gathered from many sources and in many ways. The system needs to be mapped so that decisions can be made about the sources and nature of the information required. In this sense, the whole system comes into the room through data about the diverse perspectives and assumptions of stakeholders.

Often, data gathering is undertaken directly within meetings or conferences as stakeholders share experiences and aspirations. This is ideal because it ensures that people personally communicate their own truths: there is no risk that a third party has sanitised or watered down the information. People are also required by others to back up generalisations with concrete examples. This can result in sharing others' psychological worlds and making sense of issues across organisational and cultural barriers.

However, we have found that considerable preparation can be required to create the conditions that enable people to come together in this way. Personal and organisational anxieties can create reluctance to open up to new views. An initial diagnostic phase can help to create conditions more conducive to dialogue across the system. Sometimes people have to be assisted to become free enough to explore, discover, learn, create and plan together.

This can lead to consultants, either internal or external, being asked to undertake interviews. In complex systems, this can be enormously time-consuming but can help to unfreeze previously dysfunctional assumptions about others' perspectives and attitudes. Where people are anxious, it is vital to be clear about how information will be used and that it will not be attributable to individuals.

For interviews or other means of collecting data from people across a system to be effective requires prior briefing about the reasons for the activity and, critically, its links with any other change initiatives. All too often, organisations are running several change initiatives in parallel. Where this is the case, how can the 'Mad Management Virus' be neutralised?

Integrating data gathering

After a big event, a design team is planning a number of focus groups to assess the extent to which the positive messages emerging about vision, direction and staff involvement in decision-making are percolating through to those people who did not participate in the event. In dialogue with the group responsible for overseeing all the organisation's efforts to manage change, the design team identifies a number of other initiatives that will seek to ascertain staff views about the current functioning of the organisation. Discussion with those in charge of these leads to a decision to integrate all information requirements within a single focus group process. More attention is also paid to explaining clearly to staff why information is required and how it will be used.

This short story illustrates that, although those in leadership positions may be clear about the linkages between different initiatives, this may not be the case for other people. Care to assist people to make sense of complexity is core to all aspects of whole systems development. For example, managers can be asked to make presentations to communicate the ways in which projects or activities link together. At the very least, this should ensure that those in charge are clear about the overall direction.

Sometimes this data is used directly in subsequent meetings or events; sometimes it is presented first to a steering group responsible for overseeing the development of the whole system. In the case of work in single organisations, management teams may find it helpful at this stage to think about the data and their implication for their own roles, before engaging directly with other stakeholders on the issues raised. Axelrod favours the use of 'walk throughs', in which the key messages are actively explored with people who could not participate in these events.

The anxious and dysfunctional management team

The managers of a civil service department were apprehensive about bringing all their staff together to renew values and develop a stronger corporate identity. There was fear that the lack of clarity about the department's purpose and role would be a significant impediment to the development of plans for improved working. There was evidence that many staff were demoralised and frustrated. Data were gathered that substantiated this but also pointed to the dysfunctional nature of the management team itself as a major contributor to staff dissatisfaction. The management team met to consider the data. After considerable anger was expressed at the consultants who collected the data, the team reflected more calmly. They decided to admit their failings to staff honestly in the hope that this would provide both the stimulus and the climate for improvements in working relationships.

This example illustrates the potential tensions created for those in leadership roles by whole systems development. It is easy to espouse the value of diversity and difference as a creative force. It is less easy to work constructively with disquiet or frustration on the part of others when you feel responsibility for current realities. However, if leaders are to 'hold the ring' effectively on big events or other approaches, it is vital that they recognise, reflect on and honestly articulate their thoughts and feelings about these difficulties.

There are disadvantages in data gathering being undertaken before the stakeholders come into the room together. Unhelpful tensions can be created as data gatherers act as proxies for others' views. It leaves those who have gathered the data with information that protects individual confidentiality but needs to be shared with others. It can confuse the role of the data gatherers. They may look like experts who have the solutions to problems, where, in reality, their task is to manage the processes whereby those involved make decisions about ways forward.

'The loose cannon'!

In a data-gathering exercise undertaken by consultants in a health organisation, a senior doctor is frequently described as 'a bit of a loose cannon', inclined to work separately on his own agenda to improve health, ensuring that his team does likewise and fiercely defending his territory when challenged. When this data is fed back to a big staff conference, he explodes. The ripple of amusement around the room suggests that other people see this as validation of the data. It is extremely uncomfortable for the consultants and also for the doctor.

The incident demonstrates the paradoxical nature of data gathered to inform events of this nature. On the one hand, it made it possible for a key aspect of the workings of the system to be explored so that both its positive aspects (the strength and independence of this area of clinical work) and its negative aspects (its perceived inadequate integration with other activities) were understood. It is likely that assumptions about power and the passive nature of the organisation's culture would have made it difficult for these views to be expressed without prior exploration through the data-gathering process. On the other hand, the indirect nature of that exercise conducted by consultants ran the risk that, when the system came into the room together, the data would feel inauthentic and, therefore, would not be used productively.

It is critically important to present the data in all their variety and with all their contradictions and ambiguities unresolved. This makes it most likely that the data will be treated as the authentic voice of those within the system. This will help the mutual engagement that is necessary.

Another possible option is for consultants to undertake an initial mapping of both the 'hard' and 'soft' aspects of the system. This can be communicated to a design team who can develop a range of questions for a process of collaborative enquiry with a wider range of stakeholders. Alternatively, an event can be held to undertake such an initial exploration of the issues as a precursor to bringing together a larger group of stakeholders. A detailed example of a small conference designed for this purpose follows.

Establishing key questions about mental health and mental health services as a basis for collaborative enquiry

The event aims to enable a cross section of those in positions of leadership in organisations with a stake in the improvement of the mental health of the population in a region to:

- create a shared understanding of the current state of mental health and mental health services;
- explore the realities facing attempts at improvement;
- develop a range of realistic images of a resident population with improved mental health and mental health services;
- identify the key issues to explore with a wider group of stakeholders in order that real action to improve can take place;
- agree the composition of that wider group of stakeholders with whom dialogue should take place.

The event opens with an introduction to the aims of the conference, including its position in a longer process of enquiry with stakeholders and the rationale for inviting those who were participating on this day. It is suggested that, following the conference, a cross-sectional team to design subsequent processes is constituted.

Participants are introduced to the 'graffiti wall' on which they can make suggestions about stakeholders to invite to future events. They are also asked to introduce themselves, using a similar activity to that described earlier in this chapter (page 104).

After coffee, the images of the current reality of mental health and mental health services held by those in the room are explored in the same small mixed groups and then in the whole group. This brings out the richness of participants' experiences, both positive and negative.

The next stage is an imaginative exploration of the ideal mental health system, if participants were able to implement the changes they believed to be needed. This session in small groups and in plenary creates a spirit of optimism about the significant opportunities to contribute to better lives for service users.

After lunch, an 'expert' panel, comprised of people acknowledged to have specialist knowledge about various aspects of mental health, responds to the issues emerging during the morning, sharing views of trends or developments in such areas as government policy, therapeutic regimes and societal attitudes. Participants question the panel.

In the final session, the key issues and questions about the future of mental health and mental health services for exploration with wider groups of stakeholders begin to be crystallised via a session during which participants vote to determine the most important issues or questions. There is also a review of the graffiti wall to ascertain which stakeholders should be involved in subsequent processes. The event finishes with a round-up of arrangements for the next stage, a discussion of the role of the design team charged with the detailed planning and a request for volunteers for this.

This example is not included as a template of the design of events, but rather as one way in which a cross section of stakeholders – in this case, those in formal leadership roles – can come together to decide how to improve the system within which their roles are located. You should note that experts are used once the group has developed an initial view of the significant issues, as a means of 'benchmarking' local perspectives against those commonly experienced.

It also demonstrates that what can appear to be an either/or design choice about the trade-off between a prior diagnostic phase and its incorporation into a stakeholder event can turn out to be an opportunity both to undertake an initial diagnosis and to begin to build critical leadership connections across the system.

Your views about the issues involved in gathering data on the issues to be addressed in whole systems development

You may find it helpful to explore how data about intractable problems have been gathered and used to strengthen learning about the resolution of problems currently perceived to be intractable.

- How were data gathered?
- How were key stakeholders involved in data gathering?
- How did they use the data to reach conclusions and make decisions?
- What did you learn about whole systems development through your involvement in this process?
- How would you put this learning into practice when your department or organisation faces another intractable problem?

Meetings or big events as a key means of bringing the system into the room

Getting the whole system into the room often involves large interventions or big events. These can act as a springboard from which people can create shared meanings about the history, current state and future possibilities for the improvement of the complex whole. However, whole systems development is not only achieved through large group interventions. There are other ways of ensuring that the complexity of the whole system is represented. Holographic principles can be used to prompt thinking about ways of achieving this. The essential characteristics of the system can be part of any deliberations about change, even though all those involved are unable to be directly part of the dialogue. Chapter Seven explores how this can be achieved.

SEVEN

Meeting differently: large and small group working

Question: How do you eat an elephant?

Answer: In bite-sized chunks!

At the heart of this old analogy for managing big changes lies a fallacy: that splitting a whole into parts makes the change process easier.

Consider a visual image of the elephant:

Each person sees only that part of the elephant on which they are focusing – a leg or a tusk. The whole animal is not visible. The challenge of designing whole systems development processes is to enable everyone to see the whole elephant together. Although in most cases this is an impossible aspiration, the key issue is to develop ways in which the actors can see, understand and think through their ways of working together on issues that cross organisational and community boundaries.

In this chapter we:

- examine the ways in which groups – both large and small – can meet differently to enable the principles of whole systems development to be practised;
- explore the leadership, design and logistics of big events as one key mechanism for meeting differently;

- discuss the consultancy support needed to assist these ways of working;
- encourage you to reflect and learn from personal experiences of meeting differently;
- explore the notion of 'everyone in the room together' as a metaphor for meeting differently as practised particularly through processes of action learning.

Drawing the boundaries for 'meeting differently'

The more we engage in systems thinking, the more arbitrary formal organisations seem:

- Why aren't students seen as part of a school's organisation?
- Or tenants, part of a housing department?
- Or customers and suppliers, part of a manufacturing company?

None of these can exist in isolation from the others. But so frequently, as with the internal departments of an organisation, formal boundaries quickly become walls and those beyond them adversaries. Ironically, these divisions have often been established to manage past changes, but then themselves have become barriers to progress. And traditional boundaries can so easily change – as the recent fashion for outsourcing has shown. In so many instances, what is technically inside an organisation and what is outside is relatively arbitrary.

From this perspective, it is artificial and unhelpful to design processes that are confined within the 'walls' of a single department or organisation or, indeed, at parts of the wider systems of which organisations are but one part. The whole systems approach emphasises a need, wherever possible, to seek collaborative engagement with as many relevant stakeholders across the system as possible, both within and without the formal boundaries of the organisations.

Working with the whole elephant

> Question: How together do we reach an understanding of the elephant?
>
> Answer: By recognising that we have different understandings of the elephant and that these can be used to develop a richer picture of the whole.

She may see the tail, he may see a tusk, and so on: our experiences of the 'elephant' differ. Within well-designed processes, we will be able to share perceptions and even reach some consensus, while recognising that differences in our perceptions and assumptions cause us to make sense of the issues differently. Thus, whole systems approaches to implementing strategic change involve everyone with an interest in creating more productive ways of developing and delivering products and services. Such approaches are neither top-down nor bottom-up, but participative at all levels, assisting those involved to become aligned through the development of common understandings. Everyone is involved in trying to understand and work with 'the whole elephant'.

The elephant analogy is apt because it may be that this sort of thinking and seeing is easier for those brought up with natural cycles of growth and decline, of sowing and harvest, of changes in the seasons. Those of us brought up in industrialised societies with their artificial landscapes are perhaps less likely to see these systemic relationships and more likely to see the parts rather than the whole. Much change management focuses on the world within the walls of the organisation rather than on the interrelationships between the organisation and its suppliers, customers and the wider society within which it exists. Whole systems development demands that we become less myopic, paying attention to the world as if through a wide-angle lens, so that we can see how our actions interrelate with the activities of others. The design challenge is to frame ways of working that enable this to happen.

Few of us have been trained to think *systemically*. The mental tools we acquire in education are predominantly linear and causal. We tend to narrow data down to produce answers, rather than opening up our minds to think more divergently. Most disciplines, particularly those inhabited by professionals (law, medicine and accountancy, for example), prefer to ignore knowledge outside their own boundaries.

Working together to improve primary care

A primary care organisation sees improving the quality of general practitioner services received by local residents as core to its existence. Medical models emphasise the need for better clinical treatments – ensuring, for example, that primary care services dovetail better with those of hospitals. They play down the complex factors that impact on both the quality of care and the health of the community.

The area has high numbers of single-handed practices – doctors working on their own. Many of these are members of ethnic minorities. They are working within the inner city because of their membership of these cultural or religious groups and also because it has been difficult for them to acquire a partnership in a practice that provides services to more affluent residents. Many practices are family businesses employing family members as receptionists, business managers and so on. The doctor is the gateway to decision-making often for cultural reasons of gender and ethnicity. The wider influences on health and healthcare – poverty, housing, unemployment and transport, for example – are difficult to address at practice level. Those charged with partnership working to improve health (social workers, regeneration project workers, health promotion specialists, and so on) often find it difficult to gain access to the networks that will encourage single-handed GPs with medical mindsets and small business orientations to get involved in partnership working on the broader health improvement agenda. What is needed is people with local community knowledge, who are able to understand the GPs' way of seeing the world (even if they do not agree with it). They can think through ways of influencing service improvement processes, including developing incentives to get GPs more involved, as well as by developing the capabilities of other staff working in the practices and in other parts of the healthcare system.

Working together on complex systemic issues

It may be helpful to identify some of the ways in which people can come together to work on complex systemic issues, such as those outlined here.

What do you think might be some possible ways of achieving this? The options we can identify are:

- A big event bringing together the stakeholders mentioned in the example to explore the priorities to improve the health of this community.
- An initial meeting with a small group or 'diagonal slice' of this system to think through and design ways of working with the whole.
- Initial work with the GPs to support and challenge their perceptions of the influences on the health of residents and to prepare them to work with a wider group of stakeholders.

Further ideas will be explored later in this chapter. We start by discussing the use and design of big events.

Whole systems development using big events

In our experience, organisation development has tended to take a rather pragmatic and hierarchical approach to change. Processes have been focused within the walls of single organisations, often with a cascade approach, whereby 'higher-level' issues are worked out first with the top team and then with departments or 'horizontal slices' of the organisation. This models a command and control approach to leadership and management. Chapter Four explained a more engaging and holistic set of assumptions about leadership of whole systems.

Meeting in big events

The principles underpinning big events specifically, and whole systems development approaches generally, include:

- everyone involved in a change should be an architect of it;
- everyone in the room together – on the pitch playing – as a metaphor, and as a reality.

This means that there is a need to design and manage ways in which large numbers of people can come into the room together, at big events.

Such gatherings have many advantages:

- they are a visible representation of the complexity of the whole system;
- they enable large numbers of people (several hundreds in the largest ones) to be involved in making commitments about the way forward;
- responses to system pressures can be made rapidly and flexibly and in ways that recognise the needs and interests of stakeholders. Command and control management processes are frequently slow and frustrating for those involved;
- they are 'marker' events that can become positive stories of system change on which further efforts to improve things can be built.

However, they are usually costly in terms of financial and human resources. Consultants, internal or external, are needed to manage preparation and the event itself. Everyone involved devotes time both to the event itself and to follow-through activities. A large space conducive to this sort of collaborative activity is needed and the requirements for logistical back up are complex. The very drama engendered can heighten expectations that can be difficult to meet. This is particularly the case, if, after an event, leaders revert to excluding all but the most senior people from decisions, giving instructions rather than involving, managing down the vertical columns of the organisation rather than working across internal and external boundaries. People will then view the event cynically – as a glossy performance with little underlying intention to involve them in subsequent changes. Frustration is likely to be greater than it was before.

Having weighed up the advantages and disadvantages of large events from our own experience, we believe that their rather dramatic character can be groundbreaking. They can enable much more rapid progress to be made than is the case with other, more conventional and linear, planned change efforts. They are a graphic representation of commitment to participative decision-making about complex problems that cross organisational, geographic and cultural boundaries.

Another name for big events is large group interventions (LGIs), of which there are now many varieties in use. There is no one best design and choice must be made carefully, thinking about aims, system complexity and cultural factors. At the end of this chapter is a list of references to the relevant literature. Here, we summarise some basic design principles about such occasions:

- group composition
- the organisation of physical space
- group working
- conference organisation.

Group composition

Great care must be taken to form groups in ways that assist participants both to experience the complexity and diversity of the whole system and to take decisions about ways to improve it.

In everything other than meetings involving very small numbers of people, 'max mix' or maximum mix groups are used to assist people to experience the complexity and diversity of the whole. This acts as a stimulus to creative thinking about ways of improving things for everyone.

Organisationally based or single stakeholder groups come into their own when commitments to action are needed. This recognises the different accountabilities of stakeholder groups and the specific circumstances affecting their commitments to action.

Pre-planning the composition of max mix and home groups can be a way of speeding up the dialogue between people in these forums. However, where there are considerable tensions and suspicions about the intentions of those in leadership roles, pre-planning can lead to unhelpful and often unvoiced questioning of group composition:

- Why have I been put in this group with these people?
- Why am I not in that group with those people?
- Does this mean that my input is less valued than that of some other people?

If there are dangers that pre-planning will lead to some of these unproductive and usually unfounded fears, it may be more helpful to let people form groups in a random way. This can be achieved, for example, by letting people draw numbers from a hat on arrival. However, we suggest that, as people sit down, each group is asked to check whether their group is a reasonable approximation of the diversity of the whole group. If this is not the case, people can move groups to give a better maximum mix. This can be time-consuming, but a better sense of ownership of the design assumptions underpinning the event can be given if the rationale for maximum mix groups (and later for home groups, if these are to be used) is explained briefly.

The organisation of the physical space at events

The physical space within which meetings or conferences take place has a significant influence on their effectiveness. If people sit in rows, we can expect passive/aggressive behaviour: it is difficult to communicate with the back of someone's head. Those at the front are clearly the experts with the responsibility to entertain or inform, while the rest are expected to be quiet and take notes – they cannot contribute to the best of their abilities in these situations. Genuine interchange or dialogue is unlikely. Harrison Owen, the developer of Open Space Technology, recounts how after a well-planned, though traditionally designed, conference on organisational transformation, he realised that the best conversations had occurred during the coffee breaks (Owen, 1995). This is the challenge when designing big events – to ensure that people can have the sorts of mutually engaging conversations that occur in the informal spaces of highly structured and expert-led occasions.

When we sit at square or rectangular tables, sides are clearly drawn. The odds are that we negotiate with each other. At the very best we feel separated from each other. Whoever is at the head of the table is expected to be in control or at the very least to mediate between competing parties.

For these reasons, the spirit of public learning is more likely to prevail when people sit in a circle. Circles denote inclusion, completeness and wholeness. Genuine communication, intimacy and the appreciation of the value of difference are more likely to occur in these settings. In events that aim to improve the whole system, we seat people at round tables in a room where the work of individual groups can take place in full view of other similar groups. Communication between groups is made possible by good acoustics, public address systems with roving mikes and good visibility for each group's work on flipcharts and so on.

Room organisation and other apparently trivial details of event organisation are of tremendous significance as a means of modelling the principles underpinning whole systems approaches, breaking the mould of command and control approaches to leadership and management. The room with its separate spaces and its representation of an effectively communicating whole symbolises aspirations for the workings of the whole system.

Group working

The diversity of those present at these events will result in varying levels of confidence and willingness to speak out in a large gathering. Small group work is organised to encourage everyone's contribution. We are often asked whether this means that every small group should have a facilitator. This can be counterproductive. The aim is to structure round-table discussion so that everyone is clear about the purpose and process of each activity. To facilitate this for large events, table cards with simple timed instructions for each activity are produced, indicating that everyone's voice and their skills and experiences are equally valid and valuable.

Conference organisation

In addition to table cards, much of the usual paraphernalia of conferences are needed, such as packs with programmes and name badges. These conventions relieve the anxiety of delegates, some of whom may be attending an event of this kind – much more demanding of involvement than conventional conferences – for the first time.

Successful events are generally ones where careful attention has been paid to apparently trivial details of design. Since the complexity of the event mirrors the complexity of the system, there is considerable risk that things will go wrong. Responsibility for the management of these logistics must be clearly allocated.

Preparing people to attend a staff conference

In a situation of great anxiety in an organisation whose purpose had recently been radically changed, all invitees are emailed about what to expect.

> The conference can only be part of the process of change. Some preparation has to be done. This has taken the form of discussions with all staff and with some of our major customers. We shall be presenting summaries of these to you during the conference not as a set of expert recommendations but rather to assist the conversations between you during the two days. The summaries will not identify individuals.

> We would also like all of you to do some preparatory thinking about the present workings of the organisation, including the ways in which we could all improve our work with customers. Talk with colleagues too but don't work out solutions in advance.

> It is important to stress that we, as conference managers, will provide the context and structure for the two days. You will create the content sitting at round tables with colleagues. Sometimes you will be in work groups and sometimes in more randomly constituted groups. It will be up to you to decide when to give your views personally and when to let others speak on your behalf. A definite outcome will be that you will know more colleagues by the end of the two days than you did at the beginning! We will find creative ways of sharing the conclusions of groups' deliberations not relying on boring presentations where one group after another comes to the front to read out its thoughts.

> The final product will be the result of your common work and understanding together with agreed responsibilities for follow through. This is vital. Nothing in your every day reality will change during the two days. It is likely that task forces will be established to implement the emerging thinking and aspirations for the future. The results of the conference will be your common property and will act as guarantees that you can all work together to put good intentions into action.

Steering whole systems development – the roles of leadership, design and logistics teams

In our experience, successful whole systems development is steered by four distinct, though connected, processes:

- A leadership process that enables the voices of those with power and authority in the system to be heard. This defines the questions or issues on which stakeholders should work and the 'policy givens' within which decisions must be taken to be understood.
- A design process that develops the structures within which those involved can work on the issues defined through the leadership process.
- A logistics process that enables the detailed operational implementation of the design.
- A consultancy process that supports the whole thing, but particularly assists leaders to clarify their strategic intentions and the brief for the design team.

We tend to agree with Jacobs (1994) that processes of strategic change are best served by forming four teams – one for each of these processes. This complex hierarchy recognises that the enactment of the whole systems development principle, where everyone with a stake in a system should be an architect of it, is far from straightforward to implement.

Leadership teams

As suggested earlier in this chapter, the structure of events should symbolise the desired workings of the whole system. One of the key issues is to clarify the policy and contextual 'givens'. It may be feasible for participants to challenge these, but they serve to set a framework within which different ways of doing things can be explored, developed and decided upon. To make this manifest may be achieved by round-table groups and a place in the room where leaders can address the whole gathering. In this way, both the characteristics of the leadership process and self-organising groups are visible within an event. Leaders should further demonstrate this 'freedom within frameworks' by clearly explaining their purpose, policies and aspirations in ways that enable rather than restrict action. People can make sense of the whole and their part in it with the assistance of these messages from people in positions of power and influence.

Leaders often underestimate the importance of their role. Sometimes this is because they assume, usually wrongly, that other people will understand or be able to make sense of the questions or issues that need to be addressed. They often see a design team as able to fulfil the leadership as well as the design role. Or, quite simply, the pressure of everyday work and the logistics of getting together get in the way of good intentions to lead systemic and longer-term change – the urgent pushes out the important, to quote a cliché.

A key role for the consultancy team is assisting leaders to understand and enact their roles, thinking carefully about the rationale for the changes they desire and ways of communicating this to others. The challenge for leaders can be summarised as recognising the need to balance the tension between over-prescribing the processes that will enable their aims to be met, and leaving things too wide open, increasing the sense of tension and ambiguity experienced by the design team and then, if this is not resolved, by other people.

Leaders on the stage

A leadership team had thought carefully about the ways in which it could depict its beliefs about leadership and staff involvement at a large staff conference. It wanted to enact these early on in the event. Accordingly, the chief executive interviewed each team member on a stage at the end of the conference hall, aiming in a light-hearted fashion to capture some of their qualities as people. However, this did not have the desired effect on other participants, who saw it as stage-managed and distant.

The team learnt from this and during the rest of the conference they interacted at the same level as other participants. For example, a team meeting was held in a 'fishbowl'[1] observed by, and with some interaction with, other members of staff.

Design teams

Designers must frequently grapple with the fine line between over- and under-structuring a big event. Too tight a structure may thwart the voicing, hearing and understanding of diverse views in ways that enable effective decision-making. The right amount of structure is reassuring and helps people to function in a healthy way. The dilemma is deciding how much anxiety exists and how much structure is needed. Because the design team itself is a microcosm of the system, it should be well placed to make these judgements, provided, of course, that it has developed itself to manage diversity and handle conflict constructively.

See earlier in the chapter (page 114) for a brief exploration of this aspect of the work of design teams. The rationale for, and composition of, design teams is covered in Chapter Six (pages 101-5).

Because of their composition, design teams have the advantage of credibility with those who populate the system. They are one of 'us'; they speak our language. Their planning will be assisted by their local knowledge. Their role is to develop the purpose and structure of the event in the light of the messages emerging from those in leadership roles. They do their own diagnosis of the current workings of the system and start to define aspirations for the future. This includes researching power relationships and organisational cultures.

Coming together as a group of strangers charged with the ambitious task of assisting others to make sense of complex cross-cultural or organisational issues is very daunting. At the beginning people are likely to be asking themselves and each other questions such as:

- Why have we taken this on?
- What is this task anyway?
- Where are the resources to do it?
- What does the leadership or management team want us to do?
- What are they trying to achieve anyway?
- How will other people see our role?
- How willing are others going to be to get involved?

Very skilled facilitation is needed to assist these teams to function effectively, to use their knowledge, skills and perspectives to best effect, and to feel confident about their plans. (See Chapter 6, page 104 for an introductory exercise to get a design team started.)

Design teams need time to get to know each other, to establish personal relationships that will enable them to carry out the task they have taken on. They need to feel that it is legitimate to raise their concerns. The introductory exercise is one method for such teams to voice their experiences and perspectives in ways that will enable them to work with the tensions and dilemmas of the system. Only then are they likely to be able to converse effectively with those in leadership and other roles. There can be friction between the design team and other teams as thinking progresses. For example, members of the design team will be employed within some of the organisations that comprise the system. This is likely to make it difficult for them constructively to challenge leaders in those organisations about ways of resolving previously intractable problems. Consultants can help by supporting design teams to clarify and handle the issues involved with those in leadership roles.

The consultancy team

Two of the key tasks for this team are touched on earlier in this chapter:

- Assisting leaders to clarify their role and ways of enacting it.
- Supporting designers to use their differences creatively in the development of processes that will enable leaders' intentions to be explored and worked with.

Careful contracting for consultancy support is vital. Inevitably, these processes become 'white-knuckle rides' if they are to achieve second-order or transformational change. Trust and openness between the various teams is critical. In the early stages, this applies particularly to the development of the relationship between the consultants and the leaders. If this is established, it will be possible for those in leadership roles to explore their aspirations, both common and different, and to anticipate the challenges involved in including large numbers of other stakeholders in the journey ahead.

In summary, the role of consultants, either internal or external, in supporting the whole process is significant. They can:

- enable those in leadership, design and logistic positions to clarify understanding about their roles and relationships;
- facilitate interaction between teams, reconciling purposes and helping to build confidence to drive the process;
- stimulate the development of understanding about power relationships and organisational cultures, so that learning across the system can be encouraged through the design of appropriate interventions;
- provide experience and skills in the facilitation of effective processes for working within and between small and large groups and creating the frameworks and forums to strengthen the capabilities of those in planning roles;
- judge when direction, support, guidance, facilitation and event management are required and be prepared to withdraw when others should more usefully take centre-stage roles.

This last point needs expansion. The diversity of participants means that big events require managing rather than merely facilitating. Large-scale interventions are generally designed to answer specific questions posed to the system in the room by those in leadership roles. Design teams will have thought through a detailed process to enable the voice of all present to be heard. The numbers present and their expectations create a sense of drama and anticipation. Frequently, there is anxiety because new futures can only be built if blocks to change, such as power and status assumptions, are directly challenged. For a process of public learning to occur that constructively addresses issues that may have previously been ignored is challenging and stressful for all involved.

People who run whole system events must be capable of personally managing the fine line between taking too much control of the process so that it becomes the consultants' show and abdicating all control to participants – letting a thousand flowers bloom without assisting each to understand the field within which it is growing. The role has been compared to that of the soccer umpire who, if he is caught up in the play, quickly runs backwards out of the action, hands above head indicating a determination not to get caught up again.

This is a hard balance to achieve. Those involved will benefit from training or, at least, working alongside someone more experienced. Effectiveness is assisted both by an understanding of the conceptual underpinnings of this work and by capabilities that enable participants, and design teams in particular, to do what they intend, not what the consultant thinks they should do.

Leaders meet designers

The chief executive of a voluntary organisation decided to hold a two-day staff conference with the following aims:

• to share and develop our values as a voluntary organisation;
• to acknowledge our achievements;
• to strengthen the services that we provide;
• to identify what kind of organisation we want to become in the next ten years.

A design team is established, comprised of a cross section of staff. The team is assisted by an external consultant. After getting to know each other well and working to understand the principles on which its task rests, the team shapes a draft design for the conference. A meeting is arranged with the executive team, including the chief executive, to discuss the design.

The meeting is amicable. One part of the proposed structure for the conference involves the running of a number of parallel workshops. The aim of these is to enable participants to understand more clearly the range of services that the organisation provides, to share examples of emerging successful working and to enable learning from these examples to stimulate thinking about future possibilities for the organisation. At the meeting, the chief executive and another director become very challenging of the choice of workshops. This seems to be because they have failed to listen sufficiently to the rationale for the workshops. Additionally, the director is concerned because the design team has not included any workshop about a large area of service managed by the director. The design team is nervous at this sudden challenge but then, because of the depth of thinking and planning already done, is able to articulate its reasoning clearly. Dialogue takes place unimpaired by rank and role within the organisation. Some small changes are made and both teams feel satisfied with the result.

This positive story illustrates the potential for learning but also for frustration at this point in the design of strategic change processes. In this case, the in-depth work done by the design team and supported by the consultant gave them the authority to explain why the conference should be designed in this way. Had the work been more superficial and the team less cohesive, it is likely that the greater formal power of the directors would have resulted in the design being changed. This would have been detrimental to the work in hand and, more seriously, to the commitment and motivation of the designers.

(This example also serves to illustrate another of the difficulties of the notion of 'good' or 'best practice'. The defining processes of what is to count or not count are so often shaped by the internal power politics of an organisation and/or how that organisation wants to present itself to a wider world. Many will have a vested interest in denying 'best practice' from another area, and, of course, it is always easier to do things in Cleckhuddersfax. Judgements that come top-down through this dangerously competitive environment may also be at odds with how other key stakeholders see things, especially service users.

However, not recognising and learning from good innovations and improvements in service delivery is a parallel problem. We know of one social services department that formally states that all its services for elderly people across the district are of a uniform good standard, but is very adept at directing the inspection hordes to one particular area.)

Logistics teams

The role of logistics teams should not be undervalued. Finding the right venue, hiring the right sound system, having the right-sized round tables for group work and issuing invitations at the right time are not minor details that can be left to chance. It is vital to ensure that whole systems events run seamlessly.

Learning from involvement in leading and designing big events

Run effectively, big events are stretching, challenging and 'learningful' for all involved. Leaders learn a great deal about leading; designers learn much about assisting the process of learning and change across complex systems; and consultants develop qualities to integrate action and learning across organisations, communities and cultures and to manage the consequent tensions to further the purposes of all involved.

Reflecting on experiences of conferences or big events

Think about the last time you attended a conference or large meeting in or hosted by your own organisation.

- What was its purpose?
- How was planning undertaken? Who was involved? How did they decide on the design of the event? How did they invite others to come along?
- What was the role of those in positions of power and authority at the event?
- How did participants interact with each other during the event? How were their views heard? What were the conversations about in the breaks? Were people saying things at that time that they would have been reluctant to voice in public?
- How were the themes of the meeting or conference summarised at the end?
- What were people saying as they went away?
- What action is being taken as a result of the event? How are participants informed about this? How involved are they in these outcomes?
- Did those who designed the event collectively review their learning? What was that learning? How will it be used in future?

When you reflect on some of the methods and approaches covered here, you may raise questions about their transferability into other cultures. For example, in some cultures there is a reluctance to challenge voices of authority and a preference for didactic methods. There may also be a reluctance to address history openly in some places. However, generally, most of these issues can be worked through by the design team, provided its developmental process has been thorough and sensitive to the dynamics of the system within which it is working.

Activity – reviewing the design of a large event

In Chapter Six (pages 108-10) there is a detailed design of a large event. Having reflected on your own experience, it may be helpful to think about some specific aspects of this design:

• How were decisions made about who should be invited?

There is no exact science to this. Because the aim was to hear the questions of those in leadership roles to create ownership for the subsequent process of collaborative enquiry, there was keenness to ensure that there was a good cross section of such people in the room.

• How useful is a graffiti wall?

Graffiti walls have a number of uses in large events:

• Sometimes other relevant issues occur to participants as they work on specific activities in their max mix groups. These can be flagged up on the wall and reviewed at an appropriate point.
• Sometimes information is required from participants about the potential for other follow-through work. This is the case here.
• However, it can be the case that the graffiti wall is hardly used, either for reasons of time or because people feel able to say everything in their groups. Sometimes the wall will not be used if people have doubts about whether leaders are serious about involving everyone in change.

• What is the effect of using an expert panel in a whole systems development event?

An expert panel can be useful for bringing new sources of information to strengthen whole systems working. On the other hand, the use of experts can contradict assertions that everyone's perspective is valuable and get in the way of public learning across the system.

- As a member of the design group, what do you think you would be feeling at the end of this day?
- You should have a good grasp of the perspectives of those in leadership roles. Provided you received useful training in this role, you should feel well prepared to begin to grapple with an outline design for the following stakeholder event.
- You may also feel rather tired. This is an action-packed agenda, carrying the danger that insufficient understanding is developed between these key players to clarify the most important questions for the subsequent process with stakeholders. When we were commissioned to assist with this we were faced with the need to hear the voices of leadership and to establish commitment to the approach across the system. Achieving this takes longer than a single day. However, had these people been invited to a longer event, the odds are that they would have felt unable to devote personal time to it, because of the commitment to their day-to-day work with service users.

Big events are not the only whole systems 'show in town'

At the beginning of this chapter, we addressed the question 'How can everyone look at the whole elephant together?' This question can be used to explore the various processes that can assist whole systems development. While big events bring everyone into the room together to explore the workings of the whole system, they are not the only way of doing this. We can also develop processes that, while they directly involve smaller numbers of people, focus on enabling everyone involved to see and be engaged in the dynamics of the wider system. In other words, 'everyone in the room together' can become a metaphor describing a way of working that enables the actors to see and feel the wider system. They are assisted to make collective sense of the 'world out there' and individual sense of 'the world in here' (self-knowledge) so that they can communicate and take action across the system. The focus is both on the tasks or problems with which individuals are confronted *and* the self-development of those involved. Participants are involved in a shared process of meaning that enables them to create frameworks of understanding within which to act.

Double-loop learning as a core process of whole systems development

Double-loop learning (Argyris and Schon, 1978; Argyris, 1991), in which people consciously reflect on and question their assumptions or theories-in-use, is a core process of whole systems development. It strengthens the collective capability to 'learn how to learn' within the complex networks of contemporary society. At big events, for example, by being exposed to ways of looking at the world, which differ from their own, participants come to revise their assumptions about ways of understanding and resolving intractable problems. Such exploration also occurs powerfully within smaller groups or learning sets where participants are challenged and supported to revise their assumptions about their world and capability to act within it.

Equally, processes can be designed where networks of learners from different organisations, interest groups and communities come together as 'communities of practice' (Drath and Palus, 1994) to re-vision the 'wicked' issues with which society is confronted. This is a particularly interesting and powerful way of meeting differently to change traditional and often problematic methods of working across boundaries. Since we see working in this way as a key challenge of leading whole systems change in future, it is covered in some detail in Chapter Nine.

Action learning

Action learning and the work of Reg Revans has already been introduced in Chapter Two (pages 25-6). It is a key whole systems process that enables people to meet differently in small groups in ways that can have a significant impact. It is a means of developing double loop learning capabilities. The practice of action learning within the context of whole systems working is described in the Chapter Three case study (pages 40-54).

'There can be no learning without action and no sober and deliberate action without learning.' This key axiom of Reg Revans lies at the heart of work on action learning. This perspective sees knowing as inseparable from doing, and learning as dependent on taking action. This is core to the development of learning across whole systems.

Revans (1983) argues that organisations and the individuals in them will not thrive unless processes of learning and change are integrated. He suggests that for effective change (C), the rate of learning (L) needs to be greater than or equal to the rate of change being experienced, that is:

$$L > C$$

It is sad but true that many of the people exhibiting the symptoms of workaholism identified by Roger Harrison are doing too much changing – trying to fix problems and not enough learning together about ways of resolving them.

Action learning requires everyone to work on a real problem – working and learning simultaneously. It is not about coming up with elegant solutions that other people can implement, rather it focuses on taking action and learning from it. Only by testing ideas in practice do we know whether they are effective and practical. To clarify the sorts of issues that are conducive to an action learning approach, Revans distinguishes between puzzles and problems. Puzzles have a known answer and can be solved with the help of experts. Problems have no known answers. They are dilemmas where different people in different circumstances would suggest different solutions. It is a case of using questioning insight to come up with the best way forward in the circumstances.

From this, we can see that learning consists of programmed knowledge (P), which can be applied to puzzles and questioning insight (Q), which must be applied to problems, that is:

$$L = P + Q$$

Learning to ask discriminating questions is thus at the heart of action learning. Systematic reflection is also vital. It is by replaying events, feelings and conversations that we can better understand ourselves or 'the world in here' in the context of 'the world out there'. In addition to trying to understand what happened and why, we learn to apply questioning insight to our values, beliefs and behaviours. Reflecting makes us more aware of ourselves and of our impact on others.

Action learning is not a solitary process. It is about learning from and with others who are also learning to tackle problems rather than puzzles. Revans coined the phrase 'comrades in adversity' to describe the process of working together to reveal doubts and areas of ignorance as a springboard from which to deepen insights and achieve greater clarity. In action learning, as it has developed in the UK, this collective learning takes place within a group or learning set of approximately six people. There are two aspects to this: people learn as they take action on the problem in its organisational setting and, at the same time, they learn about themselves – style, skill, attitudes, and so on. The process of taking action and that of learning are mutually reinforcing.

Action learning, therefore, can be a major contributor to whole systems development. Because it integrates problem-based learning with individual development, it has the potential to be a significant contributor to the development of individual organisations and to learning across the whole system, in which the particular organisation is but one player. This is demonstrated in the Gladwell case study in Chapter Three, where we explore the use of action learning within the facilitators' set as a vehicle for systemic learning rather than merely a process of individual development, as is the case within many management development programmes. The purpose of action learning there was the improvement of the system of local governance and service delivery in which the facilitators had important roles. Of course the work they did within the action learning set also proved a powerful stimulus to their personal development.

The following example gives a flavour of the ways in which action learning programmes that cross organisational boundaries can have a broad systemic impact.

An inter-organisational action learning programme

An action learning programme with participants from health organisations, a pharmaceutical company and other NHS suppliers is established. The participants are medical managers, doctors and other senior health professionals, researchers, managers and senior sales people from the pharmaceutical company, and senior supplies and logistics personnel from the other organisations. Individuals agree projects with sponsors from their own organisations. Guidelines for project selection have been agreed by an inter-organisational steering group:

Projects must:

- have the potential to improve relationships between participating organisations;
- enable learning and action to be integrated;
- support the personal development of individual participants – be part of their personal development plan;
- encourage the participant to venture beyond the 'walls' of their own organisations;
- focus on a problem – to which there is no known solution – rather than a puzzle for which a solution is more readily apparent.

Coaching and mentoring as whole systems processes

Coaching and mentoring of individuals can also assist the development of systemic perspectives by encouraging people to explore perspectives other than their own and, generally, to think broadly about ways of improving connections across boundaries.

The challenge to meet differently – a summary

Most people would find it instructive to calculate how many hours a year they spend in conventional meetings. This time is often spent sitting at a rectangular table with printed agendas, minutes of the last meeting and formal papers. This sort of meeting is a symbol of the command and control culture of many organisations. It enables the agenda to be managed so that all items are dealt with and all decisions recorded. However, if looked at through a whole systems development lens, such meetings often fail to ensure that:

- all voices are heard
- expertise in the group is well utilised
- everyone feels valued, and so on.

The processes of both large and small group working described here are much more likely to ensure that meetings meet the success criteria of those involved.

How could the meetings in which we spend so much of our time be more effective? We could ensure that everyone's voice is heard. A simple but important device to this end is one that is used both in big events, as described in this chapter, and in action learning. Everyone can 'check in', simply and briefly stating what they would like to get out of the meeting. The agenda can then be examined to see that it meets these aims. An effective chair can ensure that everyone stays involved.

Quaker business practice is another useful guide in this respect (see Chapter Five, pages 91-92). Meetings run as the Quakers do can create a very different climate of openness and trust from that developed in situations where the minutes have habitually been written after the meeting and circulated much later. We have all heard people say that sometimes the minutes seem to reflect a different meeting! Or, even worse, there may be suspicions that they were written before the meeting took place, since the process was designed as a rubber stamp for decisions that had already been made.

Sustaining whole systems processes and practices

In the last four chapters, we have explored ways in which whole systems development can be orchestrated. However, the evidence about the implementation of successful change (see Chapter One, pages 1-7) suggests that understanding how such processes are sustained is vital. It is to this issue that we turn in Chapter Eight.

Note

[1] Fishbowl activities have been held at training events for many years. A group of participants sit in the centre of the room observed by others while they perform a task or have a discussion. Often one seat is left empty enabling a few members of the 'audience', in turn, to join the group. At big events, this is a useful device, as in this case, for teams to work 'in camera' or for the outcomes of discussions in small groups to be shared with the larger group.

EIGHT

Follow-through and sticking with it

A friend used to tell the story of a great African river that started high in the mountains and became a rushing torrent sweeping all before it; but when it came to the plain, its momentum slowed and it split into many rivulets on the flat land. Soon it became a huge swamp and the mighty river had disappeared. Change efforts often start with great momentum, as attempts to tackle previously intractable problems, but then, as time passes and the terrain changes, energy for these efforts dissipates.

This analogy, however, can be viewed somewhat differently in whole systems terms. As those who took O level Geography will recall, it is the force of the river in its early course that creates steep valleys; as the river grows in volume, its energy disperses and it meanders to the sea. But the energy does not disappear. A feature of meandering rivers is the oxbow lake – a deep bend in the river, which becomes isolated as the river takes the shortest course. And of course, it is in the rich river floodplains and deltas that agriculture does best. So the river does what it needs to do to meet the sea, bending around obstacles, and can look very different in appearance from the mountain stream to the broad delta. But it is all part of a connected cycle of rainfall, water catchment, coastal and ocean systems.

In whole systems terms, follow-through is inextricably linked with the challenge of implementation, of getting things done and generating change in the long term. It does not have the same connotations as follow-up (the odd meeting to catch up with progress), rather it carries with it the somewhat old-fashioned virtues of persistence, resilience and sticking with it, alongside the more modern attributes of sensitivity to, and awareness of, the changing character of the environment in which we operate. So by follow-through we mean all of those activities and processes that help bring about change, translate strategy into actions and make a difference. Importantly, follow-through is not a fixed top-down process; it is an organic, dynamic process intimately connected to the circumstances and context in which the change challenge takes place.

In this chapter, we:

- introduce and develop the idea of change architecture;
- develop the links between change architectures, the Five Keys and the other important principles for leading change developed in Chapter Three (holding frameworks, middle-ground frameworks and widening circles of inclusivity);
- reiterate and develop the role and purpose of action learning within whole systems processes;

- emphasise the continuing importance of creating 'memories of the future' through scenario building and wider inclusion;
- connect to the last two chapters on the newer forms of organising and working towards local solutions with wider whole systems.

Arguably, this chapter is the most important in the book. Sustaining real long-term change seems notoriously difficult. Despite the fine rhetoric from the world of Management (and MMV), change efforts often amount to little more than restructurings, single events, disconnected initiatives and bouts of episodic 'sheep-dip' type training programmes. However, the deeper currents of organisational culture and behaviour so often stubbornly remain the same. The central idea of whole systems development is to provide more substantial routes towards sustainable implementation. But, paradoxically, this chapter is also the shortest. This is because its main purpose is to link the ideas from the previous chapters and link forward to the last two. Change architecture is the organising idea of how to do this. This chapter also anticipates some of the thinking contained in the Epilogue, where we finally pull together the core elements developed throughout the book.

Change architecture

Our first acquaintance with change architecture was provided by Rosabeth Moss Kanter in her groundbreaking book *The change masters* (1984). Change efforts so often fail because high-level executives fail 'to design and construct the new "platform" to support the innovation'. She continues:

> Corporate change – rebuilding if you will – has parallels to the most ambitious and perhaps most noble of the plastic arts, architecture. The skill of corporate leaders, the ultimate change masters, lies in their ability to envision a new reality and aid its translation into concrete terms. Creative visions combine with the building up of events, floor by floor, from foundation to completed construction. How productive change occurs is part artistic design, part management of construction.... The ultimate skill for change mastery works on ... the larger context surrounding the innovation process. It consists of the ability to conceive, construct and convert into behaviour a new view of organisational reality. (pp 278-9)

The building metaphor is a good one. Establishing change architecture involves creating purposeful and imaginative designs crafted into their own particular contexts, as well as carrying out the 'concrete' and specific framework of activities that turn design into reality. Just as there is no one best way to design and construct any building, there is no best way to lead change and construct the necessary change architecture to build and sustain it. A change architecture may be initiated from the top, but becomes so much stronger where all those involved in change can have a stake in designing both the changes taking place and the architecture for sustaining them. Essentially, it is a plan or timetable of activities that serves as a holding framework to embrace any appropriate content at any given time. Its value is in building a predictable *process* to frame an unpredictable content and detail of change.

Many, if not most, so-called whole systems interventions focus on 'big events', generating huge energy that then fades for lack of a sustaining process for implementing change over the longer term.

The change architecture does not specify the *content* of change, because this is often locally invented and not known in advance. This contrasts sharply with the predictable, one-size-fits-all targets of programmatic change. The substantive outcomes of any whole systems development process are vital and no change architecture makes sense without them. Few will bother to engage for long with the effort of arguing for and making changes if no observable effects can be seen. Yet these outcomes are often not what was specified in advance. Sometimes the effects are far greater than could have been envisaged; shifts too small to be listed as targets can transform the quality of people's engagement and have a major long-term impact.

Change architecture and equifinality

The complex systems concept of equifinality was introduced in Chapter Two (pages 24–5). In short, it is the notion that there are likely to be many equal paths to a potential destination; or many ways to skin a cat. It fits well with the idea mentioned earlier of crafting design, and it runs counter to Utopian ideas of the 'one best way' methods or techniques. The core of our argument is that change architectures need to be designed to take account of specific contexts, yet remain adaptable to both external change and that arising from the innovations being worked on. Figure 11 offers one possible configuration of activities that could be the outcome of what was both pre-designed and evolved through intentional processes of reflection, action and serendipity. For those familiar with his work, crafting change architectures fits well with Henry Mintzberg's idea of crafting strategy (Mintzberg, 1994).

Follow-through, the other Four Keys and whole systems principles

Two messages have been a recurrent theme throughout this book.

- Firstly, change is not an event; the current state of things will in most cases be the result of a long history, as well as past successes created in different circumstances. Lasting change will only be brought about over time.
- Secondly, whole systems development should not be equated with single events or large group interventions (LGIs).

Figure 10: A change architecture

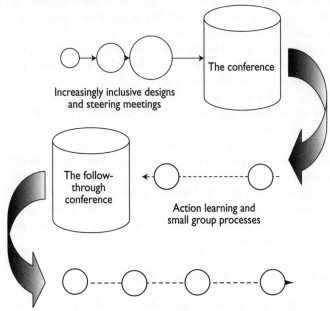

Increasingly inclusive designs
and steering meetings

The conference

The follow-
through
conference

Action learning and
small group processes

Action learning and ongoing review of progress, learning and change

From this perspective, the other Four Keys (listed below) are inextricably linked with developing change architectures and working over time to bring about sustained change.

- Leadership (Chapter Four)
- Public learning (Chapter Five)
- Valuing difference and diversity (Chapter Six)
- Meeting differently (Chapter Seven).

In perhaps his most striking organisational metaphor, Gareth Morgan talked about 'organisations as brains' (1986, pp 77-109) and introduced the idea of holographic design.

> To compare the brain with a hologram may be stretching reason beyond the limits. However, the way a holographic plate enfolds all the information necessary to produce a complete image in each of its parts has much in common with the functioning of the brain. And it is possible to extend this image to create a vision of organization where capacities required in whole are enfolded in the parts, allowing the system to learn and self-organize, and to maintain a complete system of functioning even when specific parts malfunction or are removed. (p 95)

According to Morgan, the human brain is made up of a limited number of cells arranged in repetitive units. What gives it its amazing capacity in comparison with animal life is its ability to generate such high-level and rich connectivity between cells. It is this that also creates in the human brain the capacity or space to anticipate and adjust to changing circumstances. It has built-in 'redundancy', which allows us to envision different possibilities and respond to them, to adjust and change, and, above all, both to learn and learn how to learn.

From the living complex systems perspectives developed out of our practice and theory, these are the parallel capacities we want to develop across organisations and whole systems. The development and use of the Five Keys is the route for doing this, but they need to become integral to the way of acting and not simply saved for special days, or the language talked at big events. They need to permeate the design and implementation of a change architecture that becomes the 'container' for working towards long-term, sustainable change.

Follow-through and whole systems principles

Other important principles in designing change architectures are the creation of space for leadership via holding frameworks and middle-ground frameworks; the use of action learning in the trial and implementation of agreed changes; and, finally, as change architecture connects with the organising introduced in the next chapter; the recognition that how we organise to create and deliver goods and services is itself changing, away from single, standalone organisations towards more networked forms.

Widening circles of inclusivity

What comprises the whole system? Who is included (and excluded)? What is the right boundary for this particular purpose? Getting the whole system into the room together is not possible until these questions are answered.

As the case study in Chapter Three shows, the focus was at first mainly confined to the seven pilot neighbourhoods. Yet it soon became clear that this was too limited a view. As Figure 4 in Chapter Three shows, the whole system can be defined in multiple ways as the circle of who is included widens; in this case, to the point where the big picture covered the whole of UK local government.

The notion of widening circles of inclusivity starts with the people with the problem, and moves progressively wider, with the limits set by available resources and short-term goals. There is no one system, but many, and any, bounded entity can be used as a whole or as a part of a wider whole depending upon purposes. The importance of the ability to work progressively more widely rests on Einstein's famous dictum that problems cannot be solved within their own systems but only at the level above.

Middle-ground frameworks

Middle-ground frameworks connect overall strategic direction with local knowledge and learning on the ground. In Chapter Three, the middle-ground framework was the progressive conversation over a series of meetings between the board and the facilitators' group, which allowed learning from local action to influence policy and for organisational direction to be translated into sensible local action.

In working with multiple communities and agencies, a middle-ground framework can help with the dialogue of local and professional, and can fill a temporary leadership gap created by any change. Middle-ground frameworks are holding frameworks – minimalist, loose and always being reconfigured – the process of dialogue involved being among their most useful properties.

The pivotal role of action learning

The core ideas associated with action learning have been introduced earlier (see especially Chapter Two, pages 25-6 and Chapter Seven, pages 127-9). The case study in Chapter Three (pages 40-54) describes an action-learning process as a key part of working with whole systems. There are also a number of referenced texts in these two sections for those who want to explore the ideas and theory further. For those wishing to acquaint themselves with the practice, there is only one way; to engage personally in an action-learning process or inquiry.

The central idea is that any real intractable problem or issue becomes the focus for study, inquiry, action and reflection. Individuals may come to a group, each with their own project and questions, as relative or total strangers to each other. Alternatively, a group can consist of all or many of those who have a stake in an issue and have some energy to seek improvement. In terms of whole systems and change architecture, action learning projects and groups can be thought of as a series of nodes across the system, working on the difficult or intractable problems that are being experienced. Again, employing the idea that problems cannot be solved within their own systems but only at the level above, it becomes apparent that the more richly connected action-learning groups are to each other and the hierarchy, the more likely it is that whole system improvement can take place. This also develops the whole systems brain-like potential that Morgan talks about in the process of tackling the systems' difficulties.

Two insights from the work of the quality guru, Dr W.E. Deming (for example, Deming, 1986, 1993; Deming and Watson, 1990), are also useful here. He talked about the necessity of having 'constancy of purpose' when seeking to work to improve the quality of anything; his take on 'sticking with it'. He also talked about the special role of managers. 'Workers work in the system' he would say and many of the important changes that need to be made to improve the quality of goods and services are 'boundary conditions' that only managers have the authority to change. Therefore, all need to work together. (Incidentally, for those who have not come across Deming's work, he saw no inherent contradiction between improving the quality of anything and seeking efficiency.)

Action learning, sets and facilitation

Action learning has tended to become associated with a particular format: a facilitated 'set' – a group of around six people plus a facilitator. The members of a set are likely to be managers bringing with them their individual issues to work on with each other. They are less likely to be a cross section of individuals working to solve a problem together. Increasingly, we seek to encourage organisations to engage more creatively with the spirit and principles of Revan's ideas. The use of sets and facilitators was not central to his approach. It may be better to think in terms of groups having access to particular resources and people when they need them. This is because they may decide they want help with their group process (they feel stuck) or because they need access to further knowledge or problem-solving tools that can take them forward. From their questions, they seek out the assistance of appropriate knowledge. In Chapter Seven (page 117), meeting differently makes a similar argument and demonstrates why we are reluctant to facilitate groups in larger events. This is not to reject the idea of facilitation: in many cases, for action-learning groups to get started, it may be essential. But there has been a tendency to assume a particular formatted way of working with action learning and this risks limiting its potential when working with whole systems development because it can mitigate against taking responsibility for self-organising.

Action learning: giving the work back to the people

Where organisations and whole systems face intractable issues, problems and questions, nobody knows the answers. Those in positions of high formal authority can still provide the organisation/whole system with broad overall strategic direction and start to articulate its 'adaptive challenges' (Heifetz and Laurie, 1997). According to Heifetz and Laurie:

> ... adaptive work is required when our deeply held beliefs are challenged, when the values that made us successful become less relevant, and when legitimate yet competing perspectives emerge.... We see adaptive challenges every day at every level of the workplace [And to this we can add communities as well]. Adaptive problems are often systemic problems with no ready answers. (p 124)

The leadership challenge is to encourage others to identify these adaptive challenges and then to support people as they collaborate to work on them. Making changes is difficult at any level and is often experienced by those involved as stressful. In these circumstances, leaders have to carry their own stress plus that of their people. Heifetz (1994) talks of the need for holding frameworks to contain and regulate distress. This is explored in Chapter Four on leadership. It is also the arena for giving the work back to the people. Left to themselves, they may well expect senior managers to sort out the problems, but without the knowledge and information held at these lower and local levels. And too frequently, senior managers expect that they 'should' sort out and solve the unsolvable alone to meet expectations from both above and below. These dynamics create conditions of dependency at lower levels and a flight from taking responsibility. "People tend to become passive, and senior managers who pride themselves on being problem solvers take decisive action" (Heifetz and Laurie, 1997, p 129). But this only restores the equilibrium in the short term by avoiding the underlying need for radical change and encouraging as many as possible to take on adaptive work.

> Letting people take the initiative in defining and solving problems means that management needs to learn to support rather than control. Workers for their part, need to learn to take responsibility. (p 129)

Networked action-learning processes across the whole system are the means of doing this and a vehicle for giving the work back to the people. The change architecture needs to be designed as the holding framework; an arena for sharing and networking ideas, learning, success and failure, enthusiasm and pain.

Action learning, new patterns of working and culture change

There is a further important factor to discuss – the pivotal role of action-learning processes within whole systems processes. In general, it has been useful that greater attention has been given to the role of organisational cultures ('the way we do things round here') in organisational change. The problem, however, is that it so often leads to earnest discussions about changing the culture that somehow take on a life of their own. This gets divorced from the task of putting people to work on the adaptive challenges; the deep-seated need to find new ways of providing services and solutions to intractable problems in different and hopefully in more preventative and sustainable ways. This can lead to any amount of well-intentioned effort, often in the form of ambitious vision and value statements, glossy communications, training programmes, restructurings, and so on. But so often nothing really feels the change, especially the culture.

An action learning perspective starts the other way round. People are meeting differently around the significant concrete tasks that need to be addressed to improve the systems performance. It is through the cyclical practice of this work – questioning, probing, analysing, negotiating, taking action, reflecting, collaborating – that roles, relationships and behaviours start to change and confidence is built. Cultures start to change as people work, relate and behave differently. This insight needs to be put at the centre of designing change architecture for sticking with it and moving towards long-term sustainable change.

The sequencing and purpose of different approaches to change

Beer et al (1990) provide further strong empirical support for these approaches to change. In their classic study, *The critical path to corporate renewal*, they describe similar paths taken in organisations (in the private sector in the US) that have been successful in making radical and lasting change. This is in contrast to the majority of firms in their study who were unsuccessful because of their adherence to programmatic, top-down Managerialist approaches to change. Change methods and processes are classified along two dimensions: those that focus on the individual versus the organisation as a whole and those that focus on informal behaviour versus formal organisation design. This is illustrated in Table 3.

This approach to successful change is as much applicable to working across whole systems as it is to individual organisations. It is also worth noting that there are many similarities between the 'critical path' approach and those

Table 3: Sequencing organisational interventions for learning

| | Level of focus | |
	Organisation/business unit level	Individual or team level
Change method/process seeks to modify:		
Informal behaviour	(1) Redefinition of roles, responsibilities and relationships around key business priorities	(2) Training Briefing Coaching/counselling Team building Management development programmes
Formal design	(4) Organisation structure Information systems Compensation systems Monitoring and measurement systems	(3) Performance appraisal Recruitment and selection Career planning Training needs assessment

Source: Adapted from Beer et al (1990); Wilkinson and Appelbee (1999)

pioneered in 'whole school improvement' methodologies by Michael Fullan and others (see Fullan, 1991; Hopkins et al, 1994).

Keeping an eye on the future

In Chapter Five, we talked about the need to develop collective memories of the future. In designing change processes and architectures, there needs to be continuing space for a critical mass of people to engage in thinking about working with the future. Constructing different scenarios about the future and how broad societal changes could interact in different ways and combinations within our organisations and whole systems can be a very effective way of developing new insights. Of course, we can never predict the future, but scenario building processes can allow us to test assumptions and think flexibly about different options. It helps to keep working with the gap between future possibilities and the concrete experience of now. And it will illuminate the untested, and possibly unconscious, ideas, assumptions and mental pictures that we carry from the past into our work of today. It helps balance the inherent difficulty of human existence; that life is lived forwards but understood backwards.

Scenario planning for the future of a university

The vice-chancellor's team in a leading university is thinking through more effective ways of enabling the university to respond to the competitive higher education environment of the late 20th century.

With the assistance of an external consultant, the team develops a range of future scenarios. Firstly, they do some environmental analysis, sharing their assumptions about major political, economic, technological, social and environmental influences, at international, national and local levels, which will affect the university in the next five to ten years. The group then divides to work separately on a number of scenarios for that time. One pair takes a realistically optimistic view, another a more pessimistic perspective and a third try to extrapolate from the current position. Each pair asks and answers the following questions as if they were living five to ten years into the future:

- How are we, as the vice-chancellor's team, doing in terms of fulfilling the purposes of the university?
- How effectively are we steering processes of research, teaching and programme development? What are students, sponsors and other stakeholders saying about our performance?
- What have we done together and separately that has got us to this position? What have been the critical incidents over the past five years?
- What capabilities have we demonstrated? What have been our failings?

From the results of these deliberations, the group as a whole asks:

- What do we need to do now, together and separately, to avoid the worst case and achieve the best?

In assisting the team to explore their pictures of the future, the consultant:

- encourages members to share their perceptions of the personal implications of particular organisational futures; this creates a greater sense of reality and commitment to any later decisions;
- challenges people to think about the perspectives of other stakeholders on the issues identified; this helps with the 'triangulation' of the problem;
- facilitates the team's planning of the ways in which this thinking can be shared with other members of the university, so that the sensitive political dynamics can be handled and the futures they have sketched can be enriched through the involvement of others.

From redundancy of parts to redundancy of functions

> Any system with an ability to self-organise must have an element of redundancy: a form of excess capacity which, appropriately designed and used, creates room for manoeuvre [sic]. Without such redundancy, a system has no real capacity to reflect on and question how it is operating and hence to change its mode of functioning in constructive ways. In other words, it has no capacity for intelligence in the sense of being able to adjust action to take account of changes in the nature of relations within which the action is set. (Morgan, 1986, p 98)

Fred Emery has suggested that there are two kinds of organisational or systems redundancy; redundancy of parts and redundancy of function. Redundancy of parts occurs when each part is precisely designed for a specific function, as in the classically designed 'machine' organisation. Workers pass on work to each other where it is often held until someone is free. The responsibility for quality and progress lies mainly with supervisors, progress chasers and inspectors. The MMV and the approach to Management that it fosters, with its preoccupation with targets and inspection, clearly embraces redundancy of parts (see Chapter One, page 5 and Chapter 10, pages 165-71 on the Mad Management Virus).

Redundancy of function, however, works from a very different position. Instead of adding extra parts to a system, it adds extra functions to the operating parts so that each part can take on more functions. Thus the parts are enabled to become more self-organising, flexible and adaptable, and take on responsibility for their own quality and inspection. Workers will carry skills not always in use and hence these are redundant for the time being, but they can be called into use as situations and contexts change. However, a distinction should be made between this and some kinds of multi-skilling that can exist in the machine-like organisation.

This discussion on redundancy carries the clear implication that organisations and wider systems should move towards redundancy of functions rather than redundancy of parts as they design their change architectures. But this is another way of seeing the links between action learning-based approaches to sustaining change and renewal. Essentially they are creating a greater potential for developing redundancy of function and therefore the potential for organisation and whole systems learning, change and adaptability.

The new organising

Any change architecture is constructed with an eye to understanding and exploiting the new organising that seeks to utilise the knowledge, learning and action that takes place outside, between and across formal organisations in communities of practice and networks. It is also within these frameworks that the substantive outcomes of any change process will be negotiated. Key strands in the new organising are:

- *Knowledge workers*. We are all knowledge workers now.
- *Networks*, as the organisational form of the 21st century. There is a move to networked forms in industrial, commercial and public service organisations to gain the advantages of flatness, reach and flexibility.
- *Communities of practice* (CoPs), which exist across organisational and community boundaries and are where we learn and develop our practice.
- *Social capital* as the key to successful implementation and development through dense nets of local relationships.
- *Action learning*, which is also part of the new organising. Perceived by some as a management development method, it can be the means for moving on the intractable problems of joined-up working on the ground.

These issues are discussed in Chapter Nine.

NINE

From organisations to networks

Very little is accomplished now by the single organisation acting alone. Most organisations need business partners; not only horizontally, in alliances, supply chains or joint ventures, but also vertically around relationships with users and customers. The organisational lifecycle is shorter than it was; organisations are founded, mature and die off with increasing speed. In seeking to respond to change and complexity, everyone must 'spread their bets'; have multiple options and consider more futures. Moreover, the futures of more organisations are tied to the desires and ambitions of users and consumers in their communities and neighbourhoods.

The single organisation, traditionally the site for organisational development efforts, is no longer an adequate unit of analysis. It cannot embrace the connections and relationships needed for the way in which products and services are now designed, developed, produced and delivered. This is especially so when tackling innovative solutions to intractable problems, the 'wicked issues', and in moving to more preventative and sustainable outcomes. The network, including the notions of value chain or supply chain, alliances and partnerships, is the new organisational form of the 21st century, while network organising is the new skill to be mastered by leaders and managers.

This is particularly true of public services. Although, as noted earlier, whole systems development (WSD) is not limited to this field of endeavour, the complexity and paradoxical tensions found here make it a natural site for this way of working. As Revans has observed, these tensions cannot be resolved by simple applications of science or system, and their resolution in particular demands the involvement of service users:

> But, whatever our theoretical powers, the systems we need in order to understand the public services are not to be found in the libraries and computing rooms of universities. If they are to be found at all, it will be in such social laboratories as the back streets of Gateshead, and it is there that we shall need to learn how to work. Our problem at the moment is to get ourselves invited. (Revans, 1975, p 492)

Whole systems development fits an era when organisational boundaries are loosening and becoming more complex and problematic. In giving voice to the many different interests and motivations making up an organisational field of activity, WSD builds on the earlier organisation development (OD) and learning organisation approaches. However, although many WSD methods would be recognised by OD practitioners, these earlier approaches tended to focus on helping single organisations respond to the challenges of change. Now the apparently solid noun organis*ation* seems less appropriate to describe what is happening than the more fluid verb of organis*ing*. The whole systems approach differs from what has gone before in two main ways:

- By *combining elements of practice from diverse fields*, such as organisational design, strategy management, systems thinking, organisational and community development, public and social policy.
- By *working in a new era* of rapidly changing, boundaryless, joined-up organisations, networks and communities of practice in a knowledge economy.

The argument of this chapter is that:

- We need to put whole systems development in the context of the search for a new approach to organising and that the managed network is the appropriate organisational idea for 'holding' the whole system. It is the next stage beyond change architectures.
- Industrial, commercial and public service organisations are moving to networked forms to gain the advantages of flatness, reach and flexibility. Networks are 'the organisational form of the 21st century' (Pettigrew and Fenton, 2000).

Figure 11: The emergence of the whole systems approach

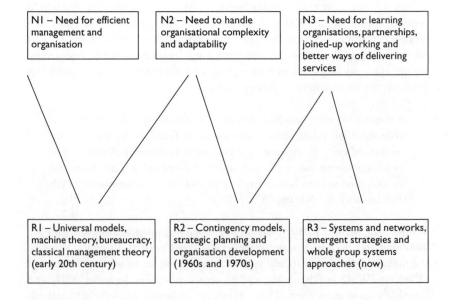

N1 – Need for efficient management and organisation	N2 – Need to handle organisational complexity and adaptability	N3 – Need for learning organisations, partnerships, joined-up working and better ways of delivering services

R1 – Universal models, machine theory, bureaucracy, classical management theory (early 20th century)	R2 – Contingency models, strategic planning and organisation development (1960s and 1970s)	R3 – Systems and networks, emergent strategies and whole group systems approaches (now)

- For 'knowledge workers' (Drucker, 1993), networks are a natural way of linking with clients, colleagues, research communities and the professional associations within which and from which their knowledge and expertise is developed and exercised. These complement and clash with the hierarchies that are so central to policy development and accountability, but that do not promote and often hinder the rapid sharing of knowledge and good practice.
- 'Communities of practice', or CoPs, are practice networks that link people with common knowledge or skills and that exist inside and outside organisational and community boundaries. CoPs are of particular recent interest because they represent reservoirs of vital know-how, and because they are the form and process by which people learn and develop their practice. Like networks, CoPs offer a complement to the order but rigidity of hierarchy.
- In particular localities and communities, CoPs and other networks can also provide vital bridging or linking capital. This is not only because of their skills and know-how but also because of their connections with other organisations and agencies. These connections are provided particularly by the 'loose ties' of networks, which reach out widely to identify and utilise remote and relevant resources when they are needed. This linking capital of access to resourceful networks and connections can add great value to people who may otherwise be struggling and disadvantaged, and help their efforts to build the social capital of local relationships, which are key to successful development.
- However, networks and CoPs have evolved in the best interests of their members. How do they serve the interests of customers, clients, users and communities as well as themselves? The nature of their engagement with these groups of people is of vital importance and is a particular focus for whole systems development work.

Knowledge working in knowledge economies

Organisations have recently been recognised as knowledge creating organisms, especially by Drucker (1993), who demonstrates the historical emergence of the relationship between knowledge and wealth creation in modern capitalism. The knowledge-based view of the organisation comes from the need to add value in competitive and technologically challenging situations. How knowledge is developed, used, traded and exchanged becomes central to the new ways of organising. As much of this knowledge is tacit rather than explicit, that is it is unwritten and intangible, held in work practices and relationships rather than being explicable in blueprint form, then the question of how best to manage the knowledge workers comes strongly to the fore.

Here creativity and productivity are likely to depend on the quality of relationships among people, and innovation is likely to depend on complex collaborations and linkages between many people involved in various specialised activities. This view of work requires a more relational concept of organisation, and one that places primary emphasis on the quality of relationships that lead to learning and innovation.

Important aspects of knowledge working include the difference between tacit and explicit knowledge and the related difference between local knowledge and official or professional knowledge. These distinctions embody power differences that are of great importance in understanding 'knowledge management'. The roots of useful explicit knowledge begin in the tacit, the personal and the difficult to articulate; and the origins of professional knowledge lie in local practice. The problems are about translation, exchange and trading. How do we share knowledge? And, having shared it, how do we use it? Who owns it and who has the right to do what with it?

Knowledge begins with a question from one person to another because they want to be able to do something. It is thus created in a dialogue of question and answer. Useful practice is best shared peer-to-peer and goes *sideways*. However, when we want to make knowledge explicit and perhaps required in codes and guidelines, then knowledge is required to go up. In this process it is 'stripped out'; it is generalised and loses context. General advice is useful and important, but only if interpreted locally. Under the pressure of accountability, performance management systems and what we earlier termed Mad Management Virus, this dislocated knowledge is 'bombed' down, not in dialogue, not to be interpreted, but as instruction or required best practice. Standing underneath the cascade it turns out to be not what is wanted – either by the user or the practitioner.

It is only recently that the mysteries of knowledge working have begun to be studied and revealed. Understandings about how knowledge works and how people work with knowledge underlie what we have called the new organising. Two aspects of this – communities of practice and managed networks – are described next. Understanding how these can harness knowledge to deliver sustainable solutions is a key task for managers and one that is central to the practice of whole systems development.

Communities of practice

> The reason I come here is because we talk about rocks. This is the only meeting in the organisation that I go to where we do that. (Geologist, Conoco)

Communities of practice, or CoPs, are working networks of people with common knowledge or skills. CoPs are vital to knowledge-based organisations, not only because they hold reservoirs of vital know-how, but because they provide the learning processes through which people acquire this knowledge. CoPs can exist inside, across and outside of particular organisational boundaries and complement the formal organisation without threatening it. A critical aspect of the CoPs idea is that knowledge is held communally rather than individually:

Researchers at the Center for Molecular Genetics in Heidelberg use photographs extensively in their work. They take pictures of radioactively-marked DNA and RNA strands using X-ray film. Their challenge is to make sense of these pictures, interpreting what the markings on the film indicate about the structure of the material and its implications for their experiments. As they pull photos from the darkroom, other people in the lab gather around to discuss what they see. These discussions frequently refer to other research, both published and current. They see the film through the eyes of one set of research findings, then another. Through these informal gatherings, the researchers think aloud together, challenge each other, try dead ends, draw metaphors from other disciplines, and use visual models and metaphors to make sense of their data and reach conclusions. Their collective know-how and knowledge of the research literature are the living backdrop for these discussions. Sometimes they talk through a procedure, looking for the meaning of a result in its minute details. Other times they focus on research findings, letting their procedures fade into the background as they compare their results to others. In these discussions, they use their knowledge of the literature and their lab know-how to think about and solve the current research problem. (Amann and Knorr-Cetina, 1989; quoted in McDermott, 1998)

In this view, knowledge is contained not only in textbooks or individual minds, but also in collective work routines, stories, specialised language, and even tools. These unwritten artefacts are the stuff of work and learning, and are also where much of the knowledge of any given CoP resides – largely tacitly, in the actual work practices. All activities are potential vehicles for sharing knowledge and learning.

This is true of all sorts of communities, not just scientific and professional ones. CoPs have been around as long as people have been learning together and the term was first used by Lave and Wenger (1991) about studies of apprenticeship. Traditionally, it was assumed that learning is one-way, from master to apprentice, but more recent interpretations suggest a widespread social process including staff, colleagues and even clients. Learning takes place in the process of interaction with all others in the workplace.

Broadening this further, everyone belongs to many communities of practice at work, at home, and in various societies and interest groups. All these groups specialise in some form of activity or work, which are also sources of learning and know-how. CoPs connected with our work are often vital in keeping us up to date and professionally viable. CoPs are very useful to individuals, but they are also collectively valuable as repositories of knowledge and learning that can only be fully experienced by becoming a member of that community. Because so much of this knowledge is tacit and hard to articulate, any practice – including that of being a member of a family or a 'local' where you live – is only fully accessible through 'apprenticeship', participation and gradual entry. This is a further reason why so much stress is placed on engagement rather than intervention (a term beloved by so many consultants and senior managers) throughout this book.

It is these characteristics that make CoPs so potentially valuable. As knowledge and its deployment increasingly differentiate firms in a market or make the difference in developing solutions to intractable problems in communities and societies, CoPs assume a vital role in and around organisations.

Meeting differently to share knowledge

However, working with peer communities requires a particular sort of approach. There are an increasing number of tasks that need the involvement and support of various communities of practice.

For example: a group of midwives began meeting informally so that they could improve the care for women and babies with HIV/Aids in their city. Having come together voluntarily to improve their practice, this group has now become influential because it has created a forum and a knowledge community that did not previously exist. The strategic health authority is now asking the group not only to advise but also to help implement policy in this important area of healthcare. Some members feel this is a step too far. How does this help women and babies?

Perhaps the best way to sabotage a peer learning and working community, which can develop this sort of bottom-up initiative, is to put early demands on it. Such people are involved on a voluntary basis; their knowledge belongs to them individually, and collectively it is community property. Like premature evaluation, making demands — that is, knowledge be made explicit, on the database, made into best practice, and so on — is the best way to kill off such initiative.

Communities of practice cannot be easily bidden or directed because their energy and enterprise is self-generated and comes from within. There are three crucial aspects of this inner life of CoPs: the level of learning energy, the quality of its social capital and the degree of self-awareness. How much energy does the CoP have for learning new things? Is it open to new knowledge and practice? The depth of social capital depends on whether people feel comfortable and trusting enough with each other to discuss the difficult problems. What would it take for a surgeon or any other skilled person to disclose doubts about his or her current level of skill in a particular area? Social capital is self-generating and developed through engagement and interaction; the more people depend upon each other, the more they are able to do so. Finally, the level of self-awareness determines how well the CoP can reflect on its own practices and identify learning needs (Wenger and Snyder, 2000).

Learning at the boundaries

Given systems, such as healthcare or biotechnology, contain any number of communities of practice. These CoPs can become very insular and self-contained, restricting access to their know-how and resisting innovation. Beyond the learning process in the CoP is the important learning that takes place at the boundaries of expertise or knowledge. Managing with CoPs includes most importantly the encouragement for these communities to maintain open boundaries and recharge their learning energies for new practice. The seeds of new practice are to be found at the boundary with other worlds or CoPs.

The very notion of community implies boundaries. Unlike formal organisations, communities of practice usually have fluid boundaries, and this helps to engage with other worlds. Because boundaries connect as well as separate, each connection offers a learning opportunity – 'civilisation develops where cultures meet'. In particular, learning at the boundary is possible because of the differences encountered there; getting to grips with these differences and understanding that there might be another way to make a car or serve a customer is the start of a change in practice. It is here, at the intersection of different ways of looking at problems and their solution, that radical or step-jump learning is likely to take place.

This provides a further insight into the medium- and long-term damage that can be done by top-down programmatic initiatives and performance Management cultures driven by the Mad Management Virus. Frequently, they press for conformity and actively limit boundary learning and networking by 'sealing the boundaries'. The awful irony is that it is the very learning and seeds of practice that would provide the longer delivery of the intended outcomes of the initiatives in the first place. Again, this is especially the case in the search for innovative solutions to 'wicked problems'. Learning at the boundary underlies the idea of action learning, which figures large as an important aspect of whole systems working, and in our suggestions for developing and working with communities of practice. However, before that, there is the second aspect of the new organising to consider.

The rise of the network

Once learning becomes crucial, it becomes clear that the single organisation is actually a poor site for learning:

> The canonical formal organisation, with its bureaucratic rigidities, is a poor vehicle for learning. Sources of innovation do not reside exclusively inside firms; instead they are commonly found in the interstices between firms, universities, research laboratories, suppliers and customers. (Powell et al, 1996, p 118)

The globalisation of commerce, the emergence of the knowledge-based firm and the advance of 'virtualisation' through information technology have prompted a new approach to organising. The solid organisation, as a physical, structured, bounded entity, is challenged and complemented by the more fluid and relational concept of 'organising'. Here the organisation is primarily a pattern of relationships and it is the quality of these connections, internal and external, that is especially important because they hold vast intangible assets of knowledge, learning, trust and social capital. The combination calls forth the network form:

> Conceived in 1993 as a response to the 1992 oil crisis, the CRINE (Cost Reduction Initiative for the New Era) initiative in the UK oil and gas industry is a joint effort involving government and key industry players representing contractors, suppliers, consultants, trade associations and others. The original goal was to achieve, by sector-wide efforts rather than individual actions, an across-the-board cost reduction of 30% for offshore developments by 1996. By 1997 the cost of field developments had fallen by 40% on a barrel/barrel basis – and attracted significant international attention and emulation. As a consequence, CRINE-based programmes are now under development or in operation in Mexico, Venezuela, India and Australia.
>
> Significantly the participants felt that the relationship was worth maintaining and set up the CRINE Network in 1997 with a new vision of international competitiveness, way beyond the original cost reduction aims, to increase its share of the non-UK market five-fold from the 1% held in 1996. CRINE's mode of operation is 'supported networking', where various forms of financial, technical and other support come from regional and national government, major operators, trade, research and academic bodies to the network of actors in the supply chain. A small co-ordinating group manages network activities and the whole is steered by a representative body of all those involved. Activities include newsletters, websites, workshops and conferences, technical projects and other initiatives. CRINE seeks to establish a learning and continuous improvement culture, encouraging dialogue and collaboration rather than confrontation between suppliers and customers. One significant initiative here is the First Point Assessment programme (FPA) which assesses and helps develop capability in the supply chain. FPA is a company employing 15 people, which has 40 major Subscribers or customers and about 2000 Registered Suppliers and which uses seconded engineers from major subscribing companies to carry out assessment and improvement work. (Bessant et al, 1999)

While not a new idea, networks are suddenly prominent as a model for organising and more broadly as a way of seeing the world. Various environmental factors combine to bring about a 'foregrounding' of the idea. Foremost among these is rapid environmental change. As Emery and Trist (1965) predicted many years ago, in turbulent environments it is not just the actors who are moving but the ground as well. In such conditions, the proper unit of analysis is not the individual firm but the network of organisations in a market.

A second important enabler is the 'living systems' view of organising now challenging the engineering model of organisations. A living system is modelled on life itself, and is complex but adaptive: "a system of independent agents that can act in parallel, develop models as to how things work in their environment, and, most importantly, refine those models through learning and adaptation" (Pascale et al, 2000, p 5). Applied to organisational life, this view suggests that self-organisation and an emphasis on learning, deals with complexity much better than top-down and linear direction.

A third factor is the rapid advance of information technology, where the internet and world wide web act as both a conceptual model and as practical enablers of networking.

What are networks?

The term is used to describe a bewildering variety of associations and relationships, ranging from geographically dispersed firms and parts of firms such as transport or information technology systems, to local, community-based organisations. Networks also describe the many local, national and international scientific, educational and professional bodies and the increasing numbers of global and largely virtual interest groups united around single issues such as pesticide control or world development. Finally, there are the billions of personal contact networks that enable and inform how we live and work today.

Relationships in the many varieties of network tend to be characterised by a high level of learning and exchange of knowledge. The contemporary organising language of subcontracting, supply chains, alliances, partnerships, interlocking ownership and so on attests to this need for inter-organisational collaboration and connectedness.

Because they are created and recreated by members' shifting interests, networks are usually more nebulous than formal organisations, the looser ones with myriads of ever-evolving connections and relationships. However, the concept of the managed network, with the implication of agreed rules and standards and some central control, fills a middle ground between formal organisation and loose kaleidoscopes of relationships.

One of the most straightforward definitions comes from the World Health Organisation:

> A network is a grouping of individuals, organisations and agencies organised on a non-hierarchical basis around common issues or concerns, which are pursued proactively and systematically, based on commitment and trust. (WHO, 1998)

As a generalisation, networks tend to be characterised by:

- people linked by common interest and ties of common goals, mutual interests, exchange and trust;

- nodes and links; nodes of individuals, groups or organisations linked by meetings, conferences, newsletters, joint projects, working partnerships and so on;
- status and authority based more on members' knowledge, usefulness, sharing and innovation, and less on formal position or qualifications;
- activities that involve working with more informal relationships within, across, and outside more formal boundaries;
- inclusion and exclusion; operating to the advantage of some people in relation to others.

The CRINE network demonstrates that, in the new organising, successful learning and joint working are never far apart. In the knowledge era, learning and the exchange of know-how have become essential to survival and development.

It is important to note that, despite all these characteristics and advantages, networks are more likely to complement than replace organisations. Networks can do things that formal organisations find difficult, but they have their own limitations, notably around stability, direction and accountability. For these reasons, the form of network that is of most interest is what looks at first sight like a contradiction – the managed network.

Managed networks

Networks are not a substitute for formal organisations, but are a way in which complex agendas can be connected for delivery. From a managerial perspective, the largely self-organising network offers a third way between the stable but slow-moving hierarchy and the creative but uncontrollable market. These three ideal types of organisation have different core operating principles: *command* in the hierarchy, *price* in the market and *relationship* in the network. They also suggest markedly different managerial styles: command and control through

Figure 12: Learning, organising and delivering are now part of the same joint enterprise

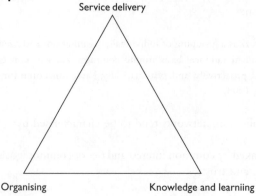

Service delivery

Organising   Knowledge and learniing

hierarchical position compared with entrepreneurial dealing using market power and the diplomacy, negotiation and influence required in networks.

In the organisational world, networks are more likely to exist alongside and to complement hierarchies and markets, rather than appear in the 'pure' version. Even so, effective network organisation practice is likely to constitute a formidable challenge to managers. This is because of the central tension between the idea of networks as free associations of people interacting together for mutual interest and the notion of 'managed networks' established to accomplish various corporate or institutional tasks.

To arrive at the managed network, the notion of a flat, decentralised structure has to be modified by the adoption of some jointly agreed, managed and accountable systems. At first, these terms seem like contradictions of the idea – introducing hierarchy into an essentially peer-based relationship. However, the network's ability to absorb variety and difference is a key factor in it being chosen as the organisational form most likely to deliver certain outcomes. For example, the notion of managed clinical networks is now central to healthcare delivery as the best chance of improving the overall quality and equality of patient access in, say, cancer services in a given geographical area.

Cancer networks

Typically, the historical development of cancer services in any given patch will display large differences in the concentration of, and access to, resources. For example, the most specialised doctors and equipment tend to be found in well-funded teaching hospitals in large cities, while in smaller urban or rural areas, these facilities do not exist to the same extent. Cancer services are particularly complex because there are so many different types; in general, the rarer the cancer, the greater the likelihood of inequality of access to treatment.

To resolve these issues, the horizontal problems of equalising access to treatment must be married to the vertical process of streamlining the 'patient pathway'. This starts with access and detection by the general practitioner, through access and diagnosis by a hospital consultant, on to treatment by surgeons, radiographers and other therapists and then back to the community, to the GP, community nursing services, hospice, private sector nursing, and so on.

Unprecedented efforts at collaboration and cooperation are required to deliver this agenda. It involves the sharing of data, the development of agreed protocols, continuing service improvements through redesign and re-engineering and the widespread negotiation changes in institutional and individual professional practices. This task contains such variety that simpler organisational forms cannot cope.

The task of the cancer networks is huge, ambitious and essential. Not to tackle it is both morally and politically unacceptable, but experience of developing general management in the NHS suggests that it is unlikely to be achieved by command and control. Yet the issue is also unlikely to be resolved by being left to the actors themselves to sort it out. Hence, the third way notion of managed networks, with boards, light-touch directors and infrastructure support, employing facilitators and service improvement teams to help bring about the changes.

Managing with networks

How a particular network is defined influences what it can do; its definition and agreed purpose determines what can be done in this relationship set, how attention is focused and how effort is directed. Managed service delivery networks may sacrifice some of the potential for learning and innovation for a more mundane quality control. Getting the management touch light enough, and shared enough, is a critical factor in realising the potentials. And however skilful the managers, networks need to find ways of sharing power and rewards with each other across organisational boundaries. There are a number of well-documented and linked dilemmas or tensions to be tackled in managing with networks. These include questions of:

- *Effectiveness*: who defines quality, effectiveness and success? And how is this decided and agreed? In a self-organising network, effectiveness is determined by the degree to which each person meets their own purpose, which in turn affects how much a network is used or activated. The more a network is used, the higher the level of connectedness, trust and social capital among the membership. In turn, the quality of these relationships affects the quality of learning, knowledge sharing and task collaboration.
- *Leadership*: how can networks be aligned and steered and find strategic direction? Should this be done by a person, a convening group or a single lead organisation acting on behalf of the whole? Leadership questions should be addressed formally and openly.
- *Governance*: what are the rules of engagement? Who is eligible to join and what are the rights and obligations? How is behaviour regulated in the network and how are conflicts resolved? Achieving good governance structures and arrangements is vital but challenging.
- *Accountability*: where does this rest? Does it devolve back to participating organisations or are there some processes inherent in the network? How is user-centred accountability achieved, in contrast to that practised in the professions or government departments? These tough questions require creative responses and hard work to resolve.
- *Systems support*: being light on overheads and infrastructure, networks may often need feeding from established sources of specialised support such as IT, human resources, finance, legal. The supply of this specialised advice may have to be reconfigured to take advantage of network forms.
- *Supportive managerial styles*: managers may need new skills in order to encourage and not inhibit the network way of working. To maximise participation and

engagement, organisational networks need to be animated and influenced, not controlled and directed.

Dealing with these issues constitutes the developmental agenda for those who wish to utilise the network form. The nature of this developmental task requires all the 'players' to play their part in arriving at agreed and simple rules for regulating their actions and relationships.

Learning to manage anew

Changes in the way organising is seen impact on notions of managing and management. While the roots of the ideas lie in the establishment of order in domestic households and later in the intervention of the professional overseer between owner and worker for the maximisation of productivity in industrial enterprises, the idea of management has developed far beyond these technical functions to a legitimisation of organisational control by a particular group of specialists (Child, 1969).

The unilateral right of managers to decide has always been challenged in attempts to make organisations more democratic. This tradition includes not only the radical notions of workers' control and industrial democracy but also the more pluralist concerns of Mary Parker Follett's championing of 'constructive conflict' (Graham, 1995) and Alan Fox's call for a 'new moral contract' (Fox, 1974). Current critiques note the inequality of voice and power in organisations by gender, race or class (Alvesson and Wilmott, 1996) and the 'inconvenience' of age, disability, ill health, poor education and unemployment for organisational efficiency (Nichol, 1984, p 45).

In addition to these critiques, the imperatives of knowledge working and the knowledge economy make many of the old distinctions less relevant, and the task of managing networks and communities of practice as part of the new organising a new and central concern for managers. The next section deals with the development challenges posed by networks and CoPs.

Developing networks and knowledge communities: guidelines, processes, roles and skills

Although they have the advantages of flexibility and variety absorption, CoPs and networks are much more fluid and slippery organisational forms. If they are to be given – as they are in the concept of managed networks – objectives, targets and responsibilities for funding, it is likely to be no simple task to 'align' all the parties to a task. In working with networks, there are a number of aspects of the process of organising that are problematic and these may need facilitation as well as direction in order to ensure that they are working effectively. These issues include:

- *Membership* – this may be hard to define. Who should be part of this discussion, and this delivery process? Managed networks have formal boundaries, but even so who in this defined patch is included? Organisations are not coterminous in their boundaries, key people may be positioned outside the boundary, while within the boundary may be some who do not want to join, and so on.
- *Roles and relationships* – these are likely to be complex, multiple and overlapping. Actors frequently appear in different hats and in different relationships. It is often hard to understand the definitions and limits, and the opportunities for confusion and misunderstanding are considerable.
- *Power and authority* – as above; power in a hierarchy is never as simple as it may look, but there is some sense of a chain of command. Here this is much weaker and power is differently distributed on different issues; you may be strong here and marginal there. Authority relationships are also hard to determine; is the board of a cancer network the apex of authority with power to direct the network, dismiss and appoint officers, and so on, or is it a general assembly of interested parties? A strong form of authority in CoPs and network is sapiential or knowledge power, but this will probably exist alongside other forms – managerial, legal, representative and personal or charismatic.

The first question is: where are the CoPs and networks relevant to our purposes and how do we work with them?

As the normal form for many professional, voluntary and community associations, first look for what exists already. Linking with existing networks and CoPs is a very different challenge to bringing together hitherto unconnected actors, but developing and nurturing knowledge communities and networks is always a process of relationship building. People need to engage spontaneously and voluntarily and early work includes getting people to attend, to agree membership and to commit to joint goals. This needs helpful facilitation and support over time.

Some key guidelines are:

- *Connect what exists*: agencies can play a valuable role in linking what already exists; communities may not be aware or connected with one another to create 'networks of networks'.
- *Animation*: boundary-crossing activities tend not to happen spontaneously. Midwifery, or helping things to get started, may be preferred to facilitation where professionals take over the process. However, "an experienced and competent collaboration manager, facilitator or convenor is an essential asset" (Huxham and Vangen, 2000, p 800).
- *Whole systems thinking*: who should be represented at which levels? This includes state, private sector and voluntary organisations, as well as user or customer involvement, which is what makes the biggest difference. The

presence of residents at a meeting of planners or diabetics at a clinicians' meeting can change the tone and terms of debate.

- *Preparation and start up*: the start-up phase is crucial and is perhaps the main factor determining the successful future of a network. Successful alliances are "highly evolutionary and [go] through a sequence of interactive cycles of learning, re-evaluation and re-adjustment" (Doz, 1996, p 55), but only if the initial conditions have been good, including agreements on purpose, common goals, leadership and governance arrangements. To be more than paper partnerships, preparation for working together is essential; people need to meet having been briefed and mandated, and able to give an organisational view.
- *Avoid contrived collegiality*: it is easy for agencies to fall into the trap of what Hargreaves (1994) and Fullan and Hargreaves (1992, p 77) have called 'contrived collegiality', where compulsion, administrative control and centralised design replace the spontaneity, discretionary and above all voluntary engagement which gives network relationships their energy and creativity.
- *Facilitate leadership, governance and accountability arrangements*: where multiple organisations and agencies own or sponsor the network, it is vital to achieve some unity and horizontal integration at the top. This may take the form of partnership boards, host or lead organisations, convenors, coordinators or more informal arrangements, but they must be able to represent the whole.
- *Encourage self-organisation*: self-interest is a powerful incentive for activity in networks and while these must balance with community interests, the more power and resources devolve to the nodes and the more rich connections take place without the centre, the greater will be self-organisation, the emergence of new repertoires and innovations, and the evolution of the network itself (Pascale et al, 2000, pp 6, 130).
- *Simple rules*: these are one of the clues to self-organisation and adaptability in complex systems. Having a lack of rules, having too many, or applying them too rigidly seems to inhibit activity; a few simple rules encourage engagement and innovation (Pettigrew and Fenton, 2000, p 99).
- *Learning from difference and diversity*: the differences between services, levels, large and small, public and private, voluntary and statutory, urban and rural, resident and professional, and so on, are a principle source for learning and innovation. At best, this gets beyond formal information to explore differences – and especially the experiences, feelings and values that inform what worked and why – that are often kept private. To acknowledge mistakes, fears and fallibilities needs a willingness to risk and trust, but in turn this level of engagement also generates that trust.
- *Learning from conflict*: when there is real honesty about differences, conflicts of purpose and interest are likely to surface. If these inevitable conflicts are suppressed, they may consequently sour relationships and sabotage effective operations. Start by inviting people to be clear about their aims and open about their differences. Negotiate common interest from a recognition of

difference, diversity and potential conflict. Although this may be painful to start with, it is most likely to lay the strongest foundations.

There are also distinctive competencies and skills associated with successful networking. These include:

- *Trading*: a readiness to trade and cross occupational, organisational, social and political boundaries to gather resources.
- *Broking*: ability to see the big picture, make connections, be credible with different groups and broker relevant partnerships.
- *Diplomacy*: strong interpersonal, communicating and listening skills; able to persuade, to act as an interpreter and sense-maker and to mediate, arbitrate and manage conflict.
- *Facilitation*: ability to animate relationships among network members, together with teaching, dissemination, mentoring and knowledge transfer skills.
- *Learning*: a high tolerance of ambiguity and uncertainty, able to reflect on and conceptualise experience; to learn quickly and adapt to changing situations.

There are also some core learning competencies for CoPs and networks if they are to realise their full potential:

- *Improving practice through sharing what we know*: encouraging new practice through connecting people; disseminating knowledge, new ideas and resources through directories, learning events, improvement fairs, and so on.
- *Learning to learn*: developing the practice of learning from reflecting on what we do and improving our joint working.
- *Organisational learning*: understanding and knowledge of how CoPs and networks work and the capacity to help people set up their own learning communities around their interests.
- *Disseminating and communicating*: informing, influencing and enthusing others, including those in hierarchies, to make sense of and understand how to manage new forms of organising and ways of working.

The way forward for whole systems development and networks

For sustained change and improvement in a world organised in networks of communities of practice, the priorities for whole systems development are to:

- help build networks and communities of practice for organising and delivery;
- sustain developmental thinking rather than focusing and becoming fixated on resistance to change;
- create top-level leadership;
- encourage leadership on the ground in local teams;

- manage the critical connections between top-down and bottom-up thinking through the development of middle-ground frameworks;
- develop partnerships across whole systems, not just partnership boards.

The first of these has already been discussed at length. Sustaining the idea of developmental thinking is an essential task, not least because the resistance to change so frequently cited by top-down change agents looks different from this perspective.

Developmental thinking and resistance to change

By including all those who need to have a voice in the change process, whole systems approaches address the problem of 'resistance to change'. This is 'big tent' or 'broad church' politics, and while this is a well-known principle in community organising and democratic politics, it is less practised in the organisational world.

To work in an inclusive way makes great demands on the courage and confidence of leaders. The fear of losing control is the reason why there is sometimes so little appetite for the leadership demanded by whole systems development processes.

> In an advertising agency, the chief executive and directors commissioned a development process for the agency to help it respond to feedback from its major customers and stakeholders. This involved collecting data via a staff survey and a conference where this data would be fed back to a large proportion of the staff. However, when the consultants submitted the design for the conference, the senior team removed all opportunities and references to 'dialogue' between the floor of the conference and the senior team. The senior team were not prepared to discuss the issues openly in public, although they were prepared to hear the views of staff. Not surprisingly, the views that were expressed from the floor were not as explicit as they might have been. The senior team concluded that people were more or less happy with how things were in the agency and that there was no need to change their own actions and behaviour.

As the Chinese say, 'the fish rots from the head' (Garratt, 1999). Whole systems development addresses some of the failings experienced with earlier designs for planned organisational change by offering a way of helping senior people share their power and learn their way forward in the company of those partners and stakeholders who also have desires and ambitions for the future. This relieves directors of the burden of having to be right first time in unpredictable circumstances, but it does demand more visible and committed leadership from the top. Lack of this sort of leadership is the biggest single obstacle to the widespread adoption of whole systems approaches.

The role of top-level leadership

Organising in networks can be thought of as a 'federation of teams'. This describes a way of working that creates local autonomy but requires continuous effort to develop a collective leadership process to steer the organisation as a whole. This concept of federation, including the subsidiarity of parts whereby they retain autonomy and independence in some affairs but cede other powers to the whole, needs to be worked through fully in each specific situation.

Disconnection between the evolving big picture ideas at the top and those of other teams in the organisation may be avoided by 'walking through' the big picture perspectives and proposed resulting actions. This involves letting others rework emerging notions so that they become increasingly widely owned. This is hard but essential work and draws on ideas about complex adaptive systems, which suggests that the development of critical connections, as well as critical mass within and beyond the organisation itself, can be built by engaging many other people in walking through the work in 'widening circles of involvement' (Axelrod, 2001).

The general point here is that, by sharing the work of the top team in an open and active way, the ideas can be enriched by others, including staff and external stakeholders. Notions such as partnership boards give opportunities to do this by building understanding and assisting people to make sense of the context in the organisational field. If it is to be meaningful for staff and capable of articulation to external stakeholders, it must be 'walked through' by all members of the management team; a key task for the top team.

This process also provides opportunities for people to enrich their understandings about personal leadership practice, both as members of the whole organisation collective and as leaders of relatively autonomous teams. This collaborative learning can help create a 'container' or 'holding framework' defining the common purpose, vision, values and standards of the organisation. Within this, the federal teams can have significant autonomy; sharing and strengthening the experience of fostering, but not controlling, connections across the organisation.

Leadership on the ground – developing local capacity

A key strategic aim of managed networks and CoPs is the development of local capacity. It is normal for different members to have different views of the organisation's role and activities in this respect. From such differences can come a lively dialogue and the creativity needed to 'bottom out' a shared understanding of ways in which these critical local connections can be fostered.

Connecting top-down policy with bottom-up local problem resolution

This development of local capacity is vital if network organisations are to be able to implement joined-up services at the point of delivery and use. To do this, they must assist in the development of:

* local solutions to local problems in communities;
* top-level policy and strategy development in the organisation as a whole and in wider policy circles, such as wider confederations or government.

Connecting these imperatives is immensely challenging. It raises questions about the creation of collective power across user 'pathways' and networks and, especially in the public services, requires connections with community development agendas around regeneration and neighbourhood renewal.

Different groups can share their learning about effecting change within local communities and make connections between this and policy emerging from the top of the organisation, or from government or Europe on the issues affecting their work. All this takes time, but qualitative change does not come instantly. In early meetings, the focus might be on understanding the learning from different perspectives. Later there is a move to an action-learning focus, piloting ways of making the critical connections or creating the middle-ground frameworks that can span the gaps between bottom-up and top-down, and strengthen connections between policy creation and local implementation. It is these connections that are so vital to the development and sustenance of a useful change.

Developing partnerships across whole systems

From a managed networks perspective, partnership working takes on a much more substantial meaning with a clear emphasis on engagement with the partnership's whole system through working on the tasks of implementation. In many instances, partnership becomes identified as a partnership board or some such body. At this level, for each member of the partnership it is the priorities of their own organisation that consume their attention. So there is a tendency to feel that the partnership work is done once the initial purposes for which it was set up – meeting government requirements, drawing down special funding and so on – has been achieved. This rather misses the point. The central purpose of partnership working is to create new ways of meeting needs collectively and this can only be achieved by new ways of interfacing with service users and communities. And for this to happen it is important for those occupying positions of formal authority – the partnership board – to create the conditions for partnership working and networking at the frontline.

One of us was reviewing the effectiveness of local partnership working between social and health services, the voluntary sector and user and carer organisations in the delivery of services to elderly people both in community and institutional settings. It quickly became evident that a great deal had been achieved and a series of new and innovatory services had been provided. It was clear that staff at all levels were fully engaged and networked and that levels of user and carer satisfaction had increased considerably. The review indicated clear factors in this success:

- A core group of key people, some holding significant position power and some with extensive knowledge and personal networks, created and held between them a collective vision of the kinds of services they wanted for the town (population 40,000) and its village and rural hinterland. They created a collective memory of the future (see Chapter Five, page 88).
- They created the time and climate to do this – 'we became friends' – and to report back and review what had been done. They met differently.
- Critically, they acted as much as a team apart as a team together. They each acted with staff, both their own and in multidisciplinary groups, as though they believed their own rhetoric. They walked the talk.
- Wherever possible, they encouraged joint reviews of services by frontline staff, joint training and opportunities for networking and learning. They created the conditions for using diversity to create common ground and public learning.
- Perhaps most importantly, it was the staff who saw themselves as 'the partnership'.

Action learning networks

All these situations are natural sites for action learning (Revans, 1998). (Action learning is more fully described in Chapter Seven, pages 127-9.) Learning and action go together in networks or CoPs, which can be seen as 'sets' that mutually support and challenge each other. In the light of intractable problems and the need for joined-up sustainable development on the ground, the single organisation is generally a poor site for learning.

Working with action learning in communities of practice and networks that transcend the old organisational boundaries is an obvious way forward to tackle the challenges of joining up services and delivering top-down agendas, while allowing for local knowledge, interpretation and innovation. Uniform solutions to local development issues inevitably fail to work, but good practice can be shared and people can learn from action in tackling real problems where they occur.

Solutions emerge from engaging the relevant communities in this sort of action and learning. Development work often consists of processes to encourage networking and connections within and between different communities, including local residents and various professional communities of practice. Only in this way can the dilemmas of local freedom, as celebrated in communities, networks and CoPs, marry with the performance-managed delivery requirements of government and commerce.

TEN

Confirming cases: local problems and local solutions within whole systems

At 3.00am in the morning of 30 October 2000 the River Aire started to flood the Stockbridge neighbourhood of Keighley. Stockbridge is a relatively poor, ethnically mixed community. The housing stock consists of mostly Victorian terraced houses and budget-priced 1930s semis, privately owned or rented. There is also a small amount of relatively new housing built on the flood plain, both privately and housing association owned. For the most part, it is a relatively low paid community.

Some people had about an hour's warning, others none at all. By 10.00am people were arriving at the Keighley Leisure Centre (about half a mile away), where the local authority (Bradford Metropolitan District Council) had set up an emergency response centre. Some arrived without shoes and socks and many were upset and disoriented by the experience. There was also a growing realisation that many had no household insurance.

A total of 292 households were affected. It was to be between 6 and 12 months before people were back in their homes. Not only was this a traumatic event for individuals, it was a traumatic event for a fragile community. What happened next is a very positive story of what frontline interagency collaboration and fully involving local people, can achieve.

The story of the floods at Stockbridge illustrates how global problems are experienced locally. It is not the citizens of Stockbridge (or Bangladesh) who have created the conditions which have submerged them, but they are nonetheless the main victims and those with the greatest interest in doing something about these conditions. There is also a responsibility on the public authorities within which these events occur to ensure they also learn from the experience.

It may be said that this is a huge problem – what does it have to do with local people and local solutions? It is of course true that issues of global warming must be tackled at a global level, and questions of flood defence at a national level, but these problems are experienced essentially at a local level, and their local solution is critical to sustainable development. This chapter makes the case for whole systems development as a methodology for combining the various levels at which action is needed, with local involvement and sustainable improvements at local level where the problems are experienced.

In Chapter One we analysed the public and social policy landscape which provides the essential context for most public, private, voluntary and community endeavour. Subsequent chapters describe the development of our whole systems approach to sustainable change derived both from our own practice and the research from wider communities of practice.

Stakeholders in the future: balancing short- and long-term priorities

Chapter One identifies four dilemmas that need to be addressed in the search for sustainable solutions to difficult problems:

- top-down and bottom-up;
- consumer and citizen;
- treatment and prevention;
- consultation and involvement.

Tackling the 'wicked issues' usually requires bringing together very different stakeholders to work on understanding the causes of problems before implementing (separately and jointly) agreed ways forward. This means facilitating between groups of unequal power with often very different codes of knowledge, beliefs and interests. The longer-term benefits are high, but in the short term this often feels like a messy, anxiety-producing waste of time. Building the essential bonds of trust through holding frameworks and widening circles of inclusion can seem very unrewarding in the short run and the much overused word 'vision' comes to have real meaning.

The problem in this sort of development work is that chief executives – acting under pressure from politicians, institutional shareholders and the public fed through the media – want results now. This pressure works against the longer-term solutions that can make real difference and encourages short-term 'solutions', which frequently recycle the problems rather than tackle their systemic root causes. How can this problem be overcome?

This adds a fifth dilemma to the other four, namely the reconciling of

- short term and long term.

This chapter will address this issue using case material from our own practice. Two further confirming cases for the WSD approach are offered here, taken from the critical areas of waste management and transport, which are currently presenting as crises for urgent resolution and development. It is clear that most of our cases are taken from the public arena.

There are a number of reasons for this but the main one is because of the pressing necessity of public consultation and stakeholder representation, which are, in many cases, being pressed on authorities and institutions by legislative and other public pressures. It is no longer possible, even if they thought it desirable, for professional planners and experts to make decision based on the unexamined 'public good' as it once was. Now most of these decisions are contested and subject to many competing interests and they simply can not longer be resolved by expert fiat.

The same is increasingly true for decisions affecting private sector organisations, many of which are involved as partners and contractors with the cases discussed below. However, at this point in time the private sector company is still ruled by a dominant stakeholder – the shareholder – to whom, in limited liability companies, there is a legal duty to maximise the returns. There have been various efforts to promote the concept of stakeholding in the commercial environment, perhaps most notably by the Cadbury (1992) report on corporate governance and the subsequent Royal Society of Arts project 'Tomorrow's Company'. However, as 'shareholder value' has re-asserted itself, the 'stakeholder company' seems a distant prospect. The notion of the 'balanced scorecard' (Kaplan and Norton, 1992, 1993) has been more popular and seems to be gaining ground, along with the related but less popular concept of 'social audit' (Evans, 1993). These approaches commonly emphasise the importance of non-financial returns, including to employees and communities as stakeholders. If this development continues then many more commercial organisations may come to adopt WSD approaches in relation to their future strategies and decisions.

However, this still lies in the future; at the moment many concerns, both public and private appear gripped by a tendency that moves them away from inclusivity towards, what we call here the MMV or Mad Management Virus. But recovery is possible, and in the spirit of searching for prevention, it is better to analyse further the carrying 'virus'.

The Mad Management Virus (MMV)

For those impatient for the short-term delivery of results, the time and other costs associated with whole systems approaches are apparently wasteful and anxiety provoking. The investment in trust building and the creation of 'social capital' is of no immediate provable benefit. On the other hand these same people are often aware that short-term solutions offer little hope of a longer-term improvement. To reduce waiting list targets, hospitals may treat easier, less urgent cases rather than more urgent cases; to meet government targets, some teachers concentrate their efforts on the few students perceived to be on the borderline of achieving five GCSEs, to the potential disadvantage of those of higher, lower and different abilities.

It often seems that management has become obsessed with top-down numerical target setting, inspection and audit. It is as though the theory and practice of management has become infected by a kind of Mad Management Virus (MMV). This purports to offer simple solutions to complex problems; it produces programmed solutions to barely understood local problems and relies heavily on command and control from the top.

The MMV sounds and feels tough; it offers a spurious certainty in an uncertain and unstable world. The need for new systems to bring about change and improvement hardens into an over-reliance on the mechanistic which betrays an underlying belief that people are not to be trusted to do this on their own. For those actors caught up in these worlds the MMV inevitably begets its own rewards and it makes perfect sense to concentrate on what gets rewarded and easily counted.

Of course, most people do their best to uphold the integrity of what they do in the public interest. But to do this they spend increasing amounts of time managing the system upwards to do 'the right thing' while trying to manage their own feelings of frustration and lack of voice in tackling those issues that could lead to longer-term sustained improvements. The search for certainty in an uncertain world by those in formal authority frequently adds to the burdens of those struggling to deliver on the frontline. The MMV makes it hard for those at the top to listen to voices from below, despite the rhetoric to consult. Criticism can be dismissed as 'resistance to change', 'the forces of conservatism', 'producer self-interest' and so on, and of course it might well be just this. This is what makes good leadership so problematic.

However the MMV does produce all sorts of lunacy at the frontline and there are some typical symptoms. Here is a true story however apocryphal it might sound.

Several inspectors call

A colleague works for an LEA (local education authority) now being run by a private company. As an experienced management developer and organisation development practitioner, she was running a leadership development programme for head-teachers. During one of the session, two inspectors arrived and joined the group. One was there to inspect the teaching and learning process and the other was there because he was a trainee inspector. Later they were joined by two more inspectors whose job was to inspect the other two inspectors. Although this seemed bizarre enough, the gathering of inspectors was not complete, because they were then joined by a fifth inspector who was there to do 'quality assurance'.

What effect did this have on the proceedings? "Well", says our colleague, "this doesn't seem to occur to them. The participants, who are themselves teachers and well versed in the hazards of inspection, do their very best to speak and behave in ways that they know the inspectors will want to hear. It does deter them from exploring some issues more deeply and personally while the inspectors are there, but they can revert to normal after they leave. The participants' first concern is to make sure that, as a comrade in adversity, they put on the best act possible to do me a good turn with the inspectors."

Do the inspectors understand the impact of their own intervention into the situation? Or are they so steeped in the internal self-reinforcing logic of the

MMV that they can only see the king's clothes and the hierarchy's shilling? For the inspected, this is transparently a charade and is told on as a cracking good story, but it is clearly not so obvious to those with the biggest influence in the situation.

As we noted in Chapter One, programmatic change frequently impoverishes rather than enriches, but the costs are felt at the frontline and are largely hidden from those making the decisions. The costs of building up networks of trust may deter some from working with whole systems approaches, but the pursuit of quick results through top-down injunctions often results in spiraling costs of audit, inspection and compliance.

The magic of numbers

"If you can't measure it, you can't manage it" is a shibboleth of modern management, which provides an incubating environment for the MMV. According to David Boyle, the current British Government has:

> introduced about 8,000 targets or numerical indicators of success during its first term of office. We have NHS targets, school league tables, environmental indicators – 150 of them at last count – and measurements covering almost every area of professional life or government, all in the name of openness, accountability and democracy. (Boyle, 2002, p 22)

Numbers are highly useful, but are nonetheless abstractions. The danger is that people do what the targets tell them, rather than what is actually necessary. We have already referred to the perverse effects of counting exam results and hospital waiting lists. Boyle adds that:

> Hospitals are ordering more expensive trolleys and reclassifying them as 'mobile beds', to sidestep the target that no patient should stay on a hospital trolley for more than four hours. I also know of at least one local authority that achieves government targets for separating waste – at great expense – but then simply mixes it all up again in landfill. Scotland Yard figures that showed it had recruited 218 people from ethnic minorities between April and September 2000 turned out to include Irish, New Zealanders and Australians. The useful figure was four. (Boyle, 2002, p 23)

Numbers are useful in taking 'a count' of things, but they do not tell us much about the meaning of these things. While indicators are intended to be a means for achieving human ends, they become ends in themselves. In cricket, the evidence suggests that better results are achieved by those who keep their eye on the ball not the scoreboard; and the cricket scorecard only has real meaning to those who understand the intricate nuances of the game. Boyle reminds us of the "18th-century mathematical prodigy Jedediah Buxton who, asked if he had enjoyed a performance of Richard III, could say only that the actors had spoken 12,445 words" (Boyle, 2002, p 22).

W. Edwards Deming, who was a world-class statistician, was deeply concerned about the applications of numbers to the improvement of human systems, but said that 'you can never measure' the most important things that improve the working of these systems. The numbers give us an all-important benchmark or 'baseline assessment' against which to measure our efforts, but they cannot give us the efforts.

In the public services, there is an exploding auditing culture which drains time and resources away from service delivery (Power, 1994; Caulkin, 2002a). Much of this has been installed in the name of transparency and accountability. But so many performance management and auditing systems assume that organisations operate like simple machines, whereas they are better likened to complex living systems. The effect then is to produce a whole series of perverse effects. Where the MMV is incubating expect some of the following symptoms:

- attempts to portray and massage the figures in a favourable light, and public and attendant media disputes about falling standards;
- one department seeking to improve its figures at the expense of another – sub-optimism;
- increasing levels of distrust: this is because the mere existence of some of these systems implies that people cannot be trusted in the first place and their operation will compound this, hence the growing pressure to inspect inspectors and to inspect the inspectors of inspectors who inspect the remaining frontline workforce (as in the example on page 168);
- cultures in which doing frontline work is stripped of freedom to act to improve services to customers and to prevent the search for improvement and innovation;
- lowered staff morale, increasing absenteeism, and staff turnover and retention problems;
- the simplistic pursuit of efficiency through such exercises as reducing the costs of cleaning hospital wards simply to displace costs elsewhere in the form of increased infections;
- concentrating on what can be counted rather than on what is important;
- management by remote control.

The new language and alchemy of management

With this increasing shift to abstraction comes the language to match. It is the language of management and plans, rather than doing, managing and planning. It takes on an abstract, almost ghostlike reality of its own, disconnected from "reflective practice, rooted in the active local, concrete and specific" (Caulkin, 2001b, p 10).

This world of 'Management' barely connects with the world of doing except to foist a host of seemingly meaningless additional tasks on those at the frontline and deflecting time and attention away from concrete activity. When new initiatives are announced they are accompanied by 'tough new targets and robust performance management systems'. Not 'systems' of course really, just another word for procedures but lifted from a different paradigm.

'Management', and its discourse is becoming an increasingly abstract entity that can be dropped onto the top of any kind of organisation in the attempt to run them by remote control, with little knowledge of the real working contexts and the work of 'managing'. Consider for example this job advertisement:

> This key role manages corporate planning and performance processes within a Best Value framework to drive business improvement. Operating at a strategic level, the successful candidate will be required to manage the corporate planning function and a performance review framework, including Best Value and developing key systems processes.

The job is for the head of corporate development for a police force. Presumably driving business improvement is something to do with providing more effective policing (Protherough and Pick, 2002).

This kind of Management speak is often accompanied by assumption of the superiority of private sector methods and private sector 'disciplines'. The latter term has increasingly become a euphemism meaning that any work done through the private sector will automatically be cheaper and better than that done in the public domain. As a general rule of course, there is little evidence for this or for the superiority of this genre of Management abstraction in general. But part of the insidiousness of this language, and of public discourse belonging to the MMV, is that it places itself outside the area of any empirical testing or evidence. This is not an arena in which 'what works is what counts'. It is only when international comparisons are made that we start to discover that Britain, which has so much academic Management training and development compared with other European nations, has lower overall productivity and, in key areas, poorer public services (Calkin, 2002b).

A typical presenting symptom of the language strand of the MMV is those gatherings of managers and policy officers, at which one or two people appear to be trying to outdo each other in the number of times they can chant 'best practice, best practice, best practice...' like demented daleks. Of course, as with the pursuit of efficiency, the desire to learn from best practice is not an inherently bad idea. The problem starts when the *concept is divorced* from any kind of contact with concrete doing seen in its systemic context. We have sought to show through this book, and especially in Chapter Nine, that transferring learning and innovation is a complex issue that involves networked learning and working through whole systems understandings and approaches. Once this is divorced from concrete 'doing', the term best practice simply becomes another slogan of this empty Managerial rhetoric.

The wrong kind of 'systems thinking'

Another subtle way in which MMV operates is through confusion around the application and use of systems analysis. The systems approaches that we have found to be useful are those which can broadly be described as belonging to soft systems theory (for instance, see Checkland, 1981). From this perspective, people are sentient, sense-making, purposeful actors with their own unique biographies and attributes. Thus, they interpret and interact with the other people and situations of which they are both part and help to shape. For most of us this tallies with our personal experiences in our 'organisational' and other lives.

But the MMV is imprinted with a hard engineering systems model, taken from the field of cybernetics. Central to this is the notion of negative feedback used in engineering control systems.

> The prototypic example ... is a central heating system. You set a target in terms of room temperature, and a regulator in the system measures the actual room temperature and compares it with that target. If the actual temperature is below the target, the regulator turns the boiler on and pumps heat into the room. It operates on the basis of negative feedback, with the machine doing the opposite of the gap that has been detected. It's self-regulating in the sense that it removes differences and keeps the machine working efficiently in achieving its target.
>
> That idea, which is perfectly sensible in relation to central heating systems, has been applied to people and has colonised thinking about organisations.... It treats our minds as essentially mechanistic devices.... Negative feedback has become an extremely powerful principle in thinking about organisations, about policy and about what it means to manage. Indeed, it is what control is understood to be about. (Stacey, 2002, p 50)

Thus, control, negative feedback and fear have become the essential tools of Management when 'hard' engineering systems theory is applied to the world of human organisation and interaction. This may be fine for those who use others around them as little more than extensions of their central heating systems, but can be pretty alarming for the rest of us. Stacey quotes a spokesman for the Department of Health as saying, "Nothing galvanises people like comparing them with others and exposing their inadequacies" (2002, p 50). This is of course quite the reverse of how staff are expected to treat patients (with respect and dignity) or teachers to develop children (building their self-worth and esteem) for example.

This use and abuse of numbers, language and systems theory helps maintain the illusion that everything can be controlled by remote centralised Management, uncontaminated by the concrete experience of doing and operational reality.

And the wrong kind of quality

Another essential component of the MMV has been its ability to completely reverse the quality philosophies, theories and practices that had been developed with much effect. Previous reference has already been made to this (see for example page 6). So much of quality assurance has simply become part of 'hard' engineering control and inspection regimes, and entirely severed from its original roots. Where Deming talked about a philosophy of 'profound wisdom' (Mauro, 1992), it might now be more appropriate to talk in terms of 'monumental stupidity' in the context of some approaches to quality assurance.

Living with MMV

Given the dominant Management paradigm that is now so unthinkingly accepted by many politicians and their civil servant and policy advisers, there is little alternative to learning to live with the MMV and seek to allay its more damaging impacts. We have to use its language and number games to penetrate policy and implementation intentions, and to engage in conversation about them. It is an irony that, when there has been so much good policy intention to understand the bigger picture, deal with causes rather than effects and to 'join up', that so much of the armoury of implementation operates from an opposite alien, mechanistic framework. In the meantime we hope that those wanting to lead change – from any position in organisations and communities – keep their immune systems healthy and develop whole systems approaches to implementation so far as they are able.

Local solutions within whole systems: work in progress 1: Frontline interagency collaboration with the flood-affected people of Stockbridge, Keighley

In accordance with Bradford Metropolitan Council's disaster emergency plan, Graham Thompson (Bradford Area Social Services Manager for older people in the Keighley area) was given the lead role from that first morning in responding to the crisis. This involved working closely with the Council's emergency planning team, other council departments and external agencies, senior council officers and the local MP and ward councillors. Reflecting on the experiences of the first few days, Graham, with his development manager Maria Wilkinson, developed some guiding principles for the relief efforts. In effect they can be seen as the minimum critical specification for responding to the crisis (see Chapter Two: Minimum critical specification, page 24). They formed the foundation for the rest of the response, which lasted for the best part of a year. Effectively it was decided:

- to set up a small full-time core team of people who would liaise and bring in all the other agencies who were already, or needed to be, involved;

- for the core team to have a continuous daily presence at the Victoria Hall leisure centre, including weekends, to respond to residents' needs, questions and anxieties;
- to pay particular attention to residents' experiences and needs, and to use this as the basis for action (people were brought into, or near to, the core team who were thought to be able to do this, rather than seek to impose predetermined professional solutions);
- to go to great lengths to communicate and involve residents and appropriate agency staff, and to seek to build trust, especially through the core team and with the assistance of a central telephone enquiry service and social services communications staff;
- to seek answers to residents' questions as soon as possible after they were asked;
- to work with other council services and other agencies to ensure residents' needs were dealt with as constructively as possible.

The key actions and events that followed were:

- Every affected person who could not find their own alternative accommodation was found somewhere by the first evening and had transport arranged. Nobody had to be housed at Victoria Hall.
- Everybody in need was provided for the first night with essential personal toiletries and medical advice if required.
- Meals were provided at the leisure centre for the first three weeks following the flood from that first day.
- Advice or information that would assist the recovery process was made available.
- Meetings, coordinated by Graham Thompson, were held every day for the first four weeks and thereafter on a less frequent basis. Attendance in the first few days was as high as around 400 people of all ages.
- Eight editions of the 'Flood information bulletin' were produced and distributed between 3 November and 11 December 2000.
- Many agencies and organisations were brought in, involving around 500 staff and volunteers, including 12 departments of Bradford Council, Yorkshire Electricity, Transco, British Telecom, Yorkshire Water, the Environment Agency, police, health (acute and primary care trusts), fire services, Royal Mail, benefit agencies, and a range of local businesses, voluntary groups, ward and other councillors, the MP and many others.

The first few public meetings, held at the leisure centre in the immediate aftermath of the crisis, had particular significance. People were confused and angry, and there was considerable expression of this, mainly focused on Graham Thompson, the coordinator. Andrew Abbott, who was later to become Chair of the Stockbridge Neighbourhood Development group, said, with much agreement from other members of the Group:

"It is embarrassing to remember how some of us behaved then. And Graham just took it all and remained completely unruffled. He was incredible. We were upset and confused and out to blame someone. I have apologised since! We quickly learned that the best way forward came through collaboration and that people were there to help us. When we had questions that couldn't be answered immediately, they always came back with answers as soon as possible. We see so many of these staff as friends now."

Within a few days, the mood had changed and new beginnings were created. High levels of trust started to be built between residents themselves, between agencies solving problems together and between agencies and residents. Graham Thompson had created a framework, a way of meeting, in which emotions and anger could be expressed and in which residents and the staff involved could collectively begin the work of rebuilding lives, property, the local environment and the community itself.

It also enabled a productive relationship between the Environment Agency, especially the Area Flood Defence Manager, David Wilkes, and residents to start planning for improved flood defences. In the beginning, the Agency was a major target for complaints about the inadequacies of both flood defences and the flood warnings. Residents are now much better informed about the complex world within which the Environment Agency operates in order to secure scarce resources for making improvements, and are much better placed to have an influence on this and flood warning systems.

A big problem that came to light on that first day was that many people had no insurance cover. Nearly half the households affected had no contents cover and about a quarter had no buildings cover. An independent trust fund was set up, supported by Bradford Metropolitan District Council and a number of banks, building societies and other organisations. Most of the money was distributed to meet the needs of those without insurance cover. (This was quite contentious for some of those who had kept up with their insurance.) Again, similar core principles of working were applied. The same core team provided most of the servicing to Trust members. By now they had extensive knowledge of what happened and its impact locally, and high levels of trust with local people through the processes of working that had been set up and through numerous home visits. It was also decided to approve one building contractor, supervised by the Council's Environmental Protection Service, and one local provider for white goods and one for carpets. The latter two were within walking distance, recognising that many residents did not have cars. This was done to build partnership and trust in the supply of services and goods.

Residents, with support and encouragement from the local ward councillors, the MP and Bradford Council's Keighley Area Panel staff, set up their own Neighbourhood Development Group and are currently actively rebuilding their community and infrastructures in continuing partnership with key agencies. In fact, some residents have expressed the view that a lot of good came out of the flooding because the processes that followed to 'rebuild' Stockbridge has been so helpful in enabling people to meet and connect with each other and revive a community spirit that had previously scarcely existed.

Work in progress

Through the experiences and close links with the Environment Agency in particular, residents have become much more aware of the causes and increasing risks of flooding. What had been a stretch of river carrying water down one side of their neighbourhood is now seen as part of a living system in which a whole host of decisions being taken upstream can impact on their lives. Changing moorland and forestry management methods, agricultural practices and urban developments have all been increasing the speed with which water runs off the land into streams and rivers, contributing to sharper peaks and troughs in flows. They are concerned about how these decisions are taken, especially through the planning processes of local authorities upstream, and also how floodwaters can be increasingly held on flood wash plains.

The Environment Agency is sponsoring a project to bring together flood-affected people from different locations along both the Rivers Aire and Calder, both to help them share experiences and longer-term concerns about flood prevention. While Stockbridge is having new defences built at the time of writing, in a number of other localities, where fewer people were affected, there is little realistic chance of defences being built. The focus has to be on alleviating causes of flooding and on flood prevention.

The project is also exploring ways in which public planning agencies and key land users can be brought together to address these issues with those most affected by the consequences. As yet these interagency and inter-stakeholder connections do not exist and will need to be built. The Environment Agency is also seeking to explore and learn more fully how it can best work with communities and other stakeholders, both in dealing with the aftermath of floods and, just as importantly, in their long-term prevention.

There around five million people living in two million houses built on river flood plains in the UK. Despite Environment Agency warnings, planning permissions are, for the most part, given. Increasing rainfall and higher sea levels, due to global warming and increasingly rapid water 'run-off' due to changing agricultural and land use practices, are leading to the growing risks of flooding with the traumatic consequences that this has on people's lives. The work following the flood at Stockbridge is a heartening example of what can be achieved when agencies and local people work together. Of particular importance in this situation was the support of the local authority for local people to get together to influence how things develop in their community in the future. But this needs to be developed towards integrated working on a much wider scale to embrace an integrated approach to river basin management and flood prevention. It is a huge task for which the lateral connections and networks currently barely exist, although a further spur for this will be the implementation of the European Water Framework Directive requiring integrated river basin management (EU Water Framework Directive, 2000).

Improving performance locally

'Local solutions to local problems' is an increasingly popular slogan. It does offer an attractive narrative to counter the worst of the centralising and programmatic tendency. But in itself it is not enough. From the whole systems perspective, local systems are always embedded in, and engaging with, wider systems.

Anybody with responsibility for complex and diffuse systems is bound to be concerned about highly variable performances across delivery units in similar environments. Why do the performances of hospitals or police forces in comparable locations vary so much? And why, despite all the rhetoric of best practice, does there seem to be so much reluctance on the part of poorer performers to learn from better performers?

From the whole systems perspective, much more effort needs to go into understanding the causes for why systems operate as they do. This involves using all the intelligence of all those who are part of the system. In Deming's terms, those who work in the system need to understand the causes of variation within that system so that things can be improved. Deming condemned top-down, parachuted-in solutions as "endless tampering" and pointed out that they frequently make things worse in the long run (Walton, 1990, pp 24, 163; see also Deming, 1993, pp 194-209).

To protect against the most virulent features of the MMV, we need to integrate the vertical imperative for change, accountability and performance, with the lateral connecting up of all those with a stake in a given local problem and its solution. Longer-term improvements are often best delivered through local engagement and locally-driven solutions. However, although they are essential to sustainable change, local resources and energies are rarely sufficient on their own. Long-term sustainable change requires the simultaneous engagement of both local and wider systems. This is for two reasons: first, because of the performance requirements and standards; second, and even more importantly, because changes are often required in these wider systems in order to enable the local changes.

Working for local solutions within wider systems is the antidote to the MMV. Such processes seek to engage human passions and intelligence for shared goals of improvement towards human ends and purpose. Numbers, tools and techniques are employed as means towards these ends and as the servants of human ambitions, not the masters.

The Stockbridge case illustrates what can happen when all those with a stake in an issue, or problem, come together to work towards its amelioration. It also shows the various stages that often must be experienced – from community anger and denial at the start to building the longer-term connections of trust. When we look at the wider issues of flood prevention and integrated river catchment management we begin to see the scale and complexity of the work that needs to be done. It involves changes in the practices of so many different parties – those involved in uplands management, agriculture, planning, property development, building, architecture and landscape architecture, the agencies of government and local government, the Environment Agency and so on. All have impacts on both the growth of the problem – the increasing speed with which rain finds its way into rivers – and in its potential amelioration.

Longer-term, sustainable improvements to so many of these bigger intractable problems involve widespread changes in both public and institutional/ stakeholder practices and behaviour. Policy rhetoric towards joined-up solutions and modernisation is high, but so much of the practice of Management keeps the focus in the curative dimension – 'end of pipe solutions' with their attachment to top-down targets – rather than searching for upstream prevention in the first place. Our work is increasingly involving us in these issues across a wide spectrum of areas such as health improvement, clinical and other networks, regeneration, rural recovery post foot and mouth disease, partnership working, local strategic partnerships (LSPs), neighbourhood and community planning and so on.

In the remainder of this chapter, we explore two further examples in which long-term improvements are dependent on the development of further local solutions within whole systems. The two cases chosen – waste management and multi-modal transport – are examples of issues that are central to quality of life, and are consequently of great public and political interest and concern. They are also both areas in which old systems, built up over many years, are now nearing collapse. Belatedly, we realise how much we have come to rely upon the legacy of the past, and how little we have done to fundamentally modernise and develop these systems. What has been done so far has been partial, piecemeal and inadequate. The challenges posed here for all stakeholders – and that means all of us – are substantial and instructive.

Local solutions within whole systems: work in progress 2: The case of strategic waste management

The UK's waste management problem is one that is now growing beyond the remedy of traditional solution and to which no panacea is in sight. In short it is an intractable problem, which is of vital public importance. A whole systems approach to it offers a way forward, and will require the development of levels of collaboration and cooperation beyond what currently exists.

The problem

As noted in Chapter One, Britain generates a huge amount of waste, which is growing alarmingly at around 3% a year. The traditional form of disposal is landfill, which is now increasingly challenged by European directives, government policy and public opposition to new sites. Incineration is a tempting alternative and offers the attraction of generating electricity and heat – energy recovery. Replacing big burial with big burn apparently offers an attractive answer to the question of what to do with the burgeoning waste mountain. It is not dependent on changes in the behaviour of the millions of commercial and public organisations and households who generate waste. But there are also high levels of public protest about the building of new incinerators due to fears about the toxicity of both fly ash (what goes into the atmosphere) and bottom ash and its disposal (what is left behind).

The organisational system for waste management is one of Byzantine complexity. It is split between collection authorities, disposal authorities, land planning authorities, the private sector waste industry (who are now mostly responsible for disposal sites) and the Environment Agency's regulatory and advisory roles. In areas of two-tier local government, collection is at the district level, disposal at the county level. Land planning is done from county planning departments, who are likely to perceive themselves as having their own independent regulatory function over the waste disposal function in their own council. Regional assemblies also have a developing role to play and are now required to produce regional waste strategies to provide the regional overview and to inform regional planning guidance. They do this via regional waste technical advisory bodies (RWTABs) that consist of officers from constituent local authorities and the Environment Agency. RWTABs are required to consult widely on their strategies and to subject them to sustainability appraisals. They report to elected councillors who, in turn, represent the component local authorities. This returns an element of democratic accountability into the strategic waste management system.

The way forward

The UK government's strategy, 'Waste 2000', embraces three very useful tools for analysing the issue of wastes (DETR, 2000):

- the waste hierarchy;
- the proximity principle;
- best practicable environmental option (BPEO).

The waste hierarchy illustrated below, shows that minimisation is the best preventative measure – not producing so much waste in the first place. This suggests the reduction of packaging and using more compostable materials.

Minimisation
Reuse
Recycle, Compost
Energy Recovery (incineration)
Landfill

Increasingly, manufacturers will become responsible for the ultimate disposal of their products via reuse and recycling. Another alternative to landfill and incineration is the separating of domestic waste at source into recycled and compostable materials. However, this option depends on massive changes of public behaviour, collection methods and the development of markets for recycled waste streams (recyclates). This will probably need appropriate financial incentives to bring such changes into being.

The second concept is the proximity principle, which is the idea that waste should be disposed of as near as possible to the point of generation. The third tool is the best practicable environmental option (BPEO), which is intended to be

> the outcome of a systematic and consultative decision-making procedure, which emphasises the protection and conservation of the environment.... The BPEO procedure establishes, for a given set of objectives, the option that provides the most benefits or the least damage to the environment as a whole, at acceptable cost in the long term as well as the short term. (European Commission, 1988)

The application of these tools requires that, in practice, each waste stream must be analysed separately and its disposal judged according to both local and regional circumstances. For instance, incineration may continue to be the best option for disposing of medical and some other wastes; for other hazardous wastes, regional facilities will be required; for municipal waste, counties will need to cooperate closely across boundaries depending on population settlement, the extent of recycling and so on. In sparsely populated rural areas the BPEO may suggest that direct landfill of municipal domestic waste is still the best option because of the length of transportation journeys required for relatively small amounts of recyclates and the added difficulties in this context of establishing local recycling markets.

The central problem at the moment is that public consultation and protest focuses around land use planning decisions – the siting of incineration and landfill sites as well as civic amenity sites ('the tip') and waste transfer stations. These are, in effect, 'end of pipe' decisions and result from upstream strategic waste decisions, or often the lack of them. For instance, the Environment Agency is required to consult the public over the granting or otherwise of licensing applications for building incinerators, but in practice it is unable to deal with vast bulk of objections because they relate to matters beyond its remit and lie in the bailiwick of other stakeholders, for example, the call for more recycling and minimisation as an alternative to incineration.

To move up the waste hierarchy, apply the proximity principle and seek the BPEOs will require levels of system collaboration and cooperation quite beyond what currently exists. This collaboration must involve industry and the public at household and neighbourhood levels. It needs to engage all those environmental and community groups that have a stake in advocating environmental and community improvement. It also requires the government to provide appropriate legislative and fiscal incentives to promote minimisation and recycling markets.

No amount of top-down target setting for individual agencies across these systems will produce the radical shift needed. The challenge is to create new 'holding frameworks', which link the different parties and interests both laterally and vertically to find common ground and agree appropriate roles and relationships. For example, it will be to little avail if collecting authorities significantly increase their levels of recycling through public education and engagement, if there are no corresponding developments in local markets for recyclates, or the disposal authority becomes heavily committed to incineration. As David Boyle notes above, it is likely that more collecting authorities will reach their recycling targets, but then have to remix for disposal. This is an outcome that would further serve to lessen public trust in public institutions.

What is encouraging however is that there is evidence of the different parties coming together 'in the same room' to explore and start to work on these issues. Many of these people would previously have seen each other as antagonists. This is an essential start, but a great deal more needs to be done to build the social capital and the capacity to enable people to meet differently: to establish common ground, to take action and to learn from this. It needs up-front investment in time, living with uncertainty and the anxiety involved with doing things differently and meeting differently. It requires new holding frameworks and spaces to learn and network together. It invites the linking of locally-sought solutions in local systems, within wider county and regional systems, which in turn support and are supported by managed learning networks (see Chapter Nine).

Local solutions within whole systems: work in progress 3: Multi-modal approaches to transport

There are many interesting parallels between the issues raised around strategic waste management and those emerging in the search for new solutions to transport problems. In what may be looked back on as a simpler, less joined-up world, the planners could decide what to do with the big issues of transport systems or public housing, just as they did with where to develop the big landfill sites. These were the big 'Fordist' solutions and there was little local public opposition, let alone European directives and government policies favouring more sustainable solutions.

The problem

From the 1960s onwards improvements in transport have been dominated by the performance of the car, the interests of car users, and the provision of motorways and dual carriageways. It has been the era of 'predict and provide' – predict the future demand for car use and attempt to provide the appropriate road space. From the 1970s onwards there have also been greater levels of public protest and environmental lobbying against the building of new roads. The aspiration of public policy to predict and provide finally disappeared by the 1990s.

At the same time, congestion increased steadily and public transport was seen as expensive and inefficient. Hopes that congestion could be eased by people switching to public transport seemed remote. The response of the Government has been to launch a series of 'multi-modal' transport studies along significant transport corridors (DETR, 1998). The possibilities that road congestion could be eased through the provision of the old 'big' Fordist solution – more motorways and dual carriageways centrally planned and delivered – were largely abandoned. The search was now on to find ways of reducing traffic volumes and the need to travel, and to find better ways of increasing the capacity of the travel/transport infrastructure as a whole with smaller-scale sustainable solutions.

The way forward

There have been great efforts to involve the public and stakeholders' views in identifying local issues and possible solutions. Those involved include transport and road users and their organisations, local interest groups, transport and environmental pressure groups, transport providers, business groups and organisations, local authorities and so on. Again, people who, in the past would have regarded each other as protagonists – 'the enemy', have been coming together to analyse the problems and look towards solutions.

The types of things that people want to see and where they can find common ground are:

- increasing the carrying capacity of the existing infrastructures, especially rail;
- integration of bus and rail services to make local connections easier; greater reliability of services;
- creating cordon schemes in which drivers have to pay to bring cars into congested areas;
- taxing employers' provision of parking spaces and increasing the cost of parking in congested areas;
- developing tramway and light railway systems;
- provision of more, safer cycle routes and trains that can carry bicycles;
- better safe and illuminated routes for walking;
- improved bus services, especially rural provision;
- lessening the need to use the car, influencing public attitudes and behaviours;
- making minor road modifications to improve and/or restrict traffic flows as appropriate;
- being much more aware of the transport and traffic-generating consequences of planning decisions around the siting of new housing, shopping centres,

commercial developments and estates, and public buildings such as hospitals, leisure centres and so on;
• finding alternatives to the school run – the walking bus.

But again, as with river catchment management, sustainable waste management and many other parallel issues, the implementation issues are likely to be hugely challenging. What is becoming increasingly clear to the range of stakeholder groups involved in these kinds of studies – local authorities, transport providers and users, environmental and campaigning groups, communities – is that implementation would require levels of collaboration and agreement far in excess of the way 'the system' currently works. For instance, increasing car-parking charges, cordon changes and moves to curb the growth in car usage are central planks in some emerging strategies, but the decisions are largely in the hands of individual local authorities. Would politicians at local, regional or national levels have the stomach for making and sticking with apparently difficult and perhaps unpopular decisions? What happens when the various elements for an integrated scheme depend on a number of contiguous local authorities, transport operators and the bodies to cooperate, and one or more refuse to do so? Linked to this, and perhaps most difficult of all, is the potential for public 'education', attitude and behaviour change in relation to use of the car and public transport.

Conclusion

There is a parallel need to create the social and 'holding' infrastructures that are capable of the necessary vertical and lateral integration. Just as the village or neighbourhood can address recycling locally, so they can look at travel and transport issues. Counties and regions are as dependent on their local activities as are the localities on them for providing the social and planning infrastructure, resources, and the wider-scale changes that only they can do, to make more local solutions possible. Essentially we are talking about evolving and interlocking forms of new local governance. It will require local government in particular to see its role as being much bigger than the provider of range of services; it will also require ways of working, leading and meeting that mediate and link hierarchies, networks and markets.

Epilogue

As noted at the outset, this book is based on a dialogue between the four of us, which has developed over the past six or seven years. Our prime motivation has been to understand and to improve our practice in a new area of work that brings together the hitherto disconnected activities of organisation development, community development and public service development.

We are excited by the emerging possibilities of the work, and this includes being sometimes downcast by the difficulties, complexities and depredations of what we have called Mad Management Virus. We have been sustained by working with many creative and engaging people, whose commitment and learning is infectious and encouraging.

The aim of the book is to help people in organisations work effectively as part of a wider system of local communities, partner organisations, myriad networks and external relationships. While there are no simple prescriptions here, we provide a framework to help people make sense of this new world of practice, without oversimplifying the complexity in the situation.

The various elements of our thinking and practice can be assembled in a synthesis that provides not so much a model, but more of a 'retro-fit' framework. This framework for whole systems development emerges as grounded theory in particular contexts, and has three components: context, process and outcomes.

Whole systems development operates within a *context* of change defined by the underlying *policy dilemmas* and *values* that guide the work. The dilemmas provide the outer context; the values the inner. Within this context, the *process* of whole systems development work is defined by the Five Keys, and the *outcomes*

Figure 13: A retro-fit framework for whole systems development

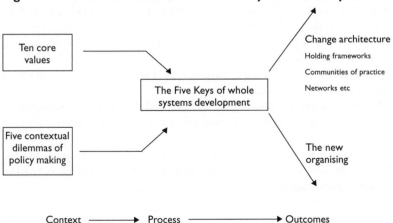

of this process are the substantive and specific *outcomes* of the particular task and the holding framework of the change architecture.

A brief recapitulation of these elements serves as a summary of our argument.

Ten core values of whole systems development

Over time, we have developed a number of values in respect of our own activities. Some of these are personal values held over many years; others are more recent and stem from the experience of whole systems development work. As ever, we offer these ten core values in the spirit of learning rather than as 'ten easy steps for consultants engaged with whole systems projects'. As stated in the Prologue, these are:

• optimism
• empathy and humility
• tenacity and courage
• learning
• whole systems perspective
• local knowledge
• local solutions
• building social capital
• celebrating small steps
• long-term focus.

Values are basic. Unless they are right – for you, for the others involved, for the situation – then however sophisticated the methodology, however skilfully implemented, it will not work. People smell bad faith.

Successful whole systems development depends on working in a way that expresses these values; for example, begin by listening to the community:

• Approach situations with humility – from 'not knowing', rather than from the presumption of expertise.
• For things to change, those concerned must learn to speak from the heart as well as from the head.
• It is important to understand the value of local knowledge and how it can fit with expert or professional knowledge.
• The process combines action with learning and the story that emerges is an account of learning, and not a cause–effect change intervention.

Where there are strong pressures to provide solutions, it is not easy to hold to values of this sort. However, without them, the Five Keys can become mere mechanical prescription.

Five contextual policy dilemmas

Whole systems processes are powerful and proven tools for sustainable change, but this only happens if the underlying dilemmas are surfaced and confronted. Effective whole systems working involves the reconciling of at least five dilemmas:

* top-down and bottom-up
* consumer and citizen
* treatment and prevention
* consultation and involvement
* long and short term.

Reconciling top-down and bottom-up

Famously set out by Douglas McGregor's theory X and Y (McGregor, 1961), this polarity is as old as history. Hierarchy and order are needed along with diversity and integration. Top-down targets and inspection regimes can feed pessimistic assumptions of human nature, while whole systems development takes a more optimistic, high-trust view of human potential and capacity to implement the changes people really want to happen. Yet these poles always have to be balanced:

> ... it is almost always a cruel deception, especially in more formal organisations when leaders say that all have equal voices and that hierarchy does not exist. The important question here, is of course, the balance between the two; the extent to which formal authority is seen as legitimate, legal, accountable and transparent, and is used to give direction, leadership and support to the horizontal ties of the wider civic society. It is the horizontal networks of civic society that give this legitimacy to vertical authority. It in turn needs to foster this by serving to strengthen its source. (Wilkinson and Appelbee, 1999, pp 55-6)

Over-reliance on top-down change initiatives in complex systems is likely to increase distrust and work against joining up on the ground. Whole systems methodologies work in the uncomfortable space where top-down collides with the horizontal and networked world of implementation. Restraining the top-down impulse in order to create virtuous cycles of hope, collective innovation and pride of purpose is what this book is about.

Improving services to customers and citizens

The agendas of consumers and citizens are not mutually exclusive. Collective effort between service agencies and neighbourhood groups can produce many benefits, but short-term service delivery imperatives tend to obscure longer-term agendas. There are huge potential gains from communities, service users and providers working together, but it does require long-term investment in both community and interagency capacity.

Both poles of this dilemma need support, but the citizen pole needs radical institutional change, for machine-like organisations cannot implement complex agendas for local improvements.

Curative and preventative approaches

Curative approaches deal with presenting problems; preventative ones aim at underlying causes. These are also not mutually exclusive; prevention may be better than cure but it is often harder to implement. Prevention has led to huge strides in public health and human longevity, the eradication of smallpox for example, but it often involves difficult and long-term strategies:

> A *public good*, such as clean air or safe neighbourhoods, can be enjoyed by everyone, regardless of whether he contributes to its provision. Under ordinary circumstances, therefore, no one has an incentive to contribute to providing the public good, and too little is produced, causing all to suffer. (Putnam, 1993, pp 163-4)

Moving towards prevention usually requires behaviour change: better diet improves health; observing speed limits keeps down road deaths; recycling lessens the changes of environmental degradation and creates jobs for others.

Consulting and involving people

Consultation or involvement or both? The route through this dilemma lies in confronting tough questions such as:

- What is meant by the terms consultation, participation, involvement and empowerment, as used by all those concerned?
- Why are people being asked to contribute?
- What differences will this consultation or involvement make?
- When organisations consult, are they really only doing it to conform to higher authority?

'Consultation fatigue' sets in easily and leads to widespread disillusionment and cynicism, blocking the flow of local knowledge and solutions. The participatory tools intended to empower people can actually maintain their exclusion from decisions and action. Community capacity building, neighbourhood renewal and sustainable change all need people to support each other's efforts. The relationship between the delivery agencies and citizens has to be fundamentally altered for effective joined-up action on the ground.

Short and long term

This fifth dilemma is covered in Chapter Nine and is brought to prominence by Mad Management Virus. Under pressure from politicians, institutional shareholders and the press, chief executives demand results NOW. This encourages the short-term fixes that frequently recycle the problems rather than tackle systemic causes and work against longer-term solutions that can make a real difference.

How can this be overcome? Tackling the 'wicked issues' usually requires diverse stakeholders to work together on understanding problems before implementing (separately and jointly) agreed ways forward. In the short run, the facilitation of diverse and frequently conflicting groups with unequal power and varying agendas is often a messy, time-consuming business. In the longer term, the benefits of building this trust and social capital, through such processes as holding frameworks and widening circles of inclusion, can be very high. Hanging on for this requires courage, persistence and that overused notion, 'vision'.

The Five Keys

The Five Keys are at the centre of our model, but they do not stand alone. Applied in the context of these policy dilemmas, and in the light of the values we espouse, the practices embodied in the Five Keys can provide a powerful means of working across the whole system. They provide an antidote to the action hero model of leadership, and, together with the keys of public learning, diversity, meeting differently and follow-through, can encourage people to come together across the barriers and boundaries of organisations and communities. The Five Keys of whole systems development are introduced in Chapter Two and dealt with in some detail in Chapters Four to Eight:

- leadership
- public learning
- diversity
- meeting differently
- follow-through.

The Five Keys are at the heart of what we do, because they describe the processes that can help people move from the complex predicaments characterised by multiple-policy dilemmas towards some useful and sustainable changes.

The fifth key, 'follow-through', is often the most difficult to sustain in practice. There is no neat dividing line between this and the change architecture that assembles useful tools and concepts for framing long-term sustainable change. The notion of change architecture indicates the need for a future perspective that frames, but does not fix, the way forward. The change architecture proposes a timetabling of processes and activities to support and bring about changes over the longer term. A change architecture can support all and any specific change outcomes.

Substantive change outcomes

The change architecture does not specify the *content* of change, because this is often locally invented and not known in advance. This contrasts sharply with the predictable, one-size-fits-all targets of programmatic change.

The substantive outcomes of any whole systems development process are vital and no change architecture makes sense without them. Few will bother, long to engage with the effort of arguing for and making changes if no observable effects can be seen.

Yet these outcomes are often not what was specified in advance. Sometimes the effects are far greater than could have been envisaged; shifts too small to be listed as targets can transform the quality of people's engagement and have a major long-term impact.

Change architecture for sustainable change

Change architecture is created by those involved in a particular change process to sustain the initiative over the longer term. Essentially, it is a plan or timetable of activities that serves as a holding framework to embrace any appropriate content at any given time. Its value is in building a predictable *process* to frame an unpredictable content and detail of change.

Many, if not most, so-called whole systems interventions focus on 'big events', generating huge energy that fades away for lack of a sustaining process for implementing change over the longer term. But whole systems development is a long-term process of change and change architecture realises the Fifth Key of follow-through via widening circles of inclusivity within multiple, overlapping systems.

Other important principles in change architecture are creating the space for leadership via holding frameworks, middle-ground frameworks and the use of action learning in the trial and implementation of agreed changes. Finally, change architecture connects with what is called here the new organising; the recognition that how we organise to create and deliver goods and services is itself changing, away from single, standalone organisations towards more networked forms.

Widening circles of inclusivity

What comprises the whole system? Who is included (and excluded)? What is the right boundary for this particular purpose? 'Getting the whole system into the room together' is not possible until these questions are answered.

The notion of widening circles of inclusivity starts with the people with the problem, and moves progressively wider, with the limits set by available resources and short-term goals. There is no one system, but many, and any bounded entity can be used as a whole or as a part of a wider whole depending on purposes. The importance of the ability to work progressively more widely rests on Einstein's famous dictum that problems cannot be solved within their own systems but only at the level above.

Middle-ground frameworks

Middle-ground frameworks connect overall strategic direction with local knowledge and learning on the ground. In Chapter Three, the middle-ground framework was the progressive conversation over a series of meetings between the board and the facilitators' group, which allowed learning from local action to influence policy and for organisational direction to be translated into sensible local action.

In working with multiple communities and agencies, a middle-ground framework can help with the dialogue of local and professional, and can fill a temporary leadership gap created by any change. Middle-ground frameworks are holding frameworks (minimalist, loose and always being reconfigured), the process of dialogue involved being among their most useful properties.

The new organising

Any change architecture is constructed with a view to understanding and exploiting the new organising, which seeks to utilise the knowledge, learning and action that takes place outside, between and across formal organisations in communities of practice and networks. It is also within these frameworks that the substantive outcomes of any change process will be negotiated. As noted in Chapter Eight, the main dimensions of the new organising are:

- *Knowledge workers*. We are all knowledge workers now.
- *Networks*, as the organisational form of the 21st century. There is a move to networked forms in industrial, commercial and public service organisations to gain the advantages of flatness, reach and flexibility.
- *Communities of practice* (CoPs), which exist across organisational and community boundaries and are where we learn and develop our practice.
- *Social capital* as the key to successful implementation and development through dense nets of local relationships.
- *Action learning*, which is also part of the new organising. Perceived by some as a management development method, it can be the means for moving on the intractable problems of joined-up working on the ground.

Local solutions to local problems

A key aim of the new organising is the development of local capacity, which is vital if network organisations are to be able to deliver joined-up services at the point of use. To do this, local people must assist in the creation of strategy development in both the organisation as a whole and in wider policy circles, such as confederations or government.

Connecting these imperatives is immensely challenging. It raises questions about the creation of collective power across user pathways and networks and, especially in the public services, requires connections with community development agendas around regeneration and neighbourhood renewal.

Different groups can share their learning about effecting change within local communities and make connections between this and policy emerging from the top of the organisation, or from government or Europe on the issues affecting their work. This takes time, but qualitative change does not come instantly. In early meetings, the focus might be on understanding the learning from different perspectives. Later there is a move to an action-learning focus, piloting ways of making the critical connections or creating the middle-ground frameworks, which can span the gaps between bottom-up and top-down, and strengthen connections between policy creation and local implementation. It is these connections that are so vital to the development and sustenance of a useful change.

Action learning

All these situations are natural sites for action learning (Revans, 1998). Learning and action go together in networks or CoPs, which can work as sets mutually to support and challenge each other.

In the light of intractable problems and the need for joined-up sustainable development on the ground, the single organisation is generally a poor site for learning. Working with action learning in communities of practice and networks that transcend the old organisational boundaries is an obvious way forward. Uniform solutions to local development issues inevitably fail to work, but good practice can be shared and people can learn from action in tackling real problems where they occur.

Solutions emerge from engaging the relevant communities in this sort of action and learning. Through this process, the local freedom of action of communities, networks and CoPs can be married with the performance-managed delivery requirements of government or other stakeholders.

Finally

Without the full participation of all those involved, change programmes quickly run out of energy. The history is one of bright starts that fade. To work for action and learning to improve local people's lives requires us to be without illusions about the forces of 'dynamic conservatism' where systems 'fight like mad to stay the same':

> ... established social systems absorb agents of change and de-fuse, dilute and turn to their own ends the energies originally directed towards change.... When processes embodying threat cannot be repelled, ignored, contained or transformed, social systems tend to respond by change – but the least change capable of neutralising or meeting the intrusive process. (Schon, 1971, pp 49-50)

However, alongside the consistently impressive forces for dynamic conservatism, there are always many splendid individual and collective examples of action and learning to be found in complex systems. Learning systems can only develop if people are able to sustain their self-identities, while at the same time learning and changing to become more of what they wish to be.

Bibliography

Ackoff, R. (1981) *Creating the corporate future*, New York, NY: John Wiley & Sons.

Alvesson, M. and Wilmott, H. (1996) *Making sense of management: A critical introduction*, London: Sage Publications.

Argyris, C. (1991) 'Teaching smart people to learn', *Harvard Business Review*, vol 69, no 3, May-June, pp 99-109.

Argyris, C. and Schon, D. (1978) *Organisational learning: A theory in action perspective*, Reading, MA: Addison Wesley.

Asch, S. (1956) 'Studies of independence and conformity', *Psychological Monographs*, no 416, quoted in Weisbord (1992), pp 21-2.

Attwood, M. (1994) *Developing organisations across boundaries*, Bristol: NHS Training Directorate.

Audit Commission (2001) *Change here! Managing change to improve local services*.

Axelrod, R. (1990) *The evolution of cooperation*, Harmondsworth: Penguin.

Axelrod, R. (2001) 'Why change management needs changing', Reflections; *The SoL Journal*, Spring, vol 2, no 3, pp 46-57. Cambridge, MA: published by the MIT press for the Society of Organizational Learning.

Bales, R. (1950) *Interaction process analysis*, Reading, MA: Addison Wesley.

Bateson, G. (1972) *Steps to an ecology of the mind*, San Francisco, CA: Aronson.

Beer, M., Eisenstat, R. and Spector, B. (1990) *The critical path to corporate renewal*, Boston, MA: Harvard Business School Press.

Bessant, J., Kaplinsky, R. and Lamming, R. (1999) *Using supply chains to transfer learning about 'best practice'*, London: report to the Department of Trade and Industry, January.

Binney, G. and Williams, C. (1997) *Leaning into the future: Changing the way people change organizations*, London: Nicholas Brealey.

Bion, W. (1961) *Experience in groups*, New York, NY: Basic Books.

Blanchard, K., Zigarmi, P. and Zigarmi, D. (1990) *Leadership and the one minute manager*, Glasgow: Fontana/Collins.

Boyle, D. (2002) 'The storming of the accountants', *New Statesman*, 21 January, pp 23-4. See also by Boyle, D. (2002) *The tyranny of numbers: Why counting can't make us happy*, London: Flamingo, Harper Collins.

Brewer, G. (1999) 'The challenge of interdisciplinarity', *Policy Sciences*, no 32, pp 327-37.

Brickell, P. (2000) *People before structures*, London: Demos.

Bunker, B. and Alban, B. (1997) *Large scale interventions: Engaging the whole system for rapid change*, San Francisco, CA: Jossey Bass.

Cadbury, A. (1992) *Report of the committee on the financial aspects of corporate governance*, London: Gee.

Capra, F. (1983) *The turning point: Science, society and the rising culture*, New York, NY: Bantam.

Capra, F. (2002) *The hidden connections – A science of sustainable living*, London: Harper Collins.

Carlisle, J. and Parker, R. (1991) *Beyond negotiation*, Chichester: John Wiley & Sons.

Caulkin, S. (2001a) 'Too complicated for words', *The Observer*, Business Section, p 10, 2 December.

Caulkin, S. (2001b) 'Why are UK prices the sixth highest in the world?', *The Observer*, 24 June.

Caulkin, S. (2002a) 'A mess in theory – a mess in practice', *The Observer*, Business Section, p 9, 13 January.

Caulkin, S. (2002b) 'Too many sums don't add up', *The Observer*, Business Section, p 8, 12 May.

Checkland, P. (1981) *Systems thinking, systems practice*, Chichester: John Wiley & Sons.

Child, J. (1969) *British management thought*, London: Allen & Unwin.

Christie, I. and Worpole, K. (2000) 'Changing places – changing lives', discussion paper for Groundwork, Groundwork.

Cooke, P. and Morgan, K. (1998) *The associative economy*, Oxford: Oxford University Press.

Dalton, P. and Dunnett, G. (1992) *A psychology for living: Personal construct theory for professionals and clients*, Chichester: John Wiley & Sons.

Dannemiller-Tyson Associates (1994) *Real time strategic change: A consultant's guide to large scale meetings*, Ann Arbor, MI: Dannemiller-Tyson Associates.

De Geus, A. (1999) *The living company*, London: Nicholas Brealey.

Deming, W.E. (1986) *Out of crisis*, Cambridge: Cambridge University Press.

Deming, W.E. (1993) *The new economics for industry, government, education*, Cambridge, MA: Massachusetts Institute of Technology, Centre for Advanced Engineering Study.

DETR (1998) 'The Transport White Paper; A New Deal for Transport Better for Everyone', London: The Stationery Office.

DETR (2000) 'The Department for the Environment, Transport and the Regions. National Waste Strategy 2000: England and Wales Part 1', Cm 4693-1, May, London: The Stationery Office.

Dixon, N. (1994) *The organisational learning cycle: How we can learn collectively*, London: McGraw-Hill.

Dixon, N. (1997) 'The hallways of learning', *Organizational Dynamics*, Spring, pp 23-34, Maidenhead: McGraw-Hill.

Doz, Y. (1996) 'The evolution of cooperation in strategic alliances: initial conditions or learning processes?', *Strategic Management Journal*, Special issue 17, Summer, pp 55-84.

Drath, W. and Palus, C. (1994) *Making common sense, leadership as meaning making in a community of practice*, Greenboro, North Carolina: Center for Creative Leadership.

Drucker, P. (1993) *Post-capitalist society*, Oxford: Butterworth Heinemann.

Emery, F. and Trist, E. (1965) 'The causal texture of organizational environments', *Human Relations*, vol 18, pp 21-32.

Emery, M. and Purser, R. (1996) *The search conference: Theory and practice*, San Francisco, CA: Jossey Bass.

European Commission (1988) 'The Twelfth Report Best Practicable Environmental Option', Cm 310.

EU Water Framework Directive (2000) 'Establishing a Framework for Community Action in the Field of Water Policy', Directive of the European Parliament and of the Council, 2000/60/EC.

Evans, R. (1993) *Social auditing and business growth*, Gateshead: Traidcraft.

Fillingham, D. (2002) 'Take five', *Health Service Journal*, vol 112, no 7, 7 February, p 27.

Fox, A. (1974) *Beyond contract: Work, power and trust relations*, London: Faber.

Fullan, M. (1991) *The new meaning of educational change*, London: Cassell.

Fullan, M. and Hargreaves, A. (1992) *What's worth fighting for in your school? Working together for improvement*, Buckingham: Open University Press.

Garratt, R. (1999) *The fish rots from the head*, London: Harper Collins.

Graham, P. (1995) *Mary Parker Follett: Prophet of management*, Boston, MA: Harvard Business School Press.

Hargreaves, D. (1994) *The mosaic of learning*, London: Demos.

Harrison, R. with Dawes, G. (1994) 'Barriers to learning in the organization', in R. Harrison, R. Boot, J. Lawrence and J. Morris (eds) *Managing the unknown*, London: McGraw-Hill.

Hastings, C. (1993) *The new organization: Growing the culture of organizational networking*, Maidenhead: McGraw-Hill.

Heifetz, R. (1994) *Leadership without easy answers*, Cambridge, MA: Belknap Press.

Heifetz, R. and Laurie, D. (1997) 'The work of leadership', *Harvard Business Review*, vol 75, no 1, January/February, pp 124-34.

Heisenberg, W. (1958) *Physics and philosophy*, New York, NY: Harper Torchbooks.

Heller, R. (2001) 'Why the centre cannot hold; things fall apart under the meddling of Blair Ltd's experts', *The Observer*, 12 August.

Hilmer, F. and Donaldson, I. (1997) *Management redeemed: Debunking the fads that undermine our corporations*,

Hopkins, D., Ainscow, M. and West, M. (1994) *School improvement in an era of change*, London: Cassell.

Huxham, C. and Vaugas, S. (2000) 'Ambiguity, complexity and dynamics in collaboration', *Human Relations*, vol 53, no 6, pp 772-805.

Jacobs, R. (1994) *Real time strategic change: How to involve an entire organisation in fast and far-reaching change*, San Francisco, CA: Berrett Koehler.

Johnson, T. (2001) *Profit beyond measure; Extraordinary results through attention to work and people*, London: Nicholas Brealey.

Jones, The Rt Revd, Bishop of Liverpool (2001) *The Guardian*, 29 August.

Kaplan, R. and Norton, D. (1992) 'The balanced scorecard: measures that drive performance', *Harvard Business Review*, 70(1), January/February, pp 71-9.

Kaplan, R. and Norton, D. (1993) 'Putting the balanced scorecard to work', *Harvard Business Review*, 71(5), September/October, pp 134-47.

Lave, J. and Wenger, E. (1991) *Situated learning: Legitmate peripheral participation*, London: Sage Publications.

Leadbeater, C. (2000) *Living on thin air*, London: Viking.

Leavitt, M. (1994 [1986]) *Quaker faith and practice: The book of Christian discipline of the yearly meeting of the Religious Society of Friends*.

Louis, M.R. (1995) 'In the manner of friends: learning from Quaker practice for organisational renewal', *Journal of Organisational Learning*.

McCrone, J. (2002) 'Network culture', book review of Capra, F. (2002) *The hidden connections: A science for sustainable living*, London: Harper Collins, in *The Guardian* Review Section, 3 August.

McDermott, R. (1998) *Knowing is a human act: How information technology inspired, but cannot deliver knowledge management*, Boston, MA: McDermott & Co.

McGregor, D. (1961) *The human side of enterprise*, New York, NY: McGraw-Hill.

Maturana, H. and Varela, F. (1980) *Autopoesis and cognition: The realisation of the living*, London: Reidl.

Mauro, N. (1992) *A perspective on Dr Deming's theory of profound knowledge*, The British Deming Association.

Menzies, I. (1960) 'A case study in the functioning of social systems as a defence against anxiety', *Human Relations*, vol 13, pp 21-5.

Mintzberg, H. (1994) *The rise and fall of strategic planning*, Hemel Hempstead: Prentice-Hall.

Morgan, G. (1986) *Images of organization*, London: Sage Publications.

Moss Kanter, R. (1984) *The change masters*, London: Unwin Paperbacks.

Mulgan, G. (1997) *Connexity – How to live in a connected world*, London: Chatto & Windus.

Murray, R. (1999) *Creating wealth from waste*, London: Demos.

Nichol, B. (1984) *John Child's history of British management thought*, occasional paper no 8, Manchester: Department of Adult & Higher Education.

O'Shea, J. and Madigan, C. (1997) *Dangerous company: The consultancy powerhouses and the businesses they save and ruin*,

Owen, H. (1992) *Open space technology*, Potomac, MD: Abbott Press.

Owen, H. (1995) *Tales from open space*, Potomac, MD: Abbott Press.

Panos Institute (1987) 'Towards sustainable development', Nordic Conference on Environment and Development, Stockholm, May, London: Panos Institute.

Pascale, R. (1991) *Managing on the edge – How successful companies use conflict to stay ahead*, Harmondsworth: Penguin.

Pascale, R., Millemann, M. and Goija, L. (2000) *Surfing the edge of chaos: The laws of nature and the new laws of business*, London: Texere.

Pedler, M. (1997) 'Interpreting action learning', in J.G. Burgoyne and M. Reynolds (eds) *Management learning: Integrating perspectives in theory and practice*, London: Sage Publications.

Pedler, M. (2002) 'Accessing local knowledge: action learning and organizational learning in Walsall', *Human Resource Development International*, vol 5, no 4, forthcoming.

Pettigrew, A. and Fenton, E. (2000) *The innovating organisation*, London: Sage Publications.

Pollard, W. (1986) 'The leader who serves', in W. Pollard, M. Goldsmith and R. Beckhard (eds) *The leader of the future*, San Francisco, CA: Jossey Bass.

Powell, W., Koput, K. and Smith-Doerr, L. (1996) 'Interorganisational collaboration and the locus of innovation: networks of learning in biotechnology', *Administrative Science Quarterly*, no 41, pp 116-45.

Power, M. (1994) *The audit explosion*, London: Demos.

Protherough, R. and Pick, J. (2002) *Managing Britannia*, Edgeways Books.

Putnam, R. (1993) *Making democracy work: Civic traditions in modern Italy*, Princeton, NJ: Princeton University Press.

Reason, P. (2002) 'Justice, sustainability and participation', Inaugural lecture, University of Bath, January, www.bath.co.uk-maspur/papers/inaugurallecture.pdf.

Revans, R. (1969) 'The enterprise as a learning system', in R. Revans (1998) *ABC of action learning*, London: Lemos & Crane, pp 124-34.

Revans, R. (1975) 'Helping each other to help the helpless', in R. Revans (1998) *The origins and growth of action learning*, Lund: Studentlitteratur, pp 467-92.

Revans, R. (1980) *Action learning: New techniques for managers*, London: Blond & Briggs.

Revans, R. (1982) *The origins and growth of action learning*, Bromley: Chartwell-Bratt.

Revans, R. (1998) *ABC of action learning*, London: Lemos & Crane, pp 124-34.

Scase, R. (2001a) *Britain in 2010*, Oxford: Capstone Publishing.

Scase, R. (2001b) 'Why we're so clock wise; companies' refusal to trust their staff is turning us into a disaffected nation – and is costing us dear', *The Observer*, 26 August.

Schon, D. (1971) *Beyond the stable state*, New York, NY: Random House.

Selznick, P. (1957) *Leadership in administration: A sociological interpretation*, New York, NY: Rowe, Peterson & Co.

Senge, P. (1990) *The fifth discipline*, Century Business, London: Century Press.

Shapiro, E. (1996) *Fad surfing in the boardroom: Reclaiming the courage to manage in an age of instant answers*, Oxford: Capstone Publishing.

Stacey, R. (2002) 'The impossibility of managing knowledge', *Royal Society of Arts Journal*, 2/6, pp 49-51.

Taylor, M. (1995) *Unleashing the potential: Bringing residents to the centre of estate regeneration*, York: Joseph Rowntree Foundation.

Thayer, H.S. (1982) P*ragmatism: The classic writings*, Indianapolis, IN: Hackett.

Trist, E. and Bamforth, K. (1951) 'Some social and psychological consequences of the longwall method of coal getting', *Human Relations*, vol 4, pp 3-38.

von Bertalanffy (1968) *General systems theory: Foundations, development, applications*, New York, NY: Braziller.

Walton, M. (1990) *Deming management at work*, London: Mercury Books.

Weisbord, M. (1987) *Productive workplaces: Organizing and managing for dignity, meaning and community*, San Francisco, CA: Jossey Bass.

Weisbord, M. (1992) *Discovering common ground: How future search conferences bring people together to achieve breakthrough innovation, empowerment, shared vision and collaborative action*, San Francisco, CA: Berrett Koehler.

Weisbord, M. and Janoff, S. (1995) *Future Search: An action guide to finding common ground in organizations and communities*, San Francisco, CA: Berrett Koehler.

Wenger, E. and Snyder, W. (2000) 'Is your organization ready for communities of practice?', *Harvard Business Review*, vol 78, no 1 January/February, pp 139-45.

Wheatley, M. (1999) *Leadership and the New Science*, San Francisco, CA: Berrett Koehler.

WHO (World Health Organisation) (1998) 'Health promotion glossary', Geneva: WHO/HPR/HEP/98.1.

Wilkinson, D. (1997) 'Whole system development – rethinking public service management', *International Journal of Public Sector Management*, vol 10, no 7, pp 505-33.

Wilkinson, D. and Appelbee, E. (1999) *Implementing holistic government – Joined-up action on the ground*, Bristol: The Policy Press.

Wilkinson, D. and Pedler, M. (1996) 'Whole systems development in public service', *Journal of Management Development*, 15/2, pp 38-53.

Zimmerman, B., Lindberg, C. and Plsek, P. (2001) *Edgeware, insights from complexity science*, Texas: VHA INC.

Index